HOLLOW PALACES

An Anthology of Modern Country House Poems

Hollow Palaces

An Anthology of
Modern Country House Poems

Edited and Introduced by
Kevin Gardner
and
John Greening

Illustrated by
Rosie Greening

LIVERPOOL UNIVERSITY PRESS

First published 2021 by
Liverpool University Press
4 Cambridge Street
Liverpool
L69 7ZU

British Library Cataloguing-in-Publication data
A British Library CIP record is available

ISBN 978-1-80085-674-5

Typeset by Carnegie Book Production, Lancaster
Printed and bound by CPI Group (UK) Ltd, Croydon CR0 4YY

Contents

Acknowledgements   xiii

Foreword
    Sir Simon Jenkins   xxvii

Introduction: 'Amid Great Chambers and Long Galleries'
    John Greening   1

Introduction: A Brief Historical Tour of Country House Poetry
    Kevin Gardner   5

List of Illustrations
    Rosie Greening   19

Poems

Insiders   23

JOHN BETJEMAN	*Castle Howard*	24
JOHN CROWE RANSOM	*Romance of a Youngest Daughter*	25
ELIZABETH DARYUSH	*Still Life*	26
VITA SACKVILLE-WEST	*Sissinghurst*	27
CLIVE WILMER	*The Manor House*	30
U. A. FANTHORPE	*Owlpen Manor*	31
PETER PORTER	*Dorothy Osborne in the Country*	32
FLEUR ADCOCK	*Peter Wentworth in Heaven*	33
STUART HENSON	*Twilight*	34
ROBERT MINHINNICK	*Daisy at the Court*	36
R. S. THOMAS	*Plas Difancoll*	38
PETER BENNET	*The Ballroom at Blaxter Hall*	40
CHARLES CAUSLEY	*Sir Frederick*	41
STEVIE SMITH	*The Grange*	42
GREGORY WOODS	from *Sir Osbert's Complaint*	44
W. H. AUDEN	*A Household*	48
JAMES FENTON	*A Vacant Possession*	50
ROBERT LOWELL	*Milgate*	52
W. B. YEATS	*Coole Park, 1929*	54
ANNE RIDLER	*Song to Mark a Boundary*	55

FREDA DOWNIE   *The Topiarist*   56
ESTHER MORGAN   *Mistress*   57
PHILIP GROSS   *Service*   58
CRAIG RAINE   *Baize Doors*   59
SHEILA WINGFIELD   *Song of a Past Scullery-Maid*   60
SEAMUS HEANEY   *Servant Boy*   61

Ghosts & Echoes   63

U. A. FANTHORPE   *Haunted House*   64
ROBERT GRAVES   *The Pier-Glass*   65
SIEGFRIED SASSOON   *While Reading a Ghost Story*   66
JANE GRIFFITHS   *A Haunted House*   67
JEAN SPRACKLAND   *In the Castle*   69
NEIL POWELL   *The Ruined Garden*   70
P. J. KAVANAGH   *Walmer Castle*   71
KIERON WINN   *In Blenheim Park*   72
RORY WATERMAN   *Shrine for a Young Soldier,*
                            Castle Drogo   73
LOUIS MACNEICE   *Soap Suds*   74
JOHN MASEFIELD   *Blown Hilcote Manor*   75
BRIAN JONES   *That House*   77
RENNIE PARKER   *Acton Burnell*   78
LAURENCE BINYON   *The House that Was*   79
ROLAND MATHIAS   *Prospect of Ditchley*   80
C. DAY LEWIS   *Tapestries*   81
ESTHER MORGAN   *House-keeping*   82
ROBERT CONQUEST   *Houghton House*   83
GLEN CAVALIERO   *Blue Bedfordshire*   85
EDMUND BLUNDEN   *At Mapledurham*   86
DAVID WRIGHT   *Canons Ashby*   87
DEREK MAHON   *Penshurst Place*   88
ALISON BRACKENBURY   *Wilton Park*   88
J. C. HALL   *Alfoxton*   89
JON STALLWORTHY   *Elm End*   90
ROBERT GRAVES   *A Country Mansion*   93
EDITH SITWELL   *Colonel Fantock*   95
SACHEVERELL SITWELL   from *Bolsover Castle*   98
SIEGFRIED SASSOON   *In Heytesbury Wood*   99
MIMI KHALVATI   *These Homes*   100
T. S. ELIOT   from *Burnt Norton*   102

Rites & Conversions 105

RENNIE PARKER	*Tresham's Fancy*	106
JANE GRIFFITHS	*Lyveden New Bield*	107
GEORGE SZIRTES	*At Colwick Park*	109
GILLIAN CLARKE	*A Banquet at Middleton*	110
SARAH SALWAY	*The Young Duchess Walks with Mr Brown To Discuss Improvements*	111
JOHN BETJEMAN	*County*	113
TONY WILLIAMS	*Great Edwardian*	115
HILARY DAVIES	*Metamorphoses*	116
ESTHER MORGAN	*Care-taking*	118
KIT FAN	*Ripley Eels*	119
TED HUGHES	*Wycoller Hall*	120
HENRY REED	*The Changeling*	123
DEBORA GREGER	*A Property of the National Trust*	125
MICHAEL VINCE	*Great Good House*	126
ELIZABETH BARTLETT	*Corpus Christi*	127
RICHARD MURPHY	*Family Seat*	128
ANNE BERKELEY	*Revesby*	129
RORY WATERMAN	*Flensby Hall Day Spa*	130
JOHN FOWLES	*At a Country-House Hotel*	131
HERBERT LOMAS	*Ridge-Foot House*	132
ROGER GARFITT	*The Space*	133
JAMIE MCKENDRICK	*Name-Tag*	134
JOHN GREENING	*A Huntingdonshire Nocturne*	135
THOMAS HARDY	*The Children and Sir Nameless*	136
TONY CONNOR	*October in Clowes Park*	137
ROY FULLER	*Newstead Abbey*	139
GEORGE SZIRTES	*Rest on the Hunt*	141

Fixtures & Fittings 143

LAURENCE LERNER	*The National Trust*	144
BERNARDINE EVARISTO	*Parson's Castle, Birr, Ireland*	147
PENELOPE SHUTTLE	*Swarthmoor Hall, Cumbria*	148
PETER REDGROVE	*Enýpnion*	149
RORY WATERMAN	*53° 09'33.17" N, 0° 25'33.18" W*	150
ROGER CALDWELL	*Late Elizabethan*	151
SIEGFRIED SASSOON	*Cleaning the Candelabrum*	153
PETER SCUPHAM	*The Old Bell-board*	154
PENNY BOXALL	*The King's Bed*	155

WILLIAM VIRGIL DAVIS	*Tapestry*	156
PENELOPE SHUTTLE	*The Gunroom*	156
GREY GOWRIE	*Aspects of a Novel*	157
KATHLEEN RAINE	*A Valentine for John and Margaret*	160
ROY FULLER	*Knole*	162
PETER BENNET	*Artemis Before a Prospect of Blaxter Hall*	163
MICHAEL HAMBURGER	*Real Estate*	164
GILLIAN CLARKE	*Plumbing*	167
LAURENCE WHISTLER	*A Charm for Blagdon*	168
JOHN GURNEY	*Greenhouses*	168
ELISABETH SENNITT CLOUGH	*The Washstand*	169
SYLVIA TOWNSEND WARNER	*Mr Gradgrind's Country*	170
HARRY GUEST	*Eighteenth-Century Blocks*	171
PENNY BOXALL	*The Laird's Lug*	173
LAWRENCE SAIL	*Guidelines*	174
TONY HARRISON	*Stately Home*	176
SEAN O'BRIEN	*Water-Gardens*	177
PETER SCUPHAM	*Fore-edge Painting*	179
ANTHONY THWAITE	*The Property of the Executors*	180

Loyalties & Divisions 183

DOUGLAS DUNN	*Gardeners*	184
DOM MORAES	*Craxton*	186
JOHN GREENING	*The Cedars at Highclere*	188
MICHAEL HAMBURGER	*Conservatism Revisited*	190
ESTHER MORGAN	*Bone China*	191
BERNARDINE EVARISTO	*Emma*	192
PETER DIDSBURY	*Mappa Mundi*	194
GEOFFREY GRIGSON	*Stately Home*	196
FLEUR ADCOCK	*Unexpected Visit*	197
GEORGE BARKER	*Stanzas on a Visit to Longleat House in Wiltshire, October 1953*	198
ALAN JENKINS	*Two Versions of Pastoral*	200
C. DAY LEWIS	*Landscape*	202
ROY FULLER	*At a Warwickshire Mansion*	203
GLYN HUGHES	*Landscape Poem*	205
PATIENCE AGBABI	*The Doll's House*	206
SIMON ARMITAGE	*The Two of Us*	209
OSBERT SITWELL	*Lord and Lady Romfort*	211
HILARY DAVIES	*The Jacobean Mansion*	213

BRIAN JONES	*At Great Tew*	214
PAUL WILKINS	*In Darley Abbey Park*	216
W. B. YEATS	*Coole and Ballylee, 1931*	217
JOHN MCAULIFFE	*Swans*	219
JOHN MONTAGUE	*Woodtown Manor*	220
MICHAEL HARTNETT	*A Visit to Castletown House*	221
JULIET AYKROYD	*The Owner Instructs the Master Mason*	223
THOMAS HARDY	*A Man*	224
GEORGE MACKAY BROWN	*Elizabeth Sweyn, Widow, at Her Writing Desk in the Hall*	226
DEREK WALCOTT	*Ruins of a Great House*	229
GEOFFREY GRIGSON	*The Landscape Gardeners*	231

Arrivals & Departures

		233
JOHN BETJEMAN	*Death of King George V*	234
RUTH PADEL	*Downe: The Extreme Verge of the World*	235
ROBERT LOWELL	*Fall Weekend at Milgate (3)*	236
ROBERT MINHINNICK	*The Mansion*	237
SIEGFRIED SASSOON	*A Stately Exterior*	238
FREDA DOWNIE	*An East Wind*	239
PETER SCUPHAM	*Effacements*	240
DEREK MAHON	*The Woods*	241
W. B. YEATS	*In Memory of Eva Gore-Booth and Con Markiewicz*	243
WENDY COPE	*Lissadell*	244
CAHAL DALLAT	*Final Movement*	245
LOUIS MACNEICE	*Order to View*	246
RUTH BIDGOOD	*Manor House*	247
SARAH SALWAY	*The Conjuror's Trick*	248
PETER LEVI	*The Lakes at Blenheim*	249
GEORGE MACBETH	*Somewhere*	250
GEOFFREY HILL	*The Laurel Axe*	252
CORINNA MCCLANAHAN SCHROEDER	*Letter of Notice to the Country House*	253
ROBERT MINHINNICK	*A Kind of Jericho*	254
SYLVIA TOWNSEND WARNER	*The Old Squire*	256
PHILIP GROSS	*The Chaos*	257
TAMAR YOSELOFF	*The Library*	258
EAVAN BOLAND	*The Break-up of a Library in an Anglo-Irish House in Wexford: 1964*	259

THOMAS HARDY	*The Old Workman*	260
KEN SMITH	*After Mr Mayhew's Visit*	261
GILLIAN CLARKE	*A Sad Story*	261
ROLAND MATHIAS	*Orielton Empty*	262
ROSANNA WARREN	*Interior at Petworth: From Turner*	263
SHEILA WINGFIELD	*View*	265
ROBERT SELBY	*St Botolph's*	266
EDMUND BLUNDEN	*The Ornamental Water*	267

Dreams & Secrets 269

JOHN GURNEY	*The Belvedere*	270
JOHN FULLER	*The Duke's Pagoda*	271
ROY FULLER	*Youth Revisited*	272
KATHERINE MANSFIELD	*Night-Scented Stock*	274
PAULINE STAINER	*Oxnead Hall, Norfolk*	276
WALTER DE LA MARE	*The Dwelling-Place*	277
JOHN GREENING	*Erddig*	279
PENELOPE SHUTTLE	*Osterley Park: Summertide Trees*	280
PETER REDGROVE	*Tapestry Moths*	281
JAMES REEVES	*Greenhallows*	283
JAMES BROOKES	*The English Sweats*	286
JOHN CLEGG	*Meteor*	287
SARAH SALWAY	*Three Riddles*	288
THOMAS HARDY	*Architectural Masks*	289
JANE DRAYCOTT	*Up at the House*	290
JOHN HEATH-STUBBS	*Send for Lord Timothy*	291
JANE YEH	*The Body in the Library*	293
GAVIN EWART	*The Owl Writes a Detective Story*	294
GLYN MAXWELL	*The Uninvited*	296
JOHN GREENING	*Greenway House*	297
VICKI RAYMOND	*The Hidden*	298
ROBERT SHEPPARD	*The Blickling Hall Poem*	299
KATHARINE TOWERS	*Furlongs*	300
GREVEL LINDOP	from *Shugborough Eclogues*	301
ALUN LEWIS	*Lines on a Tudor Mansion*	302
MICHAEL RIVIÈRE	*Felbrigg*	303
GLEN CAVALIERO	*Ha-Ha*	304
LISA KELLY	*Saltatorium*	305
SIMON ARMITAGE	*The Manor*	306
W. B. YEATS	*Ancestral Houses*	307
TOBY MARTINEZ DE LAS RIVAS	*England*	309

Outsiders 311

JEREMY HOOKER	*Avington: The Avenue at Dawn*	312
KATHERINE GALLAGHER	*Knebworth Park*	313
ALEX WONG	*The Landowner*	314
JANE DRAYCOTT	*Open Gardens Scheme*	315
DAVID ASHBEE	*Open Day at Stancombe Park*	316
FREDA DOWNIE	*Open to the Public*	317
DOUGLAS DUNN	*In the Grounds*	318
MARTYN CRUCEFIX	*Our Weird Regiment*	319
GEOFFREY GRIGSON	*Haydn, in a Neo-Gothic Mansion of the National Trust*	321
ANNE BERKELEY	*Britannia*	322
LACHLAN MACKINNON	*Staying with Friends*	323
EMILY GROSHOLZ	*After the Revolution*	324
G. S. FRASER	*Brockham End House*	326
PATRICIA BEER	*Stourhead*	327
LOTTE KRAMER	*At Burghley House*	328
THOM GUNN	*The Inherited Estate*	329
ROBERT LOWELL	*Domesday Book*	331
WILLIAM SCAMMELL	*Higham Hall*	333
CHARLES TOMLINSON	*Inheritance*	334
PHILIP GROSS	*In the Formal Garden*	336
REBECCA WATTS	*Ickworth*	337
NEIL POWELL	*Knole*	338
ROBERT MINHINNICK	*J.P.*	339
ANNE BERKELEY	*Moonlight*	340
ANDREW MOTION	*Breaking*	341
SYLVIA PLATH	*The Manor Garden*	343
WALLACE STEVENS	*The Plain Sense of Things*	344
STUART HENSON	*Asleep in the Orangery*	345
DAVID CLARKE	*To a Stately Home*	346
AGATHA CHRISTIE	*To a Cedar Tree*	347

| Notes on the Poets and Poems | 349 |
| Gazetteer of Houses | 379 |

Index of First Lines	395
Index of Titles	401
Index of Poets	405

Acknowledgements

Thanks are due to Simon Armitage, Neil Astley, Rosie Bailey, Jack Baker, Rafaella Barker, Sarah Baxter, Les Bell, Hannah Binymin, Margi Blunden, Katie Butler, Roger Caldwell, Abhrajyoti Chakraborty, Renuka Chatterjee, Emma Cheshire, John Clegg, Jane Commane, Martyn Crucefix, Hilary Davies, Gordon Dickerson, Jane Draycott, Jane Ewart, Suzanne Fairless-Aitken, Victoria Fox, John Fuller, Roger Garfitt, Georgia Glover, Rebecca Goss, Debora Greger, Philip Gross, Harry Guest, Eileen Gunn, Sally Gurney, Paul Hartle, Jeremy Hooker, Elizabeth Hughes, Mimi Khalvati, Joanna Kramer, Edwin Lerner, John Lucas, Glyn Mathias, Harriet Moore, Esther Morgan, Andrew Motion, Ruth Padel, Alex Pepple, Neil Powell, David Pryce-Jones, Robin Ravilious, Sharon Rubin, Jan Scammell, Mary Scott, Peter Scupham, Michael Schmidt, Penelope Shuttle, Jean Sprackland, Sarayu Srivatsa, Beau Sullivan, Lesley Thorne, Ann Thwaite, Anthony Thwaite, Katharine Towers, Tony Ward, Rosanna Warren, Julia Wilde, and Clive Wilmer for promptly answering queries, allowing us to adjust minor details and in many cases offering very helpful background material and offering new leads. Thanks too for the invaluable help and guidance offered by librarians Lorraine Mariner and Will René at the National Poetry Library in the Southbank Centre. The editors are especially grateful to Simon Jenkins for so swiftly providing us with an introduction, to Graham Gardner for editorial and research assistance, and to Rosie Greening for responding so positively to her father's request for illustrations.

This project was supported in part by funds from the Baylor University Research Committee and the Vice Provost for Research. Thanks is due to Dr Kevin Chambliss, Vice Provost for Research, and the staff of the Office of Sponsored Programs, for their assistance in providing a University Research Grant to support this project, without which it is unlikely that it could have been completed. Thanks is also due to Interlibrary Services at Moody Memorial Library for facilitating an inordinate number of requests to borrow books. Inexpressible thanks are due to Lois Avey for her patient assistance with innumerable payments for licensing fees.

At Liverpool University Press, we are especially grateful to our editor Christabel Scaife, our anonymous external reviewers, and the members of our design and production team, especially Rachel Clarke, Lucy Frontani, Lydia Osborne, Siân Jenkins, and Sarah Warren.

Every effort has been made to contact the copyright holders of the poems that comprise this collection. In the case of oversight, the copyright holder is encouraged to contact the publisher so that appropriate arrangements can be made. The editors and publishers would like to make the following acknowledgements for permission to reproduce copyrighted material. Permission credits are listed alphabetically by poem title; if a source has provided more than one poem, those poems are listed together in one credit line. Permission credits from Farrar, Straus and Giroux are grouped together at the end.

'Acton Burnell' and 'Tresham's Fancy' by Rennie Parker were published in *Secret Villages* (Flambard Press, 2001) and are reprinted by kind permission of the author.

'After Mr Mayhew's Visit' by Ken Smith appears in *Collected Poems* (Bloodaxe Books, 2018). Reproduced with permission of Bloodaxe Books.

'After the Revolution' by Emily Grosholz is from the series 'England', published in *The Stars of Earth: New and Selected Poems* (Word Galaxy Press, 2017).

'Alfoxton' by J. C. Hall (*Long Shadows: Poems 1938–2002*, 2003) is reprinted by kind permission of John Lucas and Shoestring Press.

'Artemis Before a Prospect of Blaxter Hall' and 'The Ballroom at Blaxter Hall' by Peter Bennet appear in *Border* (Bloodaxe Books, 2013). Reproduced with permission of Bloodaxe Books.

'Asleep in the Orangery' by Stuart Henson was first published in *Under the Radar* and is reprinted by kind permission of the author.

'Aspects of a Novel' by Grey Gowrie (*Third Day: New and Selected Poems*, 2008) is reprinted here by kind permission of Carcanet Press Limited, Manchester, UK.

'At a Country-House Hotel' by John Fowles appears in *Selected Poems*, ed. Adam Thorpe (Flambard Press, 2012), and is reprinted by kind permission of J. R. Fowles Ltd.

'At a Warwickshire Mansion', 'Knole' and 'Newstead Abbey' by Roy Fuller (*Collected Poems 1936–1961*, 1962), are reprinted by kind permission of John Fuller on behalf of the Estate of Roy Fuller.

'At Burghley House' by Lotte Kramer was first published in Great Britain in 1994 by Hippopotamus Press in *The Desecration of Trees* by Lotte Kramer, copyright © 1994 by Lotte Kramer.

'At Colwick Park' and 'Rest on the Hunt' by George Szirtes appear in *New and Collected Poems* (Bloodaxe Books, 2008). Reproduced with permission of Bloodaxe Books.

'At Great Tew' and 'That House' by Brian Jones (*New and Selected Poems*, 2013) are reprinted by kind permission of John Lucas and Shoestring Press.

'At Mapledurham' by Edmund Blunden is reprinted from *After the Bombing* (Macmillan, 1949).

'Avington: The Avenue at Dawn' by Jeremy Hooker (*Master of the Leaping Figures*, 1997) is reprinted by kind permission of the author.

'Baize Doors' by Craig Raine appears in *Rich* (Faber & Faber, 1984) copyright © Craig Raine.

'A Banquet', 'Plumbing' and 'A Sad Story' by Gillian Clarke (*Making Beds for the Dead*, 2004) are reprinted here by kind permission of Carcanet Press Limited, Manchester, UK.

'The Belvedere' by John Gurney was published in *English* in 1985 and is reprinted by kind permission of Sally Gurney.

'The Blickling Hall Poem' by Robert Sheppard appears in *Turns* (Ship of Fools Press, 2003) and is reprinted by kind permission of the author.

'Blown Hilcote Manor' by John Masefield is reprinted courtesy of The Society of Authors as the Literary Representative of the Estate of John Masefield.

'Blue Bedfordshire' and 'Ha-Ha' by Glen Cavaliero (*The Flash of Weathercocks: New and Collected Poems*, 2016) copyright © Glen Cavaliero are reprinted by kind permission of Dr. Paul Hartle on behalf of the Estate of Glen Cavaliero.

'The Body in the Library' by Jane Yeh (*The Ninjas*, 2012) is reprinted here by kind permission of Carcanet Press Limited, Manchester, UK.

'Bolsover Castle' by Sacheverell Sitwell (*Collected Poems*, 1936) is reprinted by permission of Peters Fraser & Dunlop (www.petersfraserdunlop.com) on behalf of the Estate of Sacheverell Sitwell.

'Bone China', 'Care-taking', 'House-keeping' and 'Mistress' by Esther Morgan appear in *The Silence of Living in Houses* (Bloodaxe Books, 2005). Reproduced with permission of Bloodaxe Books.

'Breaking' by Andrew Motion appears in *Salt Water* (Faber and Faber, 2019) and is reprinted by permission of Faber and Faber Ltd. 'Breaking' for *Hollow Palaces* by Andrew Motion. Copyright © 1997, Andrew Motion, used by permission of The Wylie Agency (UK) Limited.

'The Break-up of a Library in an Anglo-Irish House in Wexford: 1964' by Eavan Boland (*The Historians*, 2020) is reprinted here by kind permission of Carcanet Press Limited, Manchester, UK.

'Britannia', 'Moonlight' and 'Revesby' by Anne Berkeley were first published in *The Men From Praga* (Salt, 2009).

'Brockham End House' by G. S. Fraser (*Selected Poems*, 2015) is reprinted by kind permission of John Lucas and Shoestring Press.

'Burnt Norton' and 'East Coker' by T. S. Eliot appear in *Four Quartets* (Faber and Faber, 2019) and are reprinted by permission of Faber and Faber Ltd. Excerpts from 'Burnt Norton' and 'East Coker' from *Four Quartets* by T. S. Eliot. Copyright © 1936 by Houghton Mifflin Harcourt Publishing Company, renewed

'Craxton' by Dom Moraes (*In Cinnamon Shade: New and Selected Poems*, 2001) is reprinted by kind permission of Sarayu Srivatsa on behalf of the Estate of Dom Moraes.

'Daisy at the Court', 'J.P.', 'A Kind of Jericho' and 'The Mansion' by Robert Minhinnick (*New Selected Poems*, 2012) are reprinted here by kind permission of Carcanet Press Limited, Manchester, UK.

'The Doll's House' by Patience Agbabi was commissioned in 2012 for the Ilkley Literature Festival and is reprinted by kind permission of the author. 'The Doll's House' was first officially published in *Poetry Review* in 2013 and subsequently appeared in the *Forward Book of Poetry 2014*.

'Dorothy Osborne in the Country' from *Collected Poems* by Peter Porter published by Oxford University Press, 1991, copyright © the Estate of Peter Porter; reproduced by permission of the Estate c/o Rogers, Coleridge & White, Ltd., 20 Powis Mews, London W11 1JN.

'Downe: The Extreme Verge of the World' from *Darwin: A Life in Poems* by Ruth Padel published by Vintage, reproduced by permission of The Random House Group Ltd. © 2010.

'The Duke's Pagoda' from *Collected Poems* by John Fuller published by Chatto & Windus. Reproduced by permission of The Random House Group Ltd. © 2002.

'The Dwelling Place' by Walter de la Mare is reprinted courtesy of The Literary Trustees of Walter de la Mare and The Society of Authors as their Representative.

'An East Wind', 'Open to the Public' and 'The Topiarist' by Freda Downie appear in *Collected Poems* (Bloodaxe Books, 1995). Reproduced with permission of Bloodaxe Books.

'Effacements', 'Fore-edge Painting' and 'The Old Bell-board' by Peter Scupham (*Collected Poems*, 2002) are reprinted here by kind permission of Carcanet Press Limited, Manchester, UK.

'Eighteenth-Century Blocks' by Harry Guest (*A Puzzling Harvest: Collected Poems 1955–2000*, 2002) is reprinted here by kind permission of Carcanet Press Limited, Manchester, UK.

'Elizabeth Sweyn, Widow, at Her Writing Desk in the Hall' by George Mackay Brown copyright © 2006 is reproduced by permission of John Murray Press, a division of Hodder and Stoughton Limited.

'Elm End' by Jon Stallworthy (*Rounding the Horn: Collected Poems*, 1998) is reprinted here by kind permission of Carcanet Press Limited, Manchester, UK.

'Emma' and 'Parson's Castle, Birr, Ireland' by Bernardine Evaristo are extracts from *Lara* (Bloodaxe Books, 2009). Reproduced with permission of Bloodaxe Books.

'England' by Toby Martinez de las Rivas appears in *Black Sun* (Faber and Faber, 2018) and is reprinted by permission of Faber and Faber Ltd.

'The English Sweats' by James Brookes was first published in *Sins of the Leopard* (Salt, 2013) and is used by kind permission of the author.

'Enýpnion' and 'Tapestry Moths' by Peter Redgrove are reprinted from *Collected Poems* (Random House, 2012).

'Erddig' by John Greening appears in *The Bocase Stone* (Dedalus, 1996) and is reprinted by kind permission of the author.

'Family Seat' by Richard Murphy appears in *The Pleasure Ground: Poems 1952–2012* (Bloodaxe Books, 2013). Reproduced with permission of Bloodaxe Books.

'Felbrigg' by Michael Rivière appeared in *Selected Poems* (Mandeville Press, 1984) and is reprinted courtesy of the publisher, Peter Scupham.

'Final Movement' by Cahal Dallat was first published in *Trio 7* (Blackstaff Press, Belfast, 1992) and is reprinted by kind permission of the author.

'Flensby Hall Day Spa' by Rory Waterman (*Sarajevo Roses*, 2017) is reprinted here by kind permission of Carcanet Press Limited, Manchester, UK.

'Furlongs' by Katharine Towers was first published as 'Horse and Train' in *The Violin Forest* (Happenstance Press, 2019) and is reprinted by kind permission of the author.

'Gardeners' and 'In the Grounds' by Douglas Dunn appear in *New Selected Poems 1965–1999* (Faber and Faber, 2003) and are reprinted by permission of Faber and Faber Ltd.

'The Grange' by Stevie Smith appears in *The Collected Poems and Drawings of Stevie Smith*, ed. Will May (Faber and Faber, 2015) and is reprinted by permission of Faber and Faber Ltd. 'The Grange' by Stevie Smith (S) is reprinted from *All the Poems*, copyright © 1937, 1938, 1942, 1950, 1957, 1962, 1966, 1971, 1972 by Stevie Smith. Copyright © 2016 by the Estate of James MacGibbon. Copyright © 2015 by Will May. Reprinted by permission of New Directions Publishing Corp.

'Great Edwardian' by Tony Williams appears in *The Corner of Arundel Lane and Charles Street* (Salt, 2009) and is reprinted by kind permission of the author.

'Great Good House' by Michael Vince appears in *Long Distance* (Mica Press, 2020) and is reprinted by kind permission of Leslie Bell and Michael Vince.

'Greenhallows' by James Reeves (*Collected Poems 1929–1974*, 1974) is reprinted by kind permission of Michael Irwin on behalf of the Estate of James Reeves.

'Greenhouses' by John Gurney was published in *Poetry Review* in 1990 and is reprinted by kind permission of Sally Gurney.

'Greenway House' by John Greening is used by kind permission of the author.

'Guidelines' by Lawrence Sail appears in *Out of Land: New & Selected Poems* (Bloodaxe Books, 1992). Reproduced with permission of Bloodaxe Books.

'The Gunroom' by Penelope Shuttle is reprinted from *The Child-Stealer* (Oxford University Press, 1983).

'A Haunted House' by Jane Griffiths appears in *A Grip on Thin Air* (Bloodaxe Books, 2001). Reproduced with permission of Bloodaxe Books.

'Haunted House' and 'Owlpen Manor' by U. A. Fanthorpe (*New and Collected Poems*, 2010) are reprinted by kind permission of Stephen Stuart-Smith, Enitharmon Press, and Dr. R. V. Bailey.

'Haydn, in a Neo-Gothic Mansion of the National Trust' by Geoffrey Grigson is reprinted from *History of Him* (Secker & Warburg, 1980).

'The Hidden' by Vicki Raymond (*Selected Poems*, 1993) is reprinted here by kind permission of Carcanet Press Limited, Manchester, UK.

'Higham Hall' by William Scammell appears in *Inside Story: Selected Poems* (Arrowhead Press, 2008) and is reprinted by kind permission of Jan Scammell on behalf of the Literary Estate of William Scammell.

'Houghton House' by Robert Conquest (*Collected Poems*, 2020) is reprinted with the permission of The Waywiser Press (waywiser-press.com).

'A Household' copyright © 1952 by W. H. Auden, renewed. Reprinted by permission of Curtis Brown, Ltd.

'A Huntingdonshire Nocturne' by John Greening appears in *The Home Key* (Shoestring Press, 2003) and is reprinted by kind permission of the author.

'Ickworth' by Rebecca Watts (*The Met Office Advises Caution*, 2016) is reprinted here by kind permission of Carcanet Press Limited, Manchester, UK.

'In Blenheim Park' by Kieron Winn originally appeared in the *New Statesman* in 2018. Subsequently revised, the poem is reprinted by kind permission of the author.

'In Darley Abbey Park' by Paul Wilkins (*Pasts*, 1979) is reprinted here by kind permission of Carcanet Press Limited, Manchester, UK.

'In the Castle' from *Green Noise* by Jean Sprackland published by Jonathan Cape. Reproduced by permission of The Random House Group Ltd. © 2018.

'Inheritance' by Charles Tomlinson (*Cracks in the Universe*, 2006) is reprinted here by kind permission of Carcanet Press Limited, Manchester, UK.

'The Inherited Estate' by Thom Gunn appears in *Collected Poems* (Faber and Faber, 1994) and is reprinted by permission of Faber and Faber Ltd

'Interior at Petworth: From Turner', from *Each Leaf Shines Separate* by Rosanna Warren, copyright © Rosanna Warren, used by permission of W. W. Norton & Company, Inc.

'The Jacobean Mansion' by Hilary Davies is reprinted from *In a Valley of the Restless Mind* (Enitharmon, 1997) and is used by kind permission of the author and Enitharmon Editions.

'The King's Bed' and 'The Laird's Lug' by Penny Boxall appear in *Ship of the Line* (Valley Press, 2018) and are reprinted by kind permission of the author.

'Knebworth Park' by Katherine Gallagher was originally published in *Tigers on the Silk Road* (Arc Publications, Todmorden, UK, 2000) and is reprinted by kind permission of the author.

'Knole' and 'The Ruined Garden' by Neil Powell (*Was and Is: Collected Poems*, 2017) are reprinted here by kind permission of Carcanet Press Limited, Manchester, UK.

'The Landowner' by Alex Wong (*Poems Without Irony*, 2017) is reprinted here by kind permission of Carcanet Press Limited, Manchester, UK.

'The Lakes at Blenheim' by Peter Levi (*Shadow and Bone: Poems 1981–1988*, 1989) is reprinted here by kind permission of Carcanet Press Limited, Manchester, UK.

'Landscape' and 'Tapestries' from *Complete Poems* by C. Day Lewis published by Vintage. Reproduced by permission of The Random House Group Ltd. © 2012.

'The Landscape Gardeners' and 'Stately Home' by Geoffrey Grigson are reprinted from *Collected Poems 1963–1980* (Allison & Busby, 1982).

'Landscape Poem' by Glyn Hughes appears in *Best of Neighbours: New and Selected Poems* (Ceolfrith Press, 1979), and is reprinted by kind permission of Elizabeth Hughes.

'Late Elizabethan' by Roger Caldwell (*Setting Out for the Mad Islands*, 2016) is reprinted by kind permission of John Lucas and Shoestring Press.

'The Laurel Axe' by Geoffrey Hill, from *Broken Hierarchies: Poems 1952–2013* (Oxford University Press, 2013), © Geoffrey Hill 2013, is reproduced with permission of the Licensor through PLSclear.

'Letter of Notice to the Country House' by Corinna McClanahan Schroeder first appeared online in *Crab Orchard Review* 23.3 in March 2019 and is reprinted by kind permission of the author.

'The Library' by Tamar Yoseloff appears in *Fetch* (Salt, 2007) and is reprinted by kind permission of the author.

'Lissadell' by Wendy Cope (© Wendy Cope, 2011) is printed by permission of United Agents (www.unitedagents.co.uk) on behalf of Wendy Cope and by permission of Faber and Faber Ltd. 'Lissadell' is reprinted from *Family Values* (Faber and Faber, 2012).

'Lord and Lady Romfort' by Osbert Sitwell is reprinted from *The Wrack at Tidesend* (Macmillan, 1952).

'Lyveden New Bield' by Jane Griffiths originally appeared in *The Rialto* in 1995 and is reprinted by kind permission of the author.

'The Manor' by Simon Armitage appears in *Flit* (Yorkshire Sculpture Park, 2018) and in *Sandettie Light Vessel Automatic* (Faber and Faber, 2019) and is reprinted by permission of Faber and Faber Ltd. and David Godwin Associates. Copyright © Simon Armitage.

'The Manor Garden' by Sylvia Plath appears in *The Colossus* (Faber and Faber, 2008) and is reprinted by permission of Faber and Faber Ltd. 'The Manor Garden' from *The Colossus* by Sylvia Plath, copyright © 1957, 1958, 1959, 1960, 1961, 1962 by Sylvia Plath. Used by permission of Alfred A. Knopf, an imprint of the Knopf Doubleday Publishing Group, a division of Penguin Random House LLC. All rights Reserved.

'Manor House' by Ruth Bidgood (*New and Selected Poems*, 2004) is reprinted by kind permission of Mick Felton and Seren Books.

'The Manor House' by Clive Wilmer (*New and Collected Poems*, 2012) is reprinted here by kind permission of Carcanet Press Limited, Manchester, UK.

'Mappa Mundi' by Peter Didsbury appears in *Poems* (Bloodaxe Books, 2003). Reproduced with permission of Bloodaxe Books.

'Metamorphoses' by Hilary Davies is used by kind permission of the author.

'Meteor' by John Clegg appears in *Antler* (Salt, 2013) and is reprinted by kind permission of the author.

'Mr Gradgrind's Country' and 'The Old Squire' by Sylvia Townsend Warner (*New Collected Poems*, 2008) are reprinted here by kind permission of Carcanet Press Limited, Manchester, UK.

'Name-Tag' by Jamie McKendrick appears in *Selected Poems* (Faber and Faber, 2016) and is reprinted by permission of Faber and Faber Ltd.

'The National Trust' by Laurence Lerner (*Rembrandt's Mirror*, Secker & Warburg, 1987) is reprinted by kind permission of Edwin Lerner on behalf of the Estate of Laurence Lerner.

'October in Clowes Park' by Tony Connor (*Things Unsaid: New and Selected Poems 1960–2005*, 2006) is reprinted here by kind permission of Carcanet Press Limited, Manchester, UK.

'Open Day at Stancombe Park' by David Ashbee was published in *Perpetual Waterfalls* (Enitharmon, 1989) and in *The Oxford Book of Garden Verse*, ed. J. D. Hunt (Oxford, 1993), and is used by kind permission of the author.

'Open Gardens Scheme' by Jane Draycott (*The Occupant*, 2016) Is reprinted here by kind permission of Carcanet Press Limited, Manchester, UK.

'Order to View' and 'Soap Suds' by Louis MacNeice are reprinted from *Collected Poems* (Faber & Faber, 2007).

'Ripley Eels' by Kit Fan is used by kind permission of the author.

'Romance of a Youngest Daughter' by John Crowe Ransom (*Selected Poems*, 1995) is reprinted here by kind permission of Carcanet Press Limited, Manchester, UK.

'Ruins of a Great House' by Derek Walcott appears in *The Poetry of Derek Walcott 1948–2013* (Faber and Faber, 2019) and is reprinted by permission of Faber and Faber Ltd.

'Saltatorium' by Lisa Kelly (*A Map Towards Fluency*, 2019) is reprinted here by kind permission of Carcanet Press Limited, Manchester, UK.

'Send for Lord Timothy' by John Heath-Stubbs is reprinted from *The Watchman's Flute* (Carcanet, 1979).

'Servant Boy' by Seamus Heaney appears in *Wintering Out* (Faber and Faber, 2002) and is reprinted by permission of Faber and Faber Ltd.

'Shrine for a Young Soldier, Castle Drogo' and '53° 09'33.17" N, 0° 25'33.18" W' by Rory Waterman (*Tonight the Summer's Over*, 2013) are reprinted here by kind permission of Carcanet Press Limited, Manchester, UK.

'Shugborough Eclogues' by Grevel Lindop (*Luna Park*, 2015) is reprinted here by kind permission of Carcanet Press Limited, Manchester, UK.

'Sir Frederick' by Charles Causley is reprinted from *Collected Poems for Children* (Macmillan, 1996).

'Sir Osbert's Complaint' by Gregory Woods (*Quidnunc*, 2007) is reprinted here by kind permission of Carcanet Press Limited, Manchester, UK.

'Sissinghurst' by Vita Sackville-West is reproduced with permission of Curtis Brown Group Ltd., London, on behalf of The Beneficiaries of the Estate of Vita Sackville-West. Copyright © Vita Sackville-West 1931.

'Somewhere' from *Poems from Oby* by George MacBeth, © George MacBeth 1982, reproduced by permission of Sheil Land Associates Ltd.

'Song of a Past Scullery Maid' and 'View' by Sheila Wingfield (*Collected Poems 1938–1983*, 1997) are reprinted by permission of David Pryce-Jones on behalf of the Estate of Sheila Wingfield.

'Song to Mark a Boundary' by Anne Ridler (*Collected Poems*, 1983) is reprinted here by kind permission of Carcanet Press Limited, Manchester, UK.

'The Space' by Roger Garfitt (*The Action*, 2019) is reprinted here by kind permission of Carcanet Press Limited, Manchester, UK.

'St Botolph's', from the sequence *Chevening* by Robert Selby (*The Coming-Down Time*, 2020) is reprinted by kind permission of John Lucas and Shoestring Press.

'Stanzas on a Visit to Longleat House in Wiltshire, October 1953' by George Barker was first published in *The London Magazine* 1.6 (July 1954) and is reprinted by kind permission of Raffaella Barker and Elspeth Barker.

'Stately Home' by Tony Harrison appears in *Collected Poems* (Penguin UK, 2016) and is reprinted by permission of Faber and Faber Ltd.

'The Stately Homes of England' by Noël Coward. Extracts from *The Noël Coward Song Book* © NC Aventales AG 1953, 1977 and 1980. By kind permission of Alan Brodie Representation Ltd www.alanbrodie.com and Bloomsbury Publishing.

'Staying with Friends' by Lachlan Mackinnon appears in *The Jupiter Collisions* (Faber and Faber, 2003) and is reprinted by permission of Faber and Faber Ltd.

'Still-Life' by Elizabeth Daryush (*The Last Man and Other Verses*, 1936) is reprinted here by kind permission of Carcanet Press Limited, Manchester, UK.

'Stourhead' by Patricia Beer (*Friend of Heraclitus*, 1993) is reprinted here by kind permission of Carcanet Press Limited, Manchester, UK.

'Swans' by John McAuliffe from *The Way In* (2015), reproduced by kind permission of the author and The Gallery Press, Loughcrew, Oldcastle, County Meath, Ireland. www.gallerypress.com.

'Swarthmoor Hall, Cumbria' by Penelope Shuttle is reprinted from *Lyonesse* (Bloodaxe Books, 2021).

'Tapestry' is used by permission of William Virgil Davis. It is reprinted from *Dismantlements of Silence: Poems Selected and New* (2015) and originally appeared in *The Hudson Review*.

'These Homes' by Mimi Khalvati (*Entries on Light*, 1997) is reprinted here by kind permission of Carcanet Press Limited, Manchester, UK.

'To a Cedar Tree' by Agatha Christie from *Poems* is reprinted by permission of HarperCollins Publishers Ltd. © Agatha Christie 1973.

'To a Stately Home' by David Clarke © first published in *The Europeans* by Nine Arches Press, 2019 www.ninearchespress.com.

'Twilight' by Stuart Henson (*The Way You Know It: New and Selected Poems*, 2018) is reprinted by kind permission of John Lucas and Shoestring Press.

'The Two of Us' by Simon Armitage appears in *The Dead Sea Poems* (Faber and Faber, 1995) and is reprinted by permission of Faber and Faber Ltd. and David Godwin Associates. Copyright © Simon Armitage.

'Two Versions of Pastoral' by Alan Jenkins is used by permission of Andrew McNeillie, editor of Clutag Press; another version of this poem originally appeared as 'Some Versions of Pastoral' in *Revenants* (Clutag, 2013).

The Uninvited' by Glyn Maxwell appears in *Boys at Twilight: Poems 1990–1995* (Bloodaxe Books, 2000). Reproduced with permission of Bloodaxe Books.

'Up at the House' by Jane Draycott (*The Night Tree*, 2004) is reprinted here by kind permission of Carcanet Press Limited, Manchester, UK.

'A Vacant Possession' by James Fenton is reprinted from *Yellow Tulips: Poems 1968–2011* (Faber and Faber, 2013). Copyright © James Fenton.

'A Valentine for John and Margaret' by Kathleen Raine appears in *Collected Poems* (Faber and Faber, 2019) and is reprinted by permission of Faber and Faber Ltd.

'A Visit to Castletown House' by Michael Hartnett from *Collected Poems* (2001), reproduced by kind permission of the author's Estate c/o The Gallery Press, Loughcrew, Oldcastle, County Meath, Ireland. www.gallerypress.com.

'Walmer Castle' by P. J. Kavanagh (*Collected Poems*, 1995) is reprinted here by kind permission of Carcanet Press Limited, Manchester, UK.

'The Washstand' by Elisabeth Sennitt Clough is used by kind permission of the author.

'Water-Gardens' by Sean O'Brien, from *The Drowned Book* (Picador, 2007), © Sean O'Brien 2007, is reproduced with permission of the Licensor through PLSclear.

'Wilton Park' by Alison Brackenbury (*Skies*, 2017) is reprinted here by kind permission of Carcanet Press Limited, Manchester, UK.

'The Woods' by Derek Mahon from *New Selected Poems* (2016) reproduced by kind permission of the author and The Gallery Press, Loughcrew, Oldcastle, County Meath, Ireland. www.gallerypress.com.

'Woodtown Manor' by John Montague from *Selected Poems 1961–2017* (2019), reproduced by kind permission of the author's Estate c/o The Gallery Press, Loughcrew, Oldcastle, County Meath, Ireland. www.gallerypress.com.

'Wycoller Hall' by Ted Hughes appears in *Collected Poems* (Faber and Faber, 2003) and is reprinted by permission of Faber and Faber Ltd.

'The Young Duchess Walks with Mr Brown To Discuss Improvements' by Sarah Salway is used by kind permission of the author.

'Youth Revisited' by Roy Fuller (*Selected Poems*, 2012) is reprinted here by kind permission of Carcanet Press Limited, Manchester, UK.

Reprinted by permission of Farrar, Straus and Giroux:

'The Inherited Estate' from *Collected Poems* by Thom Gunn. Copyright © 1994 by Thom Gunn. 'Servant Boy' from *Opened Ground: Selected Poems 1966–1996* by Seamus Heaney. Copyright © 1998 by Seamus Heaney. 'Wycoller Hall' from *Collected Poems* by Ted Hughes. Copyright © 2003 by The Estate of Ted Hughes. 'Domesday Book', 'Milgate' and 'Fall Weekend at Milgate: Sonnet 3' from *Collected Poems* by Robert Lowell. Copyright © 2003 by Harriet Lowell and Sheridan Lowell. 'Ruins of a Great House' from *The Poetry of Derek Walcott 1948–2013* by Derek Walcott, selected by Glyn Maxwell. Copyright © 2014 by Derek Walcott.

The stately homes of England,
  How beautiful they stand!
Amidst their tall ancestral trees,
  O'er all the pleasant land.
The deer across their greensward bound
  Thro' shade and sunny gleam,
And the swan glides past them with the sound
  Of some rejoicing stream.

Felicia Hemans,
from *The Homes of England*

Foreword

We take our houses for granted. They are our friends and familiars, our second spouses, always with us. Yet they are also our creations, the physical expressions of how we choose to live. England's great houses rank with its cathedrals, as expressions of landed wealth and public taste. They are custodians of the nation's past and present, of its memories, fashions and affections. But England's lesser houses come closer to reflecting the personality of their occupants. I remember a friend once saying he felt closer to his house even than to his garden. His house 'does what I tell it', whereas his garden gave its first loyalty to nature.

Houses are normally recorded in pictures, but a picture is of a physical thing. It conveys beauty and atmosphere, but not what a house means to those who occupy it. It cannot embrace the hopes, fears and aspirations summed up by the word 'home'. The artist's brush or the camera's lens never gives me a wholly satisfactory account of a place. Perhaps I have a verbal rather than a pictorial mind. A picture may open a window onto a place, but only onto its surface. It does not penetrate its soul.

Prose writers have long found inspiration in houses. Brontë, Dickens, James, Forster, Waugh, Wodehouse have all rummaged inside English houses big and small, variously with affection, horror and humour. We feel we know our way round Wuthering Heights, Satis House, Howards End and Brideshead, as if they were characters in their respective plots. When Wodehouse's ancient mason patted Blandings Castle with his trowel and said, 'Finished, perfect, that will do', we knew he meant for all time. These houses told the rituals and liturgies of daily life. Their form determined how those who inhabited them behaved. They were Shakespeare's stage, on which was enacted life's 'strange eventful history'.

Yet prose can go only so far. It is the rhythm of poetry that extracts the full drama of these places. I am no poet, but I am aware that poetry delves deeper than prose. It can sculpt emotions in ways that mere sentences cannot. It can lift an image off the landscape and into the imagination.

That is why this collection gives a new awareness to our appreciation of place. These poems do indeed penetrate the souls of buildings. They get closer to their unspoken meaning, for those who wish to use and visit them. They interpret and they celebrate. I may enter a great house in prose, but I always hope to leave it in poetry.

SIR SIMON JENKINS

'Amid Great Chambers and Long Galleries'

It only occurred to me once the editing of this anthology had begun that reading a poem (particularly a poem in stanzas) is not unlike the experience of walking through a series of rooms in a stately home. Indeed, some grander poets treat the stanza as a self-contained space to be paused in, marking each one with a Roman numeral, as if to remind us that in Italian a stanza is a chamber or stopping place. But even Philip Larkin, earthiest of bards, who might seem to be most at home in Mr Bleaney's digs – and who never wrote a significant country house poem – constructed his great showpieces with an eye to their interior design. Like many before (think of Larkin's beloved Hardy, who had been an architect), he wanted to make poetry readers feel as if they were moving pleasurably, thoughtfully, from room to room.

Of course, this kind of analogy is fraught with dangers, and no poet wants to have their work thought of as a repository for dusty suits of armour, prints of highland stags, worm-eaten chests of love letters. Plenty of those included here don't use stanzas at all. But there are those who have felt their own achievements were somehow mirrored by the great houses – notably, W. B. Yeats at Lissadell eulogizing the 'great gazebo', or even Wallace Stevens in his late poem 'The Plain Sense of Things' describing a 'great structure' which has 'become a minor house' with a decaying greenhouse and a sloping chimney, where 'a fantastic effort has failed'. Certainly the comparison may help explain why so long after the official era of country house poems (when to praise Lord or Lady X's property was to angle for patronage) so many of today's poets are still fascinated by them.

There are other explanations too. Country houses attract literary types because they have been the homes of literary types. Some, like Agatha Christie's Greenway, even encourage writing by offering residencies. In compiling our anthology, we have limited ourselves almost entirely to work from the twentieth and twenty-first centuries, yet the poets of the past are by no means absent: we visit Wordsworth and Coleridge's Alfoxden, William Morris's Kelmscott, Byron's Newstead Abbey, and of course Wilton House, associated with innumerable Renaissance writers. We also have poems by writers who were to the manor born (Vita Sackville-West, the Sitwells, Sheila Wingfield, Grey Gowrie) or who married into one (Robert Lowell) or who have somehow acquired one large or small (Siegfried Sassoon, Peter Scupham, James Fenton). Others (Esther Morgan, Penny Boxall) have worked in Big Houses, or have memories of growing up very close to them, or even within their grounds (Rory Waterman, Robert Minhinnick). Meanwhile, George MacBeth simply thought of himself as an aristocrat and purchased the house to match. For most, however, it will be a visit, poet drawn perhaps by poet (Edmund Blunden to Pope's Mapledurham, Derek Mahon to Sidney's Penshurst) or just going there as you or I might go, with the Bank Holiday crowds, or slipping in at the end of the season. It is the impact of such encounters with an atmosphere, a tale, an artefact, a personality, that often prompts the poem.

The fact that many of the Big Houses have either been demolished (like Yeats's Coole) or been left to crumble, naturally appeals to the elegists – i.e., to most British poets. I remember playing in Cranford Park, near Heathrow, in the 1960s among the grassy mounds where there had been a manor house until just two decades before. Even in my early teens I was aware of it, the scent of 'a rich man's flowering lawns' and a vanished order. But these islands tend to breed satirists too, and that rich man's property can be a useful target, either for political slingshots ('those bastards in their mansions' as Simon Armitage's speaker puts it in a poem from *Book of Matches*, quoted in Kevin Gardner's introduction) or for barbed social commentary about gentrification and exclusion. To Irish, Scottish and Welsh poets, indeed to a Caribbean or half-Nigerian like Bernardine Evaristo, their presence often takes on a much more threatening significance. There is undoubtedly a colonial aspect here, and it is emphasised by poets such as Derek Walcott, Douglas Dunn, Patience Agbabi and R. S. Thomas. But not all the properties outside England are owned by heartless interlopers – unless we regard Lady Gregory as one. Take Kathleen Raine's creative friends at Canna House, or George Mackay Brown's Orkney widow in her Hall, trying to be severe but overwhelmed by love.

Complex political and social forces are involved, but beneath them there is often genuine affection, which is more than simply Downton Abbey nostalgia. Country houses are collections of stories ('Dust in the air suspended / Marks the place where a story ended' as T. S. Eliot put it in 'Little Gidding', alert to double meaning and American spelling) and such houses, along with their often improbable stories, are everywhere in the British Isles. Near where my wife and I live, for example, just into rural Bedfordshire, is Melchbourne Park (*ca*. 1610) on whose lawns Glenn Miller gave some of his last concerts; the night before he disappeared he stayed at a local Victorian mansion (now a care home), Milton Ernest Hall. Nearer still, in our own village, is the one-time home of the Dukes of Manchester, now a school where I used to teach: cleaners were sure they had seen Katherine of Aragon, who died there (she interfered with a poem on my computer once too) and there were rumours of hidden hoards of Chippendale chairs from when the house was sold off. These furnished mansions furnish our own imaginations whether we approve of them or not, whether we believe the stories or not. The rituals and mysteries of life within are natural material for writers. Kazuo Ishiguro proved it with his bestseller, *The Remains of the Day*, but before him there was (still is) the country house murder tradition. Agatha Christie was herself a poet, and I am glad we were able to include something of hers to conclude the book.

Even more popular is the country house comedy, the *To the Manor Born* or *Monarch of the Glen* brand of TV sitcom (Basil Fawlty's hotel had to be called 'Towers'). If this didn't all begin with Blandings Castle, then P. G. Wodehouse is certainly the prose stylist who most successfully evoked the potential absurdity of the privileged classes. In verse, that comic muse is served by a poet who stands at the heart of our anthology: Sir John Betjeman. Betjeman, like Hardy, knew about architecture, but he also knew about audiences. My father was a civil servant and commuted to the city from near Ruislip on the Metropolitan Line. He didn't read a great deal of poetry, but his Betjeman *Collected* was always to hand. The poems appealed to the same instinct that made him reach for the cine camera as we passed any National Trust sign on our family rambles; the same instinct that made him take us to Ham House or Kenwood or Chartwell. Betjeman understood what we would now call 'Middle England' in a way that few poets have since. He recognised the widespread uneasiness with the tearing down of old buildings after World War II, then the brutalist developments of the 1960s.

In the end I come back to that analogy, since it's not only that verses are like rooms. Poetry tends to stand aloof from most people's lives just like the Big House. People admire it, but are wary of approaching too close. I like to think that Kevin and I are offering this anthology in the spirit of the Heritage Open Days scheme. Poetry's doors are open, and upon entering I predict that you will forget you ever found the prospect in any way forbidding. You will be entranced. Never mind the statue of Shakespeare in the hallway, or the schoolteacher telling you the difference between blank verse and free verse: go wherever you feel comfortable, lingering or hurrying on. Look at the pictures. Touch the furniture. Imagine the food. Try the beds. This is indeed your heritage.

JOHN GREENING

A Brief Historical Tour
of Country House Poetry

The manor wallows in the swell and sway
of woods and fields, an ark of stone
that drifts in silence with a freight
no one can own.

What's gone has no voice but the whisper
of your pen.

Philip Gross[1]

As a symbol of authority and privilege, the English country house may have achieved its greatest potency in the Edwardian era; as the power and influence of landed society waned, however, it began to haunt the literary imagination in England and beyond. The mythos was eloquently captured by architectural historian Mark Girouard:

> One shake of the kaleidoscope, and country houses seem like visions in a dream: visions bathed in sunlight, melting in the mist, or gleaming under the moon. The architecture is frozen, the trees cast long shadows, the houses hover at the end of golden glades, the fruit hangs heavy and abundant in the orchards, the flowers along the garden walks rise in spires drenched and gleaming with dew.[2]

The melancholic sense of country house society in the twilight of its significance is a common trope in modern fiction, and many instances come to mind – John Galsworthy, Henry James, Vita Sackville-West, Evelyn Waugh, L. P. Hartley, Elizabeth Bowen, Alan Hollinghurst and Sarah Waters, to name but a few. Poetic treatments are sadly less well known. And yet, as the great house was eclipsed as an institution and symbol of cultural identity and sway, poets

---

[1] 'The Spirit of the Place', *Manifold Manor* (Faber and Faber, 1989), pp. 53–54.
[2] *A Country House Companion* (Yale University Press, 1987), p. 7.

from all corners of the British Isles and its former colonies have found in its dereliction a frequent subject and theme.

But where did it all begin? The first scholars who identified and described the genre of country house poetry and compiled examples understood it to be a literary phenomenon of the seventeenth century and assigned its date of death to the Restoration, or not long thereafter. G. R. Hibbard noted in 1956, 'After 1660, this kind of poem was no longer written, because the way of life that it reflects, and out of which it grows, was on the decline. The function of the great house changed, and to this change in function there corresponded a new style of architecture'. Thus, Hibbard concluded, 'the country house poem as a distinct form comes to an end with Marvell's *Appleton House*'.[3] If the function and architecture of the country house began to evolve, however, then it is more accurate to say that the country house poem did as well. Far from dying out, the genre would develop in striking and unexpected ways.

The first known instance is Amelia Lanyer's 'The Description of Cooke-ham' (1611). This poem is a valediction, a farewell to a place of extraordinary significance and joy in the author's life, a scene of 'fleeting worldly joys that could not last' and 'dim shadows of celestial pleasures'. The crown manor of Cookham seems nearly Edenic: a place where neither men nor class distinctions exist and so cannot mar the poet's conversations with the Countess of Cumberland and her daughter, Lady Anne Clifford, under a lovely oak tree on a hilltop. Alas, Eden cannot last, and the Countess and her daughter are called away, leaving the house and landscape to mourn – and the poet to lament the class distinctions that leave her behind. Lanyer established one of the basic tropes of the country house poem, the elegiac sense of something vital now lost and irrecoverable:

Therefore sweet memory do thou retain
Those pleasures past, which will not turn again.

Lanyer's poem is something of an outlier among country house poems of the seventeenth century because the estate she describes is so private, as was her experience there. The more common pattern was not to memorialise an estate but to acclaim its great house, landscape and gardens, and to praise the noble virtues, including charity and hospitality, of the estate's lord. Family history and continuity symbolise the desire for order and hierarchy on a national level. A celebration of rural innocence and other country virtues, set against the corruptions of Town and Court, is standard, and also typically implicit is a

---

[3] 'The Country House Poem of the Seventeenth Century', *Journal of the Warburg and Courtauld Institutes* 19.1/2 (1956), p. 159. *Cf.* William A. McClung, *The Country House in English Renaissance Poetry* (University of California Press, 1977).

critique of other estates in order to advance the poet's stated values; hence the famous concluding lines of Ben Jonson's 'To Penshurst' (1616):

> Now, *Penshurst*, they that will proportion thee
> With other edifices, when they see
> Those proud, ambitious heaps, and nothing else,
> May say, their lords have built, but thy lord dwells.

The noble virtues praised by Jonson establish the essential framework of the seventeenth-century country house poem: this genre adumbrated social order and tradition, with the well-run estate functioning like a kingdom in microcosm.[4] Thus a vein of paternalistic *noblesse oblige* is meant to justify the epicureanism of the noble lord,

> whose liberall boord doth flow,
> With all, that hospitalitie doth know!
> Where comes no guest, but is allow'd to eate,
> Without his fear, and of the lords own meate.

Praise for the lord of the manor reaches its apex in Andrew Marvell's 'Upon Appleton House' (1681), though the poet's esteem for Lord Fairfax is used for the larger purpose of meditating on art, nature, society and divine will. Why must Man, among all animals, demand to live in such 'unproportion'd dwellings'? Marvell's response gives us the title of our book:

> But He, superfluously spread,
> Demands more room alive than dead.
> And in his hollow Palace goes
> Where Winds as he themselves may lose.

Marvell acknowledges that the craze of building vast and mighty estates is not only unnatural but also a Babel-like gesture 'To strain themselves through *Heavens Gate*'. In contrast, Nun Appleton is 'composed … Like Nature, orderly and near'. As he brings this very long poem to its close, Marvell concludes that Fairfax's estate reenacts divine will, when out of chaos and darkness God created the heavens and the earth. Nun Appleton is, on a smaller scale, a reflection of this divine order and will, and thus Marvell apostrophises the estate itself:

[4] Two similar excursions are Thomas Carew's *To Saxham* (1640) and Robert Herrick's *A Panegyrick to Sir Lewis Pemberton* (1648). The most complete collection of early country house poems was compiled by Alastair Fowler, *The Country House Poem: A Cabinet of Seventeenth-Century Estate Poems and Related Items* (Edinburgh University Press, 1994).

Your lesser *World* contains the same.
But in more decent Order tame;
You Heaven's Center, Nature's Lap.
And Paradice's only Map.

Anne Finch (later the Countess of Winchilsea) was among the first to see the country house as a work of art. Her poem 'To the Honorable The Lady Worsley at Long-Leate' (*ca.* 1690) challenges the poet to capture in figurative language the splendours of its grand architecture,

Which above Metaphor itts Structure reares
Thô all Enchantment to our sight appears
Magnificently Great the Eye to fill
Minut'ly finish'd for our nicest skill
Long-leate that justly has all Praise engross'd
The Strangers wonder and our Nations boast.

The poet then takes the reader past Longleat's fabled terraces, gardens, fountains and labyrinths; it is in vain, she concludes, for the poet to attempt to replicate this extraordinary beauty, for the builder has created this estate with a near divine hand: 'No syllables the most sublimely wrought / Can reach the loftier Immage of his thought'.

The earliest examples embodied a sort of 'Golden Age' quality, as if the poet sensed how rare and fleeting was this world of the English country house. But as Britain rapidly developed a speculative economy in the late seventeenth and early eighteenth centuries, the great estates and their houses evolved as well, and a rising tide of new-monied nobles inadvertently fostered the growth of a satiric vein in the genre. By the time Alexander Pope wrote his 'Epistle to Burlington' (1731), there was a new sense that the primary purpose of the country house was to create a great show of conspicuous consumption. Hospitality gives way to prodigality, and for Pope, ever conflating taste and morality, the result is Timon's hideous and unnatural villa:

Lo, what huge heaps of littleness around!
The whole, a labour'd Quarry above ground.
…
The suff'ring eye inverted Nature sees,
Trees cut to Statues, Statues thick as trees.

Although this attack appears to be directed towards false taste, Pope's primary target is pride. Timon privileges the gratification of his vanities over communal needs and social utility. Where Jonson's Penshurst embodies and sustains social order, Timon's villa ministers solely to the self-flattery of his massive ego: 'My

Lord advances with majestic mien, / Smit with the mighty pleasure, to be seen'. On a neighbouring estate, the young heir, driven by the modern taste for open vistas, cuts down all the ancient trees his father had so highly treasured. Pope's brilliant concision captures the irony of fate, as the young heir unwittingly diminishes himself even as he reduces his estate's beauty and moral significance:

> One boundless Green, or flourish'd Carpet views,
> With all the mournful family of Yews;
> The thriving plants ignoble broomsticks made,
> Now sweep those Alleys they were born to shade.

Pope's friend Jonathan Swift shared the view that a nation's values were embodied within the individual estate. In 'A Pastoral Dialogue between Richmond-Lodge and Marble-Hill' (1727), he gives voice to neighbouring Thames-side estates. These two houses ponder their fates in the reign of a new monarch who had been accustomed to visiting both houses when Prince of Wales – the one as his summer residence, the other that of his mistress. Marble Hill House imagines the gloomiest future:

> Some *South Sea* Broker from the City,
> Will purchase me, the more's the Pity,
> Lay all my fine Plantations waste,
> To fit them to his Vulgar Taste;
> Chang'd for the worse in ev'ry Part,
> My Master *Pope* will break his Heart.[5]

Swift also contributed what may have been the first country house poem of mock-praise, 'To Quilca, a Country House in No Very Good Repair' (1725). This charming but brief poem satirizes the Irish estate of Thomas Sheridan, which Swift visited on several occasions. It is a brilliant catalogue of all that a country house would ideally strive not to be:

> Let me my Properties explain,
> A rotten Cabin, dropping Rain;
> Chimnies with Scorn rejecting Smoak;
> Stools, Tables, Chairs, and Bed-steds broke:
> Here Elements have lost their Uses,
> Air ripens not, nor Earth produces:

---

[5] Marble Hill House was in easy walking distance from Pope's own villa in Twickenham. A landscaping enthusiast, Pope helped to design the gardens at Marble Hill. A fascinating account of this aspect of the poet's life is Peter Martin's *Pursuing Innocent Pleasures: The Gardening World of Alexander Pope* (Archon Books, 1984).

In vain we make poor *Sheelah* toil,
Fire will not roast, nor Water boil.
Thro' all the Vallies, Hills, and Plains,
The Goddess *Want* in Triumph reigns;
And her chief Officers of State,
Sloth, *Dirt*, and *Theft* around her wait.

The satiric turn greatly expanded the country house poem's capabilities, to borrow a term from the greatest landscaper of the age. So did both the early rise of country house tourism (a custom gently satirised in *Mansfield Park*)[6] and the rapid expansion of authorship. For instance, Mary Leapor – the daughter of an estate gardener and herself in service – would write a considerable body of poems before her untimely death at 24. One of these is 'Crumble-Hall' (1748), an impressive contribution to the evolving genre. As a housemaid in Weston Park and a kitchen maid in Edgcote House, Leapor had access to the 'below stairs' perspective that has become *de rigueur* in contemporary representations of life in the country house, from *The Remains of the Day* to *Downton Abbey*. To this she adds a Gothic element, just beginning to come into favour, to her description of the interior:

> Strange Forms above, present themselves to View;
> Some Mouths that grin, some smile, and some that spew.
> ...
> The Roof – no *Cyclops* e'er could reach so high:
> Not *Polypheme*, tho' form'd for dreadful Harms,
> The Top could measure with extended Arms.
> Here the pleas'd Spider plants her peaceful Loom:
> Here weaves secure, nor dreads the hated Broom.

Only a poet in service would take such delight in vermin, or move from the feasting tables above stairs to the blazing kitchens below, or be troubled to count the many steps she climbs throughout the house, up and down, back and forth, from state rooms to 'familiar' rooms to store rooms.

With its random Gothic features, Crumble Hall may appear to be decaying; however, Leapor insists, largely from the perspective of members of its household staff, that it is a thriving and functioning estate. There is one threat to its survival: the improvements to landscape through the vision of a Capability Brown or Humphry Repton. First she seduces us with a pastoral scene we have grown accustomed to associating with the country house ('Now to those Meads

---

[6] Guidebooks to country houses began to be published frequently in the eighteenth century. *Cf.* Jocelyn Anderson, *Touring and Publicizing England's Country Houses in the Long Eighteenth Century* (Bloomsbury, 2018).

let frolick Fancy rove'), then demonstrates that such beauty comes at great cost, and that behind such capabilities are artifice and illusions of nature for which Brown and Repton were famous: 'To clear the Way for Slopes, and modern Whims, / Where banish'd Nature leaves a barren Gloom'. Evicted tree-nymphs will haunt such estates, which will eventually be abandoned: 'Their new-built Parlour shall with Ecchoes ring: / And in their Hall shall doleful Crickets sing'.

In Leapor's vision, the destruction of nature to produce the new estate and its heralded landscapes is the Gothic seed that would preoccupy the poetic imagination of the late eighteenth and early nineteenth centuries. What follows is a sharp departure from the lively and hospitable estates in poems of the seventeenth and early eighteenth centuries. Oliver Goldsmith's 'The Deserted Village' (1770) is not strictly speaking a country house poem, but rather a consideration of rural depopulation and a study in contrast 'Between a splendid and an happy land'. With an economy based on global trade and the spoils of colonialism, the *nouveaux riches* demanded country estates in keeping with those established centuries ago by the aristocracy. These estates often enclosed common lands and depopulated entire villages. A new wave of Enclosure Acts in the late eighteenth century deprived people of access to some seven million acres once devoted to common lands, sometimes from an earnest belief that it would boost agricultural productivity, but often for no better reason than to improve the vista of the wealthy landowner.[7] In 'The Deserted Village', Goldsmith relentlessly assaults the new plutocrats of Britain:

> The man of wealth and pride
> Takes up a space that many poor supplied;
> Space for his lake, his park's extended bounds,
> Space for his horses, equipage, and hounds:
> The robe that wraps his limbs in silken sloth,
> Has robbed the neighbouring fields of half their growth;
> His seat, where solitary sports are seen,
> Indignant spurns the cottage from the green;
> Around the world each needful product flies,
> For all the luxuries the world supplies.
> While thus the land adorned for pleasure, all
> In barren splendour feebly waits the fall.

In contrast with the country house poems of the seventeenth century, where the wealth of an estate was both a reflection of social order and the means of social harmony, by the late eighteenth century an estate's wealth is a blunt instrument that turns class hierarchy into social dysfunction, drives rural

---

[7] *Cf.* G. E. Mingay, *Parliamentary Enclosure in England: An Introduction to Its Causes, Incidence, and Impact, 1750–1850* (Longman, 1997).

innocence into urban corruption, and transforms a thriving village into a hollow palace. Such a Britain may be beautiful – but so is a cemetery: 'The country blooms – a garden, and a grave'.

The moral emptiness of the country house nearly destroys the genre, particularly once the lively satire of Pope has been supplanted by the lugubrious rectitude of Goldsmith. It was time again for a stylistic transformation, and what evolved in the late eighteenth and early nineteenth centuries was a splintering into distinct traditions. In most of the examples of this period we can spot a trend towards more careful observation of specific estates, with a particular interest in the house itself, as opposed to its moral and social values or its natural setting. In one of these new developments, the poet is transformed into tourist, though nonetheless an aesthete who easily appreciates the extraordinary works of art contained within the hallowed walls of the great house. Thus Thomas Warton's 'Sonnet Written after Seeing Wilton House' (1777):

> From Pembroke's princely dome, where mimic art
> Decks with a magic hand the dazzling bowers,
> Its living hues where the warm pencil pours,
> And breathing forms from the rude marble start,
> How to life's humbler scene can I depart?
> My breast all glowing from those gorgeous towers,
> In my low cell how cheat the sullen hours!
> Vain the complaint; for fancy can impart
> (To fate superior, and to fortune's doom)
> Whate'er adorns the stately-storied hall:
> She, mid the dungeon's solitary gloom,
> Can dress the graces in their Attic pall,
> Bid the green landskip's vernal beauty bloom,
> And in bright trophies clothe the twilight wall.

Another strand presents a more objective perspective – neither enamoured with the beauty of the building nor condemnatory of the estate's economy, but more empirical in perspective and meditative in tone and theme. The ethos of the aristocratic country house already seems embalmed in history and far removed from present concerns, as in Wordsworth's 'Inscription for a Seat in the Groves of Coleorton' (1811):

> Beneath yon eastern ridge, the craggy bound,
> Rugged and high, of Charnwood's forest ground
> Stand yet, but, Stranger! hidden from thy view,
> The ivied Ruins of forlorn GRACE DIEU;
> Erst a religious House, which day and night
> With hymns resounded, and the chanted rite:

And when those rites had ceased, the Spot gave birth
To honourable Men of various worth:

…

Communities are lost, and Empires die,
And things of holy use unhallowed lie;
They perish; – but the Intellect can raise,
From airy words alone, a Pile that ne'er decays.

Henry Alford's 'Haddon Hall' (1836) is in this vein; the significance of the country house lies not in 'mirrored halls, nor roofs with gilding bright, / Nor all the foolery of the rich and vain' but in how the 'grey battlements' and 'ivy-shadowed oriels' seem to give meaning to the lives of ordinary humans.

Also in this observational vein is the poem that relates the history of the estate as a kind of microcosm of a nation's history, such as George Crabbe's 'Belvoir Castle' (1812) or (in a comical variation) the 13th canto of Lord Byron's 'Don Juan' (1823). It may have been Byron who introduced the elegiac note to country house poetry. 'On Leaving Newstead Abbey' (1807) is a personal lament for the loss of the ancestral home:

Through thy battlements, Newstead, the hollow winds whistle;
    Thou, the hall of my fathers, art gone to decay;
In thy once smiling garden, the hemlock and thistle
    Have choked up the rose which late bloom'd in the way.

His 'Elegy on Newstead Abbey' (also from 1807) expands that elegiac element: a threnody for a lost world and a noble pile decaying is the nation's loss, not just the individual nobleman's.

Hail to thy pile! more honour'd in thy fall,
    Than modern mansions, in their pillar'd state;
Proudly majestic frowns thy vaulted hall,
    Scowling defiance on the blasts of fate.

…

An abbey once, a regal fortress now,
    Encircled by insulting rebel powers;
War's dread machines o'erhang thy threat'ning brow,
    And dart destruction, in sulphureous showers.

…

Ah happy days! too happy to endure!
    Such simple sports our plain forefathers knew:
No splendid vices glitter'd to allure;
    Their joys were many, as their cares were few.

Other poems used the ballad form to reclaim English history through the symbol of the country house. Alfred, Lord Tennyson's 'The Lord of Burleigh' (1842) is a narrative poem whose affect is more Gothic ballad than chronicle. A 'village maiden' marries a nobleman and is introduced to a world of

> Parks with oak and chestnut shady,
> Parks and order'd gardens great,
> Ancient homes of lord and lady,
> Built for pleasure and for state.

Alas, she dies of shame, 'With the burthen of an honour / Unto which she was not born'. A similar approach is taken in George Walter Thornbury's 'John of Padua' (1863), a ballad of the life of the architect of Longleat, whose life is given to building that extraordinary estate earlier praised by Anne Finch:

> Two hundred feet of western front,
> And chapel and turret, and acres of roof,
> And porch, and staircase, and welcoming hall,
> And gate that would keep no beggar aloof.

Tennyson introduces a new strand of country house poem that would influence twentieth-century poets. In such poems a country house provides a backdrop for a meditation or narrative that has little to do with the realities (or even fantasies) of country house life, but which functions as a heavily symbolic setting. Great houses rise in the backgrounds of 'Audley Court' and 'Locksley Hall' (both published in 1842); in the latter, a young man expresses his anxiety about the future and makes grim prophecies about humanity and technology, modern civilisation and scientific progress. Though no action occurs in Locksley Hall, the house casts figurative shadows across the poem's speaker:

> 'Tis the place, and all around it, as of old, the curlews call,
> Dreary gleams about the moorland flying over Locksley Hall;
>
> Locksley Hall, that in the distance overlooks the sandy tracts,
> And the hollow ocean-ridges roaring into cataracts.
>
> Many a night from yonder ivied casement, ere I went to rest,
> Did I look on great Orion sloping slowly to the West.

The poem was subjected to a brilliant parody by William Bromley-Davenport. 'Lowesby Hall' (*ca.* 1853) thrills in the chase even as it prophesies that fox hunting will be 'abolished by an order of the State'. Richard Cobden and the Anti-Corn Law League will bring the ruin of the Victorian landed class and their great estates:

Saw the Landlords yield their acres after centuries of wrongs
To the cotton Lords, to whom, it's proved, all property belongs.

Queen, Religion, State abandoned, and all flags of party furled
In the government of Cobden and the dotage of the world.

We have come a long way from the seventeenth-century country house poem, which embodied and celebrated an illusion of timeless patriarchal values and social structures. The fragmenting in the nineteenth century of what had once been a relatively coherent genre would become more diffuse still in the twentieth, especially as many houses began to be converted into museums and many more fell victim to the wrecking ball. A wide variety of perspectives appears in modern examples: stately exteriors and interiors, crumbling ruins, gardens both wild and cultivated, and the voices of noble owners, servants, and curious visitors who gaze at objects both beautiful and baffling – royal beds, tapestries, bell-boards, and ha-has. The contemporary poet may even see in the country house a symbol of poetry itself, as in the opening lines of Alan Brownjohn's 'The World Outside' (1975):

When poetry was a landscape art, arranging
Syllables in a noble sweep to gaze up, the vista
Was the big house of order and seclusion, stately
Between stiffly regular lines of most proper trees.
The world kept out was the goatherds and their pipes.

The concept of order was under assault in the twentieth century: aristocratic hegemony and grand estates gave way to collectivist impulses, and neat stanzas and tidy metrical patterns gave way to freer verse forms.

In an age that witnessed the rapid decline of the country house as a culture and economy and showed remarkable indifference to its architectural heritage, a dominant tone in country house poems is elegiac. One of the saddest of these is Amy Lowell's 'Appuldurcombe Park' (1917). A pall hangs over the poem, as if an entire way of life is under a sentence of death. The speaker paces 'long, cold corridors' in a lifeless country house and sits endless, comfortless hours in her garden:

I am a woman, sick for passion,
Crumbling the beech-leaves to powder in my fingers.
The servants say: 'Yes, my Lady', and 'No, my Lady'.
And all day long my husband calls me
From his invalid chair:
…
Poor little beech leaves,
Slowly falling,

Crumbling,
In the great park.

A similar loss and lament pervade Edwin Morgan's translations of Anglo-Saxon poetry. 'The Ruin' (1952) may describe a Saxon mead-hall destroyed by invading pagan hordes, but it also evokes the ongoing demolition of country houses in that decade, when more than four hundred were destroyed: 'This wall bore well, / Moss-grey and reddened, the revolutions of kingdoms'; now, alas,

> Gigantic battlements are crumbling,
> Roofs sunk in ruin, riven towers fallen,
> Gates and turrets lost, hoarfrost for mortar,
> ... And so those halls are wastes,
> The old purple stone and the tiles and wood are lying
> Scattered with the smashed roofs.

We are reminded that the destruction of country houses, particularly wanton in the 1950s, is rooted in ancient cycles of history.[8]

For many owners, the only solution was to throw open one's doors and become a living museum. In 'Stanzas on a Visit to Longleat House' (1954 – the poem may be read in full on p. 198), George Barker vituperates against the fate of the country house in our century as the 'splendours and the miseries / Of that cold illustrious shade' are transformed into a 'fouled public nest'. Longleat in this condition would be unrecognisable to Anne Finch and George Walter Thornbury, who wrote about it in earlier ages. For others, though, the country house had become a symbol of social and economic inequity. In 'Those Bastards in Their Mansions' (1993), Simon Armitage gives voice to those angry at class division, the injustices of private property, and the snobbery of 'lords and ladies in their palaces and castles'. Here the poet is both trespasser and modern Prometheus; he confesses to having forced entry, stolen a torch, 'then given heat and light to streets and houses, / told the people how to ditch their cuffs and shackles, / armed them with the iron from their wrists and ankles'.

The dominant note sounded in modern and contemporary country-house poems is not, however, anger at class division, but is instead curiously meditative about the end of the era of the landed gentry. A common fate of

---

[8] For an account of the rampant demolition of country houses in the 1950s, see John Harris, *No Voice from the Hall: Early Confessions of a Country House Snooper* (John Murray, 1998), esp. pp. 1–31. See also *The Destruction of the Country House, 1875–1975*, eds. Roy Strong, Marcus Binney, and John Harris (Thames and Hudson, 1974), a publication deriving from the 1974 exhibition by the same name at the Victoria and Albert Museum. Also noteworthy are the writings of James Lees-Milne; his twelve diaries, published between 1975 and 2005, recount his long career at the National Trust and his vital work on behalf of country houses and their owners.

the country house is that described by William Plomer in 'Now' (1972). Here the stately home is transformed into a 'dream' of 'a lost civilization' now under assault by the rapid sociological changes of the twentieth century:

> This once quiet by-road's now a by-pass.
> Her well-built house stands well back
> half hidden by trees,
> and not yet for sale.
>
> 'Rare opportunity,'
> some agent will announce,
> 'gracious detached
> character residence of older type,
> might suit institution, requires
> some modernization,'
> having been planned for
> a lost civilization.

Perhaps in anticipation of such a sale, in 'Evening in the Park' (1983) Peter Scupham revisits 'the mansions of the dead', fallen into 'ruins ruinous' or abandoned as a 'no-man's-land of cold uncertainty'. Landscapes are in disarray as 'all the garden gods have smudged into the rain', while the interiors of the big house strike the intruder as a confusion of 'trinkets' and 'baubles': 'Back at the Hall, red drugget leads the maze: / A ghostly peepshow of embroidered rooms'.

Unsurprisingly, many stately properties are preserved only through the resources of the National Trust, English Heritage, or other conservation-minded organisations. With the whittling away of the social and economic power of the upper classes, many owners willed their houses to a preservation trust, which in turn opened them to a fee-paying public to generate revenue. Poets ask us to remember the former owners of grand estates, to imagine knowing what they knew, and what we cannot. In the transformation of the country house to a museum, the old master is a spectral presence and the casual visitor has taken his place. We can only conjecture at and fantasise about the life of lordly masters. Thus the mythmaking tendency, even from historians, that results in hyperbole:

> An informed judgment would agree that English country-house life exemplified in its day the best and most balanced kind of any in the world. ... Moreover, the country-houses all over the land, in every properly constituted parish, stood above all for *responsibility*, a responsible attitude towards people locally and on a county basis, and towards society at large.[9]

---

[9] A. L. Rowse, *Heritage of Britain* (Putnam, 1977), p. 116.

Poets, we may see, are often more willing to challenge this pastoral illusion.

Although an elegiac note prevails in modern poetic treatments, our age has brought variety to the country house poem, and comic, satiric and Gothic tones appear regularly as well. Despite their diversity of voices and perspectives, modern and contemporary poets retain one common thread with their seventeenth-century forebears. In response to the rapid sociological changes of the twentieth century, our poets reflect on the country house as an architecturally, politically and culturally potent symbol and institution, whether recalling its heyday or meditating on its eclipse. This perspective resonates with particular strength in a nation that fears its greatness has evaporated, a void filled, as historian George Lichtheim put it, with 'meanness of spirit consequent upon the relentless decline of material influence and power.'[10] The perception of this void may best account for the curious frequency of the country house in modern and contemporary poetry and the magnetic influence great houses exercise upon the poet. This imaginative potency – the same effect John Greening notes in his introduction as he recollects playing in Cranford Park as a child – was succinctly catalogued by Betjeman:

> But how well one knows the feel of the presence of a big house – the planted woods which adorn the hills, the high park wall, the lodges and gates, the avenues sweeping away to hidden private splendour, the lake, the fishponds, the ice-house, the sheltered kitchen garden, the folly on the hill, the stable clock chiming over the yard a full five minutes ahead of the church clock in the village, the hunters in the paddock, the estate cottages deep in their well-worked gardens of fruit and vegetables and flowers, the neatly ordered farms and snug stack-yards, the family arms on hatchments in the church and swinging on a sign over the village inn. Today the woods are down, ruined Army huts deface the park, the gates are sold, the park wall has fallen, the church is locked …, the kitchen garden has been ploughed, the folly has disappeared, demolishers have bought all the chimney pieces and panelling of the old house and these, like its pictures and furniture, have either been sold to America or gone to adorn the board rooms of investment trusts.[11]

To poets in such an age, the country house as a symbol of declining cultural identity and economic power has fiercely maintained its enigmatic appeal. The manor is now voiceless; only the poet's pen can revive its whispering echoes.

KEVIN GARDNER

[10] 'Post-Imperial Britain', *Commentary*, October 1966, p. 71.
[11] John Betjeman, 'Men and Buildings: Country House Heritage', *Daily Telegraph* 7 April 1958, p. 6.

Illustrations

Mullioned window	22
Mausoleum, Castle Howard	24
Fountain	35
Atlas	49
Swallow	55
Topiary	56
Staircase	62
Croquet	74
Mapledurham	86
Heytesbury	99
Parley Manor	104
Wycoller	122
Gates	132
Kimbolton	135
Newstead	140
Bell-board	142
Candelabrum	152
Canna	161
Rooks	164
Highclere	182
Obelisk	187
Tutankhamun	189
Harewood	208
Swan	218
Grandfather clock	232
Down House	235
Blenheim	249
Queen Anne's Summerhouse	268
Moth	281
Moxhull Hall	289
Ha-ha	304
Avington Park	310
Fortepiano	320
Gabled House	325
Laburnum	333
Peacock feather	335
Pears	343
Cedar	348

In my beginning is my end. In succession
Houses rise and fall, crumble, are extended,
Are removed, destroyed, restored, or in their place
Is an open field, or a factory, or a by-pass.
Old stone to new building, old timber to new fires,
Old fires to ashes, and ashes to the earth
Which is already flesh, fur and faeces,
Bone of man and beast, cornstalk and leaf.
Houses live and die: there is a time for building
And a time for living and for generation
And a time for the wind to break the loosened pane
And to shake the wainscot where the field-mouse trots
And to shake the tattered arras woven with a silent motto.

T. S. Eliot,
from *East Coker*

The Stately Homes of England,
How beautiful they stand

Noël Coward,
from *The Stately Homes of England*

Insiders

Our ancient lineage we trace
Back to the cradle of the race

Noël Coward

Castle Howard

Stay traveller! With no irreverent haste
Approach the mansion of a man of taste.
Hail, Castle Howard! Hail, Vanbrugh's noble dome
Where Yorkshire in her splendour rivals Rome!
Here the proud footman to the butler bows
But kisses Lucy when she milks the cows.

Here the proud butler on the steward waits
But shares his mistress at the castle gates.
Here fifty damsels list my lady's bells,
And a whole parish in one mansion dwells.
Chef, housekeeper, and humblest houseboy, all
In due gradation of the servants' hall,
Dependent on the slightest frown or smile
Of him who holds the Earldom of Carlisle.

But what are wealth and pomp of worldly state?
To yonder mausoleum soon or late,
Up those broad steps will go great Howard's dust –
A journey no man makes before he must.

JOHN BETJEMAN

Romance of a Youngest Daughter

Who will wed the Dowager's youngest daughter,
The Captain? filled with ale?
He moored his expected boat to a stake in the water
And stumbled on sea-legs into the Hall for mating,
Only to be seduced by her lady-in-waiting,
Round-bosomed, and not so pale.

Or the thrifty burgher in boots and fancy vest
With considered views of marriage?
By the tidy scullery maid he was impressed
Who kept that house from depreciation and dirt,
But wife does double duty and takes no hurt,
So he rode her home in his carriage.

Never the spare young scholar antiquary
Who was their next resort;
They let him wait in the crypt of the Old Library
And found him compromised with a Saxon book,
Claiming his truelove Learning kept that nook
And promised sweet disport.

Desirée (of a mother's christening) never shall wed
Though fairest child of her womb;
'We will have revenge,' her injured Ladyship said,
'Henceforth the tightest nunnery be thy bed
By the topmost stair! When the ill-bred lovers come
We'll say, She is not at home.'

JOHN CROWE RANSOM

Still-Life

Through the open French window the warm sun
lights up the polished breakfast-table, laid
round a bowl of crimson roses, for one –
a service of Worcester porcelain, arrayed
near it a melon, peaches, figs, small hot
rolls in a napkin, fairy rack of toast,
butter in ice, high silver coffee pot,
and, heaped on a salver, the morning's post.

She comes over the lawn, the young heiress,
from her early walk in her garden-wood
feeling that life's a table set to bless
her delicate desires with all that's good,

that even the unopened future lies
like a love-letter, full of sweet surprise.

ELIZABETH DARYUSH

Sissinghurst

Thursday. To V.W.

A tired swimmer in the waves of time
I throw my hands up! let the surface close:
Sink down through centuries to another clime,
And buried find the castle and the rose.
   Buried in time and sleep,
   So drowsy, overgrown,
That here the moss is green upon the stone,
   And lichen stains the keep.
I've sunk into an image, water-drowned,
Where stirs no wind and penetrates no sound,
Illusive, fragile to a touch, remote,
Foundered within the well of years as deep
As in the waters of a stagnant moat.
Yet in and out of these decaying halls
I move, and not a ripple, not a quiver,
Shakes the reflection though the waters shiver,
My tread is to the same illusion bound.
Here, tall and damask as a summer flower,
Rise the brick gable and the spring tower;
      Invading Nature crawls
With ivied fingers over rosy walls,
      Searching the crevices,
Clasping the mullion, riveting the crack
      Binding the fabric crumbling to attack,
And questing feelers of the wandering fronds
Grope for interstices,
Holding this myth together under-seas,
   Anachronistic vagabonds!

And here, by birthright far from present fashion,
As no disturber of the mirrored trance
I move, and to the world above the waters
   Wave my incognisance.
For here, where days and years have lost their number,
I let a plummet down in lieu of date,
And lose myself within a slumber
   Submerged, elate.

For now the apple ripens, now the hop,
And now the clover, now the barley-crop;
Spokes bound upon a wheel forever turning,
Wherewith I turn, no present manner learning;
Cry neither 'Speed your processes!' nor 'Stop!'
I am content to leave the world awry
(Busy with politic perplexity)
If still the cart-horse at the fall of day
Clumps up the lane to stable and to hay,
And tired men go home from the immense
    Labour and Life's expense
That force the harsh recalcitrant waste to yield
Corn and not nettles in the harvest field;
This husbandry, this castle, and this I
            Moving within the deeps,
Shall be content within our timeless spell,
Assembled fragments of an age gone by,
While still the sower sows, the reaper reaps,
Beneath the snowy mountains of the sky,
And meadows dimple to the village bell.
So plods the stallion up my evening lane
And fills me with a mindless deep repose,
    Wherein I find in chain
The castle, and the pasture and the rose.
Beauty, and use, and beauty once again
Link up my scattered heart and shape a scheme
Commensurate with a frustrated dream.
The autumn bonfire smokes across the woods
And reddens in the water of the moat;
As red within the water burns the scythe,
And the moon dwindled to her gibbous tithe
    Follows the sunken sun afloat.
Green is the eastern sky and red the west;
The hop-kilns huddle under pallid hoods;
The waggon stupid stands with upright shaft,
As daily life accepts the night's arrest.
Night like a deeper sea engulfs the land,
The castle, and the meadows, and the farm;
Only the baying watch-dog looks for harm,
And shakes his chain towards the lunar brand.
In the high room where tall the shadows tilt
As candle-flames blow crooked in the draught,
The reddened sunset on the panes was spilt,

But now as black as any nomad's tent
The night-time and the night of time have blent
Their darkness, and the waters doubly sleep.
Over my head the years and centuries sweep,
      The years of childhood flown
      The centuries unknown;
I dream; I do not weep.

VITA SACKVILLE-WEST

The Manor House

'Ramshackle loveliness' was the phrase I wrote,
then cancelled and kept free for use elsewhere:
    the whole feel of the place – as much
      the countryside as his house –

is in that sense of unachieved perfection
and slight neglect that makes for beauty. It might be
    the receding lip of a stone step
      foot-worn to a wave,

or a tie-beam, the curved thew of a bough
black with pitch, or the way each block of stone
    (crudely dressed, set on the soil
      it was dug from time out of mind)

fits so closely yet roughly against stone.
I come outside and imagine him living there,
    as the wind heaves and the loaded tree
      lurches, towards the wall,

its freight of apples. In there, he draws or writes
and apple and grey stone are in his work
    as leaves and feathers are, which seem
      (ruffled in draught, the dust

blown from their pores) fresh from creation. What
is this I feel but love for the man he was
    or must have been? The river willows
      tense hard against the wind

as I drive by a rutted track for the M4:
it is only five miles off and yet (with the river,
    clear as its source, flowing between)
      might as well be a thousand.

CLIVE WILMER

Owlpen Manor

I am folded among my terraces
Like an old dog half asleep.
The sunlight tickles my chimneys.

I have never cared for grandeur.
This narrow handcarved valley fits
My casual autocracy. But I hold

What's mine. The long, undistinguished
Dynasty of Cotswold gentlemen,
Who never married cleverly, and made

Only a modest fortune in Ireland,
Suited my fancy. Owlpens, Daunts
And Stoughtons, I charmed them to a happy

Apathy. Even Margaret, my ghost of Anjou,
Pacing my Great Chamber in her high-crowned hat,
Knowing that tomorrow is Tewkesbury,

Walks in benevolence. My floorboards creak
In their infinite adjustment to time.
I have outlasted my successor on the hill,

I am permanent as the muted roar
Of white pigeons in my barn, as the drift
Of dry leaves in my ancient garden.

U. A. FANTHORPE

Dorothy Osborne in the Country

Watching the doves in the drowned park,
Every leaf dripping its colourless wax,
The shine of water over the world's face,
I envy the slightest fish in its cold pond.
I shall take the waters of Epsom for my spleen
Among high ladies and their little dogs:
Boredom is like the great clock in the hall,
It writes the hours with unchanging face.

My suitors' wheels turn upon the drive:
Sir Entail and Sir Gravitas approach –
The one owns all a lake and half a shire,
The other is tone deaf and keeps a choir.
The wet birds still sing and dare to love.
Easy to arm against melancholy,
Hard to be true hearted at midnight
Alone in England under uncertain stars.

Fortune is a horse that must be ridden,
Fear a curtain to be pushed aside.
Birds build in soundest branches,
Precepts of love hang all about my eyes.
In a field a boy fights the wind
Whipping his kite to a corner of the sky,
The string still holds and the proud frame
Turns its cheek upon the dangerous air.

PETER PORTER

Peter Wentworth in Heaven

The trees have all gone from the grounds of my manor –
the plums, quinces, close-leaved pears –
where I walked in the orchard, planning my great speech;
and the house gone too. No matter.

My *Pithie Exhortation* still exists –
go and read it in your British Library.
I have discussed it here with your father;
he was always a supporter of free speech.

The trouble it brought me it is not in my nature
to regret. Only for my wife I grieved:
she followed me faithfully into the Tower;
her bones lie there, in St Peter ad Vincula.

I would not have gone home to Lillingstone Lovell,
if my friends had gained my release, without her,
'my chiefest comfort in this life, even
the best wife that ever poor gentleman enjoyed'.

She was a Walsingham; her subtle brother
was the Queen's man; he guarded his own back.
Any fellow-feeling he may once have cherished
for our cause he strangled in his bosom.

I was too fiery a Puritan for him.
His wife remembered mine in her will:
'to my sister Wentworthe a payre of sables'.
Not so Francis: he was no brother to us.

Well, we are translated to a different life,
my loyal Elizabeth and I.
We walk together in the orchards of Heaven –
a place I think you might find surprising.

But then you found me surprising too
when you got some notion of me, out of books.
Read my *Exhortation*, and my *Discourse*;
so you may understand me when we come to meet.

FLEUR ADCOCK

Twilight

The Fourteenth Earl is shivering,
in what the Americans would call his tuxedo,
at the lip of the fountain.
The moon is cold as justice, broken in lights:
his life in little white fragments,
winking leerily. The guests at the party
are guzzling, gossiping, fornicating
with reckless abandon: a dance through
the twilight of the aristocracy.
His mind fuddles. When did they start to be
this huge parody, this backdrop for a costume
binge shot lovingly in endless episodes
and financed by the fashion industry?

There was a girl once. He remembers
her white body. She laughed at him, decamped
with his money – or what was left
after the courts and the divorce, the bouts
with the vulturine attorney.
A nymph beckons. To reach her he must swim,
or wade at least. Her marble kiss
thrills through his teeth. Tomorrow the police
will halt their cars on the gravel.
The warrant will prove unnecessary: the last
of the guests will have dragged him,
sack-like, into the buttery, leaving
anonymously, before the questions start.
Leaving the long wet marks on the floor and
the green shape of a man on the dew-soaked grass.

STUART HENSON

Daisy at the Court

'Arithmetic and manners, start with those':
And he had left her on the stair
And gone off after partridges, small bundles
Of feathers you'd tread on before they'd move.

So this was it. A house as long as a street,
Stone lions, and the Welsh language
In a shield on the portico. One of the children
Already pawed the darkness under her skirt.

In a newspaper once she had wondered
At the Cherokee leader who claimed
The worst part of exile was having nowhere
To bury your dead. 'Yes,' she murmured,

Picturing homesickness as a white
Lily, one of those flowers grown
For the graveside, a field of lilies
Whose perfume was a secret shared only by herself.

'This isn't home,' breathed the nanny, a girl
Whom no child had sucked, thinking of
The charcoal ovens in Dean, no bigger
Than beehives, the warmer vowels:

This was foreign, even the bread was strange,
And at dinner the men came out
Of the greenhouses and looked at you when
Your back was turned. Especially the ones with wives.

And yet. There was Ivor, most often Ive,
(Christian names in this country split in half)
Who saluted every morning, except once,
When his hands were cupped for her in a nest

Of blond apricots; who had walked her down
To a corner of the long garden,
Where water was spun across terraces,
Looped and stretched over rocks, before falling

Like a roll of silk into a pool.
'This is a palace,' he had said. 'At Catterick
We slept fifty to the barrack-room
And still the windows froze on the inside:

'In the village we cut the avenue
Of elms, a hundred years old, for firewood;
There's some eat only gooseberries and milk.
But here is a place hard times don't touch.'

She had looked at him then and felt
All the ghostly answers of a sum unwritten,
As the Wolseley bit into the drive's gravel
And a man leaped out and strode towards her.

ROBERT MINHINNICK

Plas Difancoll

1

Trees, of course, silent attendants,
though no more silent than footmen
at the great table, ministering shadows
waiting only to be ignored.

Leaves of glass, full of the year's
wine, broken repeatedly and
as repeatedly replaced.
A garden ventilated by cool

fountains. Two huge lions
of stone, rampant at the drive
gates, intimidating no-one
but those lately arrived

and wondering whether they are too early.
Between hillsides the large house,
classical and out of place
in the landscape, as Welsh as

it is unpronounceable. He
and she, magnificent both, not least
in the confidence of their ignorance
of the insubordination of the future.

2

Down to two servants now and those
grown cheeky; unvisited any more

by the county. The rust of autumn
outside on the landscape and inside in the joints

of these hangers-on. Time running out
for them here in the broken hour-glass

that they live in with its cracked
windows mirroring a consumptive moon.

The fish starve in their waters or
are pilfered from them by the unpunished trespassers

from away. The place leans on itself,
sags. There is a conspiracy of the ivy

to bring it down, with no prayers
going up from the meeting-house for its salvation.

3
The owls' home and the starlings',
with moss bandaging its deep wounds
to no purpose, for the wind festers in
them and the light diagnoses
impartially the hopelessness
of its condition. Colonialism
is a lost cause. Yet the Welsh
are here, picnicking among the ruins
on their Corona and potato
crisps, speaking their language without pride,
but with no backward look over the shoulder.

R. S. THOMAS

The Ballroom at Blaxter Hall

We might be anywhere but are in one place only.
— Derek Mahon

Here is the home of lost romance,
where gilded chairs are stiffly paired,
each uppermost inverted, legs in air
to tent the dust-sheets, hammocking the dust.

The grand piano, like a catafalque
to house the still form of Despair,
is also sheeted, and attempts a groan.
The fireplace yawns. The afternoon

outside is always almost dusk,
and cocked like an enormous ear
to catch the whisper of a waterfall.
With only cobwebs to support its bulk,

a bagged and massive chandelier –
the wasps' nest of a glass-swarm – hangs prepared
to drop at once if you should call
for wine and roses, or the chance to dance.

PETER BENNET

Sir Frederick

Stiffly Sir Frederick
Stumps the green cobble-stones,
Opens the gate
By the stable door,
Hums as he strolls
In the pale of the afternoon
A faded old song
Of the First World War.

He lifts up his feet
Like a stork by the river bed,
Treads the long grass
Where the narcissi lean,
Plucks perhaps six or seven,
And at a sting-nettle
Strikes with his infantry-
Officer's cane.

Then in the library
Of his great mansion,
Books at attention
On every shelf,
Shakily signs his name
In his biography,
Serves tea and Dundee cake,
Has some himself.

Just as I drive away
I catch a glimpse of him
Dodging as best he can
Bullets of rain,
And as a thunder-clap
Bursts like a howitzer
He melts in the history
Books once again.

CHARLES CAUSLEY

The Grange

Oh there hasn't been much change
At the Grange,

Of course the blackberries growing closer
Makes getting in a bit of a poser,
But there hasn't been much change
At the Grange.

Old Sir Prior died,
They say on the point of leaving for the seaside,
They never found the body, which seemed odd to some
(Not me, seeing as what I seen the butler done.)

Oh there hasn't been much change
At the Grange.

The governess 'as got it now,
Miss Ursy 'aving moved down to the Green Cow –
Proper done out of 'er rights she was, a b. shame,
And what's that the governess pushes round at nights in the old
    pram?

Oh there hasn't been much change
At the Grange.

The shops leave supplies at the gate now, meat, groceries,
Mostly old tinned stuff you know from McInnes's,
They wouldn't go up to the door,
Not after what happened to Fred's pa.

Oh there hasn't been much change
At the Grange.

Parssing there early this morning, cor lummy,
I 'ears a whistling sound coming from the old chimney,
Whistling it was fit to bust and not a note wrong,
The old pot, whistling The Death of Nelson.

No there hasn't been much change
At the Grange,

But few goes that way somehow,
Not now.

STEVIE SMITH

from *Sir Osbert's Complaint*

For Catherine Byron

Part One

1

When a thousand coal-gas crocuses ignite like pilot lights
In the grass between the tree trunks, and the scented air excites
Both the senses and the intellect, we long for shorter nights.

2

By the time they've flickered out the air is warmer by degrees
And, depressing though the drizzle is, at least it doesn't freeze.
There's a feeling of renewal on the saturated breeze.

3

Sure enough, the afternoons become reluctant to give way
To the moment when our nanny calls us children in from play
And we dawdle by the door before relinquishing the day.

4

Not that play was what we did when out of sight and out of mind.
If a child had the effrontery to ask us, we declined.
Given books instead of playthings, we were not the playing kind.

5

The society our parents kept we mimicked in our own:
Their jejune, dogmatic arguments; that hyperbolic tone;
And the scenes we'd seen two adults act without a chaperone.

6

But our parodies were arid: we forgot to be amused.
The lampoon and the reality were hopelessly confused.
We became the very adults we'd complacently abused.

Part Two

7

A new century came in. The motorcar replaced the horse.
Every bath we took was heated by the coal mine at its source.
(The industrial's the only revolution I endorse.)

8

Oily rainbows on the fishpond, flaky cinders on the lake,
Claggy slagheaps on the skyline and domestics on the take –
Yet there's nothing in Arcadia that our gardens couldn't fake.

9

At a distance from reality the hedges lead the eye
Into Italy or ancient Greece beneath a leaden sky,
With a fountain or a temple to identify them by.

10

Though our daffodils are hardly more Italian than the Swedes,
Cultivating them is more a deed of habit than Candide's.
What would make it more Italianate would be a clump of weeds.

11

Every vista has a gist, a sort of statement of a creed,
Unbelievable in beauty but in logic guaranteed
To attract one to the factor to which all perspectives lead.

12

Never accurate, the sun-dial is a wiser judge of time
Than the most acute chronometer's mechanic pantomime.
Tempus fugit says enough, obscured by moss and hardened slime.

Part Three

13

Conversational location shaped the content of our talk.
Disagreements were concluded by a choice where footpaths fork,
The direction of our thoughts by the direction of the walk.

14

It was easy to escape whatever choking atmosphere
Was reducing them to silence in the adult stratosphere:
Any path or passageway could make an infant disappear.

15

Mother Nature, as we knew her, had an organising mettle,
Like a nanny. Telling stories to enthral us, she would settle
Our anxieties with posies. We knew nothing of the nettle.

16

I was not so much a bookworm as a bookish sort of leech,
Draining books of every corpuscle of what they had to teach.
(I had heard the mermen singing, in my daydreams, each to each.)

17

I remember with relief a play I wrote while still a child:
Not a word did it contain but what I stole from Oscar Wilde.
It was torn up by my sister, whose good taste it had defiled.

18

Though precocious as a reader, as a writer I was slow.
Masquerading as an author, I mistook the easy flow
Of my nib for wit, parading everything I didn't know.

Part Four

19

With the loyalty a Boyar feels for sullen Mother Russia,
One attempts to save one's ancestry from time's remorseless crusher.
What the Sitwells feel for Renishaw, the Ushers felt for Usher.

20

When a home's been in your family this long, you feel related
To each Godforsaken stone. And that's the very thing I hated:
Like my brother it was haunted, like my sister crenellated.

21

It's the typical estate: a country house in formal grounds,
Rambling woods, a lake to boat on, open fields to ride to hounds,
A view beyond to wooded hillsides, the horizon out of bounds.

22

Like the dynasty it serves, rough-hewn by long vicissitude,
Irrespective of the point from which its oddity is viewed,
The aesthetic of the building is by any standard crude.

23

Where you might expect a doorway, there's a brutal chimneystack,
Like a boxer's broken nose on which you dare not turn your back.
Yet the building seems defensive as if tensed for an attack.

24

Horizontal, squat, as grey as Sheffield's weather, this façade
Serves as backdrop to the lives we act out under the regard
Of the statues on the lawn, our audience and bodyguard.

Part Five

25

What with Sachy holding back, and what with Edith holding forth,
With yours truly in the middle, holding little of much worth,
We established all the habits that would mark our time on Earth.

26

We enjoyed ourselves, though sober in the thrust of our hilarity:
For such purpose as we had was to abolish a disparity
By donating Sitwell brilliance to the national culture's charity.

27

Our modernity was earnest. We conducted an impassioned
Celebration of the new – but we preferred our newness rationed.
Though mere novelty wears off, you can rely on the old-fashioned.

28

In the country we conducted our concerns by candlelight
Well into the nineteen-fifties, and kept faith with anthracite.
Reading verse through megaphones would hardly put the past to flight.

29

What we managed as a trio we could not have done apart.
We were thought of as a single beast, a Cerberus of art,
Whose three contrapuntal voices represented just one heart.

30

All for one and one for all!… I was distracted from this course
By a fourth, one David Horner. Our affair involved, perforce,
Being granted from my siblings an emotional divorce.

GREGORY WOODS

A Household

When, to disarm suspicious minds at lunch
Before coming to the point, or at golf,
The bargain driven, to soothe hurt feelings,

He talks about his home, he never speaks
(A reticence for which they all admire him)
Of his bride so worshipped and so early lost,

But proudly tells of that young scamp his heir,
Of black eyes given and received, thrashings
Endured without a sound to save a chum;

Or calls their spotted maleness to revere
His saintly mother, calm and kind and wise,
A grand old lady pouring out the tea.

Whom, though, has he ever asked for the week-end?
Out to his country mansion in the evening,
Another merger signed, he drives alone:

To be avoided by a miserable runt
Who wets his bed and cannot throw or whistle,
A tell-tale, a crybaby, a failure;

To the revilings of a slatternly hag
Who caches bottles in her mattress, spits
And shouts obscenities from the landing;

Worse, to find both in an unholy alliance,
Youth stealing Age the liquor-cupboard key,
Age teaching Youth to lie with a straight face.

Disgraces to keep hidden from the world
Where rivals, envying his energy and brains
And with rattling skeletons of their own,

Would see in him the villain of this household,
Whose bull-voice scared a sensitive young child,
Whose coldness drove a doting parent mad.

Besides (which might explain why he has neither
Altered his will nor called the doctor in),
He half believes, call it a superstition,

It is for his sake that they hate and fear him:
Should they unmask and show themselves worth loving,
Loving and sane and manly, he would die.

W. H. AUDEN

A Vacant Possession

In a short time we shall have cleared the gazebo.
Look how you can scrape the weeds from the paving stones
With a single motion of the foot. Paths lead down
Past formal lawns, orchards, notional guinea-fowl
To where the house is entirely obscured from view.

And there are gravel drives beneath the elm-tree walks
On whose aquarium green the changing weather
Casts no shadow. Urns pour their flowers out beside
A weathered Atlas with the whole world to support.
Look, it is now night and there are lights in the trees.

The difficult guest is questioning his rival.
He is pacing up and down while she leans against
A mossy water-butt in which, could we see them,
Innumerable forms of life are uncurving.
She is bravely not being hurt by his manner

Of which they have warned her. He taps his cigarette
And brusquely changes the subject. He remembers
Something said earlier which she did not really mean.
Nonsense – she did mean it. Now he is satisfied.
She has bitten the quick of her thumb-nail, which bleeds.

What shall we do the next day? The valley alters.
You set out from the village and the road turns around,
So that, in an hour, behind a clump of oak-trees,
With a long whitewashed wall and a low red-tiled roof
Peaceful, unevenly they appear again.

The square, the café seats, the doorways are empty
And the long grey balconies stretch out on all sides.
Time for an interlude, evening in the country,
With distant cowbells providing the angelus.
But we are interrupted by the latest post.

'Of course you will never understand. How could you?
You had everything. Everything always went well
For you. If there was a court at which I could sue you
I should take you for every memory you have.
No doubt you are insured against your murdered friends.'

Or: 'We see very little of Hester these days.
Why don't you come home? Your room is as you left it.
I went in yesterday, looking for notepaper,
And – do you know – the noose is still over the bed!
Archie says he will bring it out to you this summer.'

On warm spring afternoons, seated in the orchard,
The smocked, serious students develop grave doubts
About Pascal's wager. Monsieur le Curé stays
Chatting till midnight over the porcelain stove.
The last of his nine proofs lie smouldering in the grate.

I have set up my desk in an old dressing-room
So that the shadow of the fig-tree will be cast
On this page. At night, on the mountain opposite,
The beam of approaching cars is seen in the sky.
And now a slamming door and voices in the hall,

Scraping suitcases and laughter. Shall I go down?
I hear my name called, peer over the bannister
And remember something I left in my bedroom.
What can it have been? The window is wide open.
The curtains move. The light sways. The cold sets in.

JAMES FENTON

Milgate

Yearly, connubial swallows nest
in the sky-flung gutter and stop its mouth.
It is a natural life. Nettles
subdue the fugitive violet's bed,
a border of thistles hedges the drive;
children dart like minnows. They dangle
over the warm, reedy troutbrook.

It's a crime
to get too little from too much.

In mirage, meadow turns to lawn,
in the dredged cowpond, weed is water,
half-naked children beautify,
feud and frighten the squabbling ducks –
from vacation to vacation,
they broaden out to girls, young ladies,
a nightlife on two telephones.

The elderflower is champagne.

Age goes less noticed in humbler life –
the cedar of Lebanon dumbly waves
one defoliated millennial stump;
the yew row, planted under Cromwell
with faith and burnish, keeps its ranks,
unpierceably stolid, young, at ease.

August flames in the rusty sorrel,
a bantam hen hatches wild pheasant chicks,
the dog licks ice cream from a cone;
but mostly the cropped, green, sold-off pastures
give grace to the house, to *Milgate Park*,
its name and service once one in Bearsted,
till uselessness brought privacy,
splendor, extravagance, makeshift
offered at auction for its bricks –
yet for a moment saved by you,
and kept alive another decade,
by your absentminded love,

your lapwing's instinctive elegance,
the glue of your obdurate Ulster will –
Milgate,
enclosures to sun and space to cool,
one mural varied in fifty windows,
sublime and cozy, stripped of creeper,
its severity a blaze of salmon-pink,
its long year altered by our small ...
easy to run as things made to run.

ROBERT LOWELL

Coole Park, 1929

I meditate upon a swallow's flight,
Upon an aged woman and her house,
A sycamore and lime tree lost in night
Although that western cloud is luminous,
Great works constructed there in nature's spite
For scholars and for poets after us,
Thoughts long knitted into a single thought,
A dance-like glory that those walls begot.

There Hyde before he had beaten into prose
That noble blade the Muses buckled on,
There one that ruffled in a manly pose
For all his timid heart, there that slow man,
That meditative man, John Synge, and those
Impetuous men, Shawe-Taylor and Hugh Lane,
Found pride established in humility,
A scene well set and excellent company.

They came like swallows and like swallows went,
And yet a woman's powerful character
Could keep a swallow to its first intent;
And half a dozen in formation there,
That seemed to whirl upon a compass-point,
Found certainty upon the dreaming air,
The intellectual sweetness of those lines
That cut through time or cross it withershins.

Here, traveller, scholar, poet, take your stand
When all those rooms and passages are gone,
When nettles wave upon a shapeless mound
And saplings root among the broken stone,
And dedicate – eyes bent upon the ground,
Back turned upon the brightness of the sun
And all the sensuality of the shade –
A moment's memory to that laurelled head.

W. B. YEATS

Song to Mark a Boundary

for the Blands at Augop

In these tall trees warbler and wren all day
Beat boundaries of music, marking a province.
The song of birds is functional, they say:
This year at least its function is delight
For you in a new-built house, here tasting a first May.
The notes seem colour of spring made into sound:
Viridian leaves of beech, and powdery gay
Yellow of hornbeam, all that your window sees;
Green slopes and golden kingcups for the play
Of evening light, where the obedient trees
Compose a parkland picture; far away
The hills of Radnor Forest – I name them yours,
For the eye possesses what it can survey.

New come, and well come now to the birds' kingdom
This mortal nest – newcomer but no rival.
My poem too is functional: I sing
To claim your territory, and to pray
A blessing on your house, and on your stay.

ANNE RIDLER

The Topiarist

Imperceptibly his art has hedged him in
With the company of pampered shapes
And you are hedged out with bosky formality.
No, he has no room for riotous beds
Or the cold fixity of statues
Whose sapless forms he cannot pare –
And if – approaching leafy battlements,
You were to say something colourful to him
Like *Gnomes* or *Toadstools*,
There is no knowing to what lengths his tongue
May run from underneath his hat's straw brim.

Where you stand, beyond his care, days run
Footloose and dangerous with untethered forms;
But where he moves, light is shed on living order
And even darkness does not halt his slow green art –
For then the world is undoubtedly a perfect sphere
Turning easily on branchy axis – and he is no more
Than its attendant moth hovering in a well-kept universe.

FREDA DOWNIE

Mistress

There's always been someone to hide
inside hollow walls and sliding oak panels:
a divine of the heretic religion,
the family simpleton with their mooning face.

I used to frighten myself at midnight feasts
telling tales of nuns sealed up in cells
for devotion's sake, or some unspeakable sin.
When I slept, my eyes closed over their bones.

Every house contains a room that doesn't exist
where we find ourselves almost at home
behind this skim of horsehair plaster,
the roses breathing into your ear.

ESTHER MORGAN

Service

For X, in service,
    probably not lovely,
        no one's daughter
            in particular,

who lost her hours
    of daylight on her knees
        to a gritstone floor,
            never raising her eyes

but to climb to an attic
    by a back stair, glad
        of a share of a mattress,
            too knackered to dream …

for her, and all the others,
    this:
        the old scullery floor
        is cracking up.

A flagstone
    four men could not lift
        has buckled and split.
        A hundred years

it's taken it, but look,
    a mushroom!
        Pale white skin
            as soft as yours.

This is her flesh,
    a musty taste
        of earth, but sweet.
            In memory of X …

take, eat.

PHILIP GROSS

Baize Doors

She had forgotten the bellows again
and the family was due back from church.
Her mind was on the gardener's boy,

who'd left her in the lurch
the Friday before: without his reference,
leaving only a collar stud behind

at the back of a paper-lined drawer,
and that drawn length of linen blind
which curtsied gently in her hand

then vanished when she let it go.
She knew that she must be alive
by her breath on the window

when she deliberately adjusted
an hairpin, before going downstairs.
The bellows were kept in the kitchen

beyond the bottle-green baize
where the floral carpet stopped
and the stone steps started.

No one had ever fallen before.
The under-cook was broken-hearted
about the blood and slipped

a *Reynold's News* between her floor
and the opened skull. Morgan, the valet,
was dispatched for the doctor,

who turned the face to find
a phrenologist's head: the stop press
transferred backwards on the brain.

The gardener's boy was on her mind.
A pair of bellows prayed in the hearth.
The kitchen fire fell to its death.

CRAIG RAINE

Song of a Past Scullery-Maid

Let origano – so
The mistress calls wild marjoram – be
Stuck a-plenty
In my window.

Worn out by soap and scrub-brush,
And my naked feet
Bruised by stone flags,
I want the smell of the old gardener's sweet
Potting-shed: there hide my rags
And arms in its dim, earthy hush.

And when at last I go
And need some blooms to smother me,
If season's right, may parson see
They're from the wild white gean tree.

SHEILA WINGFIELD

Servant Boy

He is wintering out
the back-end of a bad year,
swinging a hurricane-lamp
through some outhouse,

a jobber among shadows.
Old work-whore, slave-
blood, who stepped fair-hills
under each bidder's eye

and kept your patience
and your counsel, how
you draw me into
your trail. Your trail

broken from haggard to stable,
a straggle of fodder
stiffened on snow,
comes first-footing

the back doors of the little
barons: resentful
and impenitent,
carrying the warm eggs.

SEAMUS HEANEY

Ghosts & Echoes

And people who come to call
Meet her in the hall.

Noël Coward

Haunted House

At six the furniture begins to fade.
Slit trenches' mouths gleam stickily along
The Axminster. Fixed bayonets look out
From cupboards. Gas and cordite tinge the air.
Hats turn to helmets as they hang. Outside
Hillocks of quicklime wait to hold the dead.

Children don't find this house by chance. A brown
Obsequious mongrel bitch seduces them
Into the magic garden, where faint smoke
Curls round the lily leaves. The oriole,
Night heron, bustard, bee-eater, composed
And friendly, eye their visitors with grace
And never move away. Strange trees extend
Embroidered hands. The air purrs with desire.

This stair promises something. Painted heads
Smile in its angles. Glowing shoulders, lace,
Arms, ringlets, sapphires, eyes, attest some force.
Concealed among the bosoms, spiky heads
Of Samurai, speared, tiger-whiskered, peer
In search of enemies twin to themselves.

At last, the lady and her room. Tea waits;
Smart bread-and-butter; polished brandysnaps;
Hands patrol teacups; angel cake presides;
Gentleman's relish sounds a richer note.
The children eat and drink. The day grows dark.
At six the furniture begins to fade.

U. A. FANTHORPE

The Pier-Glass

Lost manor where I walk continually
A ghost, though yet in woman's flesh and blood.
Up your broad stairs mounting with outspread fingers
And gliding steadfast down your corridors
I come by nightly custom to this room,
And even on sultry afternoons I come
Drawn by a thread of time-sunk memory.

Empty, unless for a huge bed of state
Shrouded with rusty curtains drooped awry
(A puppet theatre where malignant fancy
Peoples the wings with fear). At my right hand
A ravelled bell-pull hangs in readiness
To summon me from attic glooms above
Service of elder ghosts; here, at my left,
A sullen pier-glass, cracked from side to side,
Scorns to present the face (as do new mirrors)
With a lying flush, but shows it melancholy
And pale, as faces grow that look in mirrors.

Is there no life, nothing but the thin shadow
And blank foreboding, never a wainscot rat
Rasping a crust? Or at the window-pane
No fly, no bluebottle, no starveling spider?
The windows frame a prospect of cold skies
Half-merged with sea, as at the first creation –
Abstract, confusing welter. Face about,
Peer rather in the glass once more, take note
Of self, the grey lips and long hair dishevelled,
Sleep-staring eyes. Ah, mirror, for Christ's love
Give me one token that there still abides
Remote – beyond this island mystery,
So be it only this side Hope, somewhere,
In streams, on sun-warm mountain pasturage –
True life, natural breath; not this phantasma.

ROBERT GRAVES

While Reading a Ghost Story

Opening my window for a breath of air
I meet the midnight cold, and am aware
Of wind-shook trees and harmless lonely stars.
There's nothing monstrous moving; nothing mars
This friendly blustering of mid-winter gloom.
    Behind me, in the comfort of my room,
    A story I've been reading lies half read …
    Corrupt revisitation by the dead.

Old houses have their secrets. Passions haunt them.
When day's celestials go, abhorred ones taunt them.
Inside our habitations darkness dwells.
While dusk of dawn is on the unwatched stair
And lofty windows whiten strangely – there
What presence thins – with what frustrated spells?

SIEGFRIED SASSOON

A Haunted House

There are clues everywhere.
A caravan is parked
in the old parlour.
They are growing thyme
and tarragon against the wall.

Someone is out, calling
the animals. Indoors,
alcoves lead to nothing
in particular. A blocked
window above the stairs,

traces of half-timbering
over the hall. In the green
room, remains of Regency
wallpaper: fleur-de-lis
on eau-de-nil. A backdrop.

The hunt is off the scent
in the long gallery; dogs
raise their noses from a tide
of whitewashed reeds.
Nothing is only itself:

the house is a sampler.
In an early engraving
a man in a morning-coat
retreats swiftly into the hall.
The chimney is crooked already;

the curved white mermaids
over the door watch swimmingly
over the fields, which are their fields,
over the farm. The sun is setting
through the orchard; someone

is out, calling the animals.
Like drought-photography,
sun-down reveals the line
of the moat, the foundations
of a barn. And the animals,

taking the place in their stride:
an eyeful of peacocks trampling
the tarragon; sheep flowing
through the stony moat,
squaring up to the vanished

yard. The dead cats, Quince,
Olly and Ragtime are dancing
like light over bricks left out
to dry for the first building
of the hall. Doves pass over

in a loose-leaved fan;
rooks gather round the oaks
in the moat. The sky is dark
with cries; they are all out
calling the animals, but

the sun forges walls to red
umber, to burnt sienna, and tilts
at windows as if, given purchase,
it would course through the house
as through a shell, emblazoning

rafters and licking life into
the painted dogs in the gallery
until they too give tongue,
raising the roof and calling,
calling the animals home.

JANE GRIFFITHS

In the Castle

What, then, are these three things of the thing?
         – Jacques Derrida

When I visited the castle and read about what had happened there –
a nobleman tricked into meeting to sort out some differences,
the guidebook was vague on what or why,
but he was in his nightclothes, had just finished his supper,
the girl who came to clear the table was in on it,
still she felt her throat ache as she watched him unfold the note,
his eyes brightening as he read it,
he was getting tired of all this aggravation,
there might after all be something to be said for a quiet life,
she thought of warning him, but no, impossible,
so she went on loading the silver tray, a family piece,
his grandmother had brought it from the old country,
it was engraved with peacocks,
under strange weeping trees which were dropping their fruit,
if you looked closely you could see some rotting on the ground,
there was even a crown of flies over it,
and he fussed about, re-tying his robe, pomading his hair,
the mirror he used was the one I was looking into now,
scratched and blown like a winter pond thawed and refrozen,
and all the time she knew they were here,
whispering in the kitchen,
she fingered the key in her apron pocket,
and they would take the back stairs, enter without knocking,
one leading the way with a bow then stepping aside,
to let the next through with his long knife,
and it was going dark in the knot garden,
and the tea-room was closing,
they were stacking the chairs and cashing up the till,
and everything was turning away from the light,
taking this room with it,
the old duke, and those who wanted him dead,
the mirror, the girl with the key, the smoky fire in the grate,
the silver fruit devoured by flies the only token of summer –
then I thought about the lovely words dusk and November,
and all the other words,
stacked hard against the door as if they could keep it shut.

JEAN SPRACKLAND

The Ruined Garden

These are the foundations. Roots of walls
Map out the careful pattern of a home.
The great house seems so curiously small.

The south view is magnificent: the downs
Merge gently into mist, if you could see.
Now giant rhododendrons block the light
And blossom at the unresponsive sky.

Round the great lawn, ornamental trees
Have overreached themselves. A colony
Of rooks invades the intermingled boughs,
Applauds a ruined aristocracy.

Wealth and Empire, bland extravagance,
The wasteful whims and pleasures of the rich:
These are the foundations.

NEIL POWELL

Walmer Castle

Leaves of summer
Strong and green
That gusts have strewn
Across his lawn
A lower wind
Sweeps in a line
Now, neat as a windscreen-
Wiper, on.
Wellington here
Asleep in his chair
Whisped his last breath
Into east Kent air.
(His mask after death
With no false teeth in
Is unsparing, unkind.)

Dismissive, that wind
Rolls summer, a window-blind,
Up. I see out
To a yew-sheltered clearing.
See where I sit
A father with sons
Both nearly grown
Now, thinking of bronze
Masks and my own
Life, the unsparing
Wind of it.
Watching the season
Sweep round our feet
Cross as a barman
Impatient to shut.

P. J. KAVANAGH

In Blenheim Park

The statue of the first Duke of Marlborough

Shadows the shape of islands paraphrase
White racing clouds; dragonflies dart and climb
In mail of lapis lazuli and lime,
While gardeners watch a heaped-up bonfire blaze,
Joggers raise dust on ancient public ways
And pheasants flee a tractor just in time;
Pointillist light-cells in the River Glyme
Dazzle then melt into the Great Lake's glaze;
But, cast in lead, the Duke is on his column
And streaked by lumpen pigeons as they rise,
His shoulders hunched atop that soaring phallus,
With lifted torch, hip jutting, camply solemn,
Absurdly high above the trees, his eyes
Averted from his famous draughty palace.

KIERON WINN

Shrine for a Young Soldier, Castle Drogo

Easy to pick out, Gioconda-faced:
here he crouches in Oxford sepia-blue;
here in the Eton Boys' XI;
here in a family portrait, in casuals;

here in straitening khaki, moustached like a man,
clutching a bayonet proudly: Major Drewe.
'With the Angels in Heaven'.

The day the letter arrived from the Front
the butler stood silent behind the door;
the maids waited, eyes blank, and prayed for their masters
in their cluttered living room, newspapers spread with the War.

The golden child rancid in mud
and horror brought home like a catkill left
on a worn-through scullery floor.

RORY WATERMAN

Soap Suds

This brand of soap has the same smell as once in the big
House he visited when he was eight: the walls of the bathroom open
To reveal a lawn where a great yellow ball rolls back through a hoop
To rest at the head of a mallet held in the hands of a child.

And these were the joys of that house: a tower with a telescope;
Two great faded globes, one of the earth, one of the stars;
A stuffed black dog in the hall; a walled garden with bees;
A rabbit warren; a rockery; a vine under glass; the sea.

To which he has now returned. The day of course is fine
And a grown-up voice cries Play! The mallet slowly swings,
Then crack, a great gong booms from the dog-dark hall and the ball
Skims forward through the hoop and then through the next and then

Through hoops where no hoops were and each dissolves in turn
And the grass has grown head-high and an angry voice cries Play!
But the ball is lost and the mallet slipped long since from the hands
Under the running tap that are not the hands of a child.

LOUIS MacNEICE

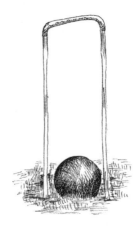

Blown Hilcote Manor

In perfect June we reached the house to let,
In remote woodland, up a private lane,
Beyond a pond that seemed as black as jet
Whereon a moorhen oared with chickens twain;
And from the first a sense of want or debt
Seemed to possess the place from ancient pain.

Then, turning Right, we had the House in view,
A red Victorian brick – with earlier stone,
Fair, but unhappy, being overgrown
With all the greenness Summer ever grew.
Above, about, the Summer sky was blue,
And drowsy doves intoned their purrilone.

But though abundant Summer shed her grace,
A look sufficed, to tell a wanderer there
That Death and Sorrow of Soul had hurt the place,
Stricken its life and plucked its glory bare.
No tick of time, no bell-chime, charmed the air;
The clock had stopped; we saw an empty case.

The House was dead, with doors and windows shut.
No chimney smoked; no broom, no bucket, plied;
Under the pampas at the border-side
A humping rabbit shewed a flash of scut.
How many Summers since the lawn was cut?
I plucked the door-bell's pull; no bell replied.

Then, as I sought another door, a sense
Startled my mind, a sense my comrade shared,
That all the House was glad, because suspense
(Long there) was finished, and a peace declared.
Blank on the uncut grass the windows stared,
But, oh, delighted souls were gazing thence.

A tall French-window in a garden room
Was latchless and ajar; we entered in.
The place seemed full of folk, expecting whom?
A Household mustered there, expecting kin ...
Someone most dear, perhaps estranged by sin,
Or lacking absolution from the tomb.

Through open doors we looked into rooms bare
All, sensibly inhabited with glee,
And happy folk seemed coming down the stair
From sunny bedrooms in eternity,
Although we might not talk with them nor see
We felt the joy they wanted us to share.

The Manor brimmed with happiness unknown
From sorrows ending and beloved return.
Death having perished, hell was overthrown,
And spirits there made festal fires burn,
And ours, too, for, did we not discern
Love, living on, not dying all alone?

Men in their misery forever pray
For any gleam, for any certain ray,
From light beyond the mirk they struggle through.
This certainty of living love we knew
At Hilcote Manor, off the Icknield Way,
On Monday, June the sixth, in 'thirty two.

JOHN MASEFIELD

That House

Remember that house. To what end
did all that brightness shine? A bitter
woman at a bland party, the man
digging out her yorkers, the worn
smiles, the dry dry sherry. And behind them
framed acres of English idyll, the totally
unhelpful Eastern smiling gods, the bronze
boy chalice-holders, the perfect tints.
Marvellous, the sweet fields Misery grazes
and is still Misery.

BRIAN JONES

Acton Burnell

History is silent, the one door
the dead can enter. They slide below
the smooth green cover, grateful at last,
cold buds split and passions make no haste.

Forgive us then our trespasses
oh moribund garden too reduced to care,
the aspect of a gothic afternoon;
white petals fall, 'the flowering of the leafe'
dark birds haul and dive in the leather-leaved wood,

a pewter sky is plated on
the four-square mansion, too held up to die,
such sadness in its self-effacing way
unnoticed in the silence of that air.

RENNIE PARKER

The House that Was

Of the old house, only a few, crumbled
Courses of brick, smothered in nettle and dock,
Or a shaped stone lying mossy where it tumbled!
Sprawling bramble and saucy thistle mock
What once was fire lit floor and private charm,
Whence, seen in a windowed picture, were hills fading
At night, and all was memory-coloured and warm,
And voices talked, secure of the wind's invading.

Of the old garden, only a stray shining
Of daffodil flames among April's cuckoo-flowers
Or clustered aconite, mixt with weeds entwining!
But, dark and lofty, a royal cedar towers
By homelier thorns; and whether the rain drifts
Or sun scorches, he holds the downs in ken,
The western vales; his branchy tiers he lifts,
Older than many a generation of men.

LAURENCE BINYON

Prospect of Ditchley

The ancient pirouette of trees
And the dropped scent of saunters done
Linger, though stiff decades of sun
Have stepped into this ride. No breeze
Now lifts Capability Brown's dead finger.

Here where the dancers cross, the arms
Of the wayfarer over berried cheek
Steeper than sticks in blood, a blown freak
Of silverweed and John's wort warms
The seed of the grass and the stiffened keeper.

The gallery of heat-haze lifts.
Gibbs's Italian is topped with leaves.
Only the grandeur of a memory grieves
Over the park and the great shifts
Of age. The upstart cormorants will not be lonely.

The face of Heythrop with stone eyes
Still looks up the ride, but the younger trees
Wander, and the wayfarers do as they please.
The crowd with blood in their cheeks surprise
The dancers. That is their last line yonder.

ROLAND MATHIAS

Tapestries

I lingered in that unfriended room
Where wind in the keyhole croons forlornly
As a woman barren of womb
Over a dusty cradle.
  I lingered. Nothing was there
  But tapestries cobwebbed and threadbare,
  Stirred by the uneasy air.

And, as I watched them, on the wall
Hound and hunter and quarry, lake and garden
And young girls playing at ball
Shook off their trance: grew dimly aware,
Remembering the delightful fingers
That wove them into life.
      And soon to me
  Those figures, ghostly and fantastical,
  Seemed a forgotten madrigal
Sung by dead lips at midnight merrily.

C. DAY LEWIS

House-keeping

You do your work in the small hours
when I am most deeply asleep,
festooning the ceilings with cobwebs,
clouding my mirrors with dust.

You sprinkle mud over the rugs,
breathe tarnish into the silverware.
In the pure shimmer of damask
rings of red wine appear.

When mist rises like the ghost of milk
you melt up the backstairs
to gas-mantled attics
where you thin into air

though I know you've been keeping this house
by the cold that I wake to,
the ashes laid in my hearth,
this silence that shifts for itself.

ESTHER MORGAN

Houghton House

1

Behind the elms, sunlight on ripe grey stone,
The blue-green grass, the slow gold of the bracken,
A glow of ruined Jacobean fluting
Whose separate bricks have weathered into one.

The towers speak pride, intellect, devotion;
The grass-floored hollow halls direct to peace:
The whole great building seems, in stone and space,
A huge machine to generate emotion.

But slow the emotions rise, and incomplete
Roused not by beauty set in stone or phrase
But by the watching ancestors who raise
The creative past, the centuries of weight

On the formulating centre of my brain,
– And then the patterns of responses die
Caught in that unpredictability
Only the verse can hold and perhaps explain.

2

It is seldom that all the conditions are present together
To harvest the heart. It is seldom that chance allows
Suitable landscape, physical well-being, weather.
      But here by the ancient house

Emotive bells of nature and mind are pealing
And I should be, and am not, in this summer prime,
Caught up in a resonance of air and feeling
      An assuaging single chime.

And the rolling turf and trees, a vigorous vista
Down to the slow sweet waters of fenland stream
Somehow today can do little more than foster
      An illusory tension of dream.

And at the carved lintel framed by this glowing view
I look half-expecting the fall of another stone
With a vague sense of fate, but of the ordinary too:
      As they might have done.

3

The emotions are truly there
But immobile, as it were.

No real tensions remain
From deeper thought or from pain:

So I take my pen and write
To focus its fading light

And the energies disperse
Through the loose dykes of a verse.

ROBERT CONQUEST

Blue Bedfordshire

Courtesy of a thirteenth Duke
the unblocked window sheds calm light
upon a hoard of Canalettos
hung for all to stare at
every day but Christmas: resourceful notables
now flog the wild where others cultivated grace.
Lay tourists in the state-rooms overlook
a monkish burying ground. They think the dead men quaint.

Yet from that window nothing's to be seen,
only the deer, the fishponds and the thrifty park
until you've reached the forest ridge
whose trees go back forever.
The great house squats alone, alone
too the solitary would-be occupant.
No interruptions, for the wall lopes on
engulfing miles. Room opens out of room.

That church, redundant in its earthwork,
would make a lordly residence. Last night up there
the bones of an apothecary's
two hundred year old wife
were laid out hex-wise on the gravel, but
she'll not come back. On Dead Man's Hill we watch
the lights roar into action where the motorway
shoots specks of gold that bug the dark for silence.

GLEN CAVALIERO

At Mapledurham

In these old country nooks, it is far from plain to see
What year the calendar has reached, or that empires disagree;
Indeed, for all we find here, we must think our dating wrong,
And, excepting the twentieth, all centuries here belong,
De Wint or Geoffrey Chaucer, young Milton or old Crome
With pencil or pen here would find themselves at home;
The nervous steps of Pope might be brushing through the grass
With as evident a presence as those ramblers who now pass.
The chaffinch who has nested in the bole of that tall pear
Might have brought off her brood when Pope's Martha glanced up there.
The vast hungry hog, the gander and the cow
Refuse all theories of time, their only time is now.
For ever fly the woodpeckers through a bright eternal glade,
And in the pond the basking pike thinks the world was quite well made.

EDMUND BLUNDEN

Canons Ashby

County of squares and spires, in the middle of England,
   Where with companions I was used to rove,
Country containing the cedar of John Dryden,
   Cedar, in whose shadow of thunder and love
I saw those Caroline lawns, and musical
I heard, inaudible, those waters fall, fall

Triumphs and miseries, last poet of a golden
   Order, and under whose laurel I desire
To plant a leaf of bay, and by whose building
   To tune irregular strings, his stronger lyre
Plunging, a swan to alight, upon a clear
Music of language I delight to hear.

Not a hundred yards from where my substance wastes
   Nightly in London, John Dryden died on tick.
The air clouded, and in his garden gusts
   Shook the cedar tree; as I watched its branches flick
In a windy prolegomenon to autumn
While a sky marshalled engines to a storm,

I no longer heard those falling waters fall,
   Silence like Iris descended from a cloud,
And lawns grew dark, as that once musical
   Shadow of a cedar faded in the loud
Shades of thunder-cumuli on the grass,
Till we left the garden empty as it was.

DAVID WRIGHT

Penshurst Place

The bright drop quivering on a thorn
in the rich silence after rain,
lute music in the orchard aisles,
the paths ablaze with daffodils,
intrigue and venery in the air
à l'ombre des jeunes filles en fleurs,
the iron hand and the velvet glove –
come live with me and be my love.

A pearl face, numinously bright,
shining in silence of the night,
a muffled crash of smouldering logs,
bad dreams of courtiers and of dogs,
the Spanish ships around Kinsale,
the screech-owl and the nightingale,
the falcon and the turtle dove –
come live with me and be my love.

DEREK MAHON

Wilton Park

Where Philip Sidney Wrote Arcadia

Why have I never read *Arcadia*?
Because I sensed doors in the dark.
For William Herbert swept a village far
out of his green and perfect park
until the starving shepherds spilled
back to his lawn, were clubbed and killed.

ALISON BRACKENBURY

Alfoxton

Suddenly (as when a road steeply rising
Shows only the sky ahead although we know
That beyond stretches all the surprising
Yet still predictable world) – suddenly below
I saw the house, just as the map foretold,
The gentle contours falling away
Through Kilve and Lilstock, fold upon fold,
To the dim vistas of Bridgwater Bay.

Alfoxton, mansion of poets, how I marvelled
To behold you then – no longer a mere name,
A place on a map to which I travelled
Under stormy August skies. Your fame
Stood firm and foursquare, bold as the beeches
That crowned the romantic park in which you stood.
I paused for the past. So a long dream rehearses
Miraculous presences, their times renewed.

The stage was set, I summoned the rightful players,
But nothing awoke; and I could only guess
How Wordsworth paced the drive in poetic labour
And Coleridge came with his fragile happiness
To talk the summer out. Or how one day
When every sensible man was safe indoors
They defied November rain and took their way
To Lynton over the bleak and dripping moors.

A golden year, not to be known again,
A poem too perfect for time to tolerate.
In a darker age I surveyed that green domain
And thought how the living always come too late.
The house lies empty, even the mice are gone,
Only a dusty sunlight haunts the rooms.
We knock. Mortality echoes back upon
Our hearts. An impossible dream consumes.

J. C. HALL

Elm End

I

Those cherubs on the gate
emasculated by the village boys
are now sole heirs to the estate.

The elms in the avenue,
planted through centuries
one for a daughter, two

for a son, within the year
will carry the timber-
merchant's mark. He walks here

sometimes on Sunday. The rings
on their trunks are numbered:
and a rip-saw sings

in his head seeing columns
of figures march and countermarch.
This Sunday comes

the snow, keeping him indoors:
but it re-vaults the avenue
and for today restores

that manhood the cherubs knew
when a lodge-keeper swung the gate
letting the phaetons through.

II

Don't worry the bell in the porch.
If its tongue is not tied
with rust, it will search

out a ghost from the scullery.
The handle demands both hands:
go in, go up. He will be

pillow-bound in the great bed
under the griffin's eye
that saw his father born, and dead,

and him conceived. His grandmother's
grandmother caged that bird
in its crest, stitching feathers

by candlelight for Charlie
riding to Waterloo.
Under her canopy

the griffin sees not the hollow
trunk, tackled by gravity, but
how far the roots stretch under snow.

III

The fires have fallen. He has drawn
the white acres up to his chin:
fingers grapple the lawn

that once they crawled on. Letting go
can be harder than holding on
or taking hold – as elms ago

the griffin's claw took hold
of these white acres. Letting go
is a language he's too old

to learn. The griffin grips
a scroll inscribed *Hold Fast*
between its talon tips.

Tonight or tomorrow
or tomorrow night
he will cease to echo

the wind in the chimney. Blinds
will be lowered. The snow
will cover his hands.

If then the bulldozer roars
at its kill, he will not hear,
nor see the road-gang's griffin flex its claws.

JON STALLWORTHY

A Country Mansion

This ancient house so notable
For its gables and great staircase,
Its mulberry-trees and alleys of clipped yew,
Humbles the show of every near demesne.

At the beginning it acknowledged owners –
Father, son, grandson –
But then, surviving the last heirs of the line,
Became a place for life-tenancy only.

At the beginning, no hint of fate,
No rats and no hauntings;
In the garden, then, the fruit-trees grew
Slender and similar in long rows.

A bedroom with a low ceiling
Caused little fret at first;
But gradual generations of discomfort
Have bred an anger there to stifle sleep.

And the venerable dining-room,
Where port in Limerick glasses
Glows twice as red reflected
In the memory-mirror of the waxed table –

For a time with paint and flowered paper
A mistress tamed its walls,
But pious antiquarian hands, groping,
Rediscovered the grey panels beneath.

Children love the old house tearfully,
And the parterres, how fertile!
Married couples under the testers hugging
Enjoy carnality's bliss as nowhere else.

A smell of mould from loft to cellar,
Yet sap still brisk in the oak
Of the great beams: if ever they use a saw
It will stain, as cutting a branch from a green tree.

... Old Parr had lived one hundred years and five
(So to King Charles he bragged)
When he did open penance, in a sheet,
For fornication with posterity.

Old Parr died; not so the mansion
Whose inhabitants, bewitched,
Pour their fresh blood through its historic veins
And, if a tile blow from the roof, tremble.

The last-born of this race of sacristans
Broke the long spell, departed;
They lay his knife and fork at every meal
And every evening warm his bed;

Yet cannot draw him back from the far roads
For trifling by the lily-pool
Or wine at the hushed table where they meet,
The guests of genealogy.

It was his childhood's pleasure-ground
And still may claim his corpse,
Yet foster-cradle or foster-grave
He will not count as home.

This rebel does not hate the house,
Nor its dusty joys impugn:
No place less reverend could provoke
So proud an absence from it.

He has that new malaise of time:
Gratitude choking with vexation
That he should opulently inherit
The goods and titles of the extinct.

ROBERT GRAVES

Colonel Fantock

To Osbert and Sacheverell Sitwell

Thus spoke the lady underneath the trees:
I was a member of a family
Whose legend was of hunting – (all the rare
And unattainable brightness of the air) –
A race whose fabled skill in falconry
Was used on the small song-birds and a winged
And blinded Destiny ... I think that only
Winged ones know the highest eyrie is so lonely.
There in a land, austere and elegant,
The castle seemed an arabesque in music;
We moved in an hallucination born
Of silence, which like music gave us lotus
To eat, perfuming lips and our long eyelids
As we trailed over the sad summer grass,
Or sat beneath a smooth and mournful tree.

And Time passed, suavely, imperceptibly.

But Dagobert and Peregrine and I
Were children then; we walked like shy gazelles
Among the music of the thin flower-bells.
And life still held some promise – never ask
Of what – but life seemed less a stranger, then,
Than ever after in this cold existence.
I always was a little outside life –
And so the things we touch could comfort me;
I loved the shy dreams we could hear and see –
For I was like one dead, like a small ghost,
A little cold air wandering and lost.
All day within the straw-roofed arabesque
Of the towered castle and the sleepy gardens wandered
We; those delicate paladins the waves
Told us fantastic legends that we pondered.

And the soft leaves were breasted like a dove,
Crooning old mournful tales of untrue love.

When night came, sounding like the growth of trees,
My great-grandmother bent to say good-night,

And the enchanted moonlight seemed transformed
Into the silvery tinkling of an old
And gentle music-box that played a tune
Of Circean enchantments and far seas;
Her voice was lulling like the splash of these.
When she had given me her good-night kiss,
There, in her lengthened shadow, I saw this
Old military ghost with mayfly whiskers –
Poor harmless creature, blown by the cold wind,
Boasting of unseen unreal victories
To a harsh unbelieving world unkind:
For all the battles that this warrior fought
Were with cold poverty and helpless age –
His spoils were shelters from the winter's rage.
And so for ever through his braggart voice,
Through all that martial trumpet's sound, his soul
Wept with a little sound so pitiful,
Knowing that he is outside life for ever
With no one that will warm or comfort him ...
He is not even dead, but Death's buffoon
On a bare stage, a shrunken pantaloon.
His military banner never fell,
Nor his account of victories, the stories
Of old apocryphal misfortunes, glories
Which comforted his heart in later life
When he was the Napoleon of the schoolroom
And all the victories he gained were over
Little boys who would not learn to spell.

All day within the sweet and ancient gardens
He had my childish self for audience –
Whose body flat and strange, whose pale straight hair
Made me appear as though I had been drowned –
(We all have the remote air of a legend) –
And Dagobert my brother whose large strength,
Great body and grave beauty still reflect
The Angevin dead kings from whom we spring;
And sweet as the young tender winds that stir
In thickets when the earliest flower-bells sing
Upon the boughs, was his just character;
And Peregrine the youngest with a naïve
Shy grace like a faun's, whose slant eyes seemed
The warm green light beneath eternal boughs.

His hair was like the fronds of feathers, life
In him was changing ever, springing fresh
As the dark songs of birds ... the furry warmth
And purring sound of fires was in his voice
Which never failed to warm and comfort me.

And there were haunted summers in Troy Park
When all the stillness budded into leaves;
We listened, like Ophelia drowned in blond
And fluid hair, beneath stag-antlered trees;
Then, in the ancient park the country-pleasant
Shadows fell as brown as any pheasant,
And Colonel Fantock seemed like one of these.
Sometimes for comfort in the castle kitchen
He drowsed, where with a sweet and velvet lip
The snapdragons within the fire
Of their red summer never tire.
And Colonel Fantock liked our company;
For us he wandered over each old lie,
Changing the flowering hawthorn, full of bees,
Into the silver helm of Hercules,
For us defended Troy from the top stair
Outside the nursery, when the calm full moon
Was like the sound within the growth of trees.

But then came one cruel day in deepest June,
When pink flowers seemed a sweet Mozartian tune,
And Colonel Fantock pondered o'er a book.
A gay voice like a honeysuckle nook –
So sweet – said, 'It is Colonel Fantock's age
Which makes him babble.' ... Blown by winter's rage
The poor old man then knew his creeping fate,
The darkening shadow that would take his sight
And hearing; and he thought of his saved pence
Which scarce would rent a grave ... That youthful voice
Was a dark bell which ever clanged 'Too late' –
A creeping shadow that would steal from him
Even the little boys who would not spell –
His only prisoners ... On that June day
Cold Death had taken his first citadel.

EDITH SITWELL

from *Bolsover Castle*

When the sun climbed high enough to see into the garden
The palaces were down and Charles had ridden far away,
The towers still were lived in, as the trees are full of doves,
But the Banquet Hall has never shone with lights again,
Empty are its windows of the glass that glowed like water
And long dead the torches that turned the glass to flame,
While the rooms stand roofless for the rain to spoil them
Each time those glancing armies rattle out from Heaven.
The long and weedgrown terrace cracks and falls on the hillside,
That once the steps led down to from the Banquet Hall
As though you left a cloud and climbed upon a steady ship,
But now is it wrecked among the gnarled trees
Soon to sink deep down to where its loose stones roll.
Through the windows of the Banquet Hall
You see the level lawns before you reach them walking round,
Down along the terrace past the riven walls,
And when you reach the corner and can see the Castle keep,
Soft is the grass without the print of horsehoofs
And empty the caves of shade below the deep leaved trees.
But Venus, down the alleys, still stands upon her shell,
She glitters through the hornbeams like those fruit boughs heaped
    with snow
And, higher than the apples, do the lofty trees stand back
To let her lover down and never tear his cloud with leaves;
Loud do the boughs ring, but not with lutes,
For a deep and rumbling murmur sounds among their very branches.

SACHEVERELL SITWELL

In Heytesbury Wood

Not less nor more than five and forty years ago
The old lord went along the ornamental ride;
For the last time he walked there, tired and very slow;
Saw the laburnum's golden chains, the glooming green
Of bowery box trees; stood and looked farewell, and sighed
For roots that held his heart and summers that he'd seen.

And then, maybe, he came again there, year by year,
To watch, as dead men do, and see – who knows how clear? –
That vista'd paradise which in his time had thriven;
Those trees to which in cogitating strolls he'd given
Perennial forethought – branches that he'd lopped and cherished:
Came, and saw sad neglect; dense nettles; favourites felled
Or fallen in gales and left to rot; came and beheld
How with succeeding seasons his laburnums perished.

'Return,' I think, 'next summer, and you'll find such change –
Walking, some low-lit evening, in the whispering wood –
As will refresh your eyes and do them ghostly good;
See redolence befriend, neglect no more estrange;
See plumed acacia and the nobly tranquil bay;
Laburnums too, now small as in the prosperous prime
Of your well-ordered distant mid-Victorian time ...'

Thus I evoke him; thus he looks and goes his way
Along that path we call the ornamental ride –
The old slow lord, the ghost whose trees were once his pride.

SIEGFRIED SASSOON

These Homes

These homes in poems –
    how large they were. Upwards
and sideways. How they housed
    in sun and gloom, those loved
unloving fathers' ghosts
    mothers medicinal as scents
that drifted in from trees
    with unusual names.

These homes had attics, tea-chests.
    Country or cathedral views
woodsmoke like epitaphs
    scrawled indelibly on air.
Air was always resident.
    Charged with the many duties
loss imposes on a habitation
    whose owners are elsewhere.

(Air must don its apron, dust
    shafts of light, shake out
camphor and cobweb, breathe
    rings on the bell.) Above all
there was singing. As if the mind
    had climbed to its highest
landing, from an upstairs room
    someone's voice.

And the house rose only
    that this voice should be
embodied, bulwarked against
    wind by walls, rooted
in nursery furniture, friendships
    only flyleaves know
married to its elements, skeleton
    and soul and carried downstairs.

For those who have no homes like
   these, no fork in the road to mark
their winding route from others'
   let the house that the song sings
into being serve as a stopping-inn
   to share a couch, pass the jug
re-sing the song that will carry
   over wilderness and mountain.

MIMI KHALVATI

from *Burnt Norton*

Time present and time past
Are both perhaps present in time future,
And time future contained in time past.
If all time is eternally present
All time is unredeemable.
What might have been is an abstraction
Remaining a perpetual possibility
Only in a world of speculation.
What might have been and what has been
Point to one end, which is always present.
Footfalls echo in the memory
Down the passage which we did not take
Towards the door we never opened
Into the rose-garden. My words echo
Thus, in your mind.
                    But to what purpose
Disturbing the dust on a bowl of rose-leaves
I do not know.
                Other echoes
Inhabit the garden. Shall we follow?
Quick, said the bird, find them, find them,
Round the corner. Through the first gate,
Into our first world, shall we follow
The deception of the thrush? Into our first world.
There they were, dignified, invisible,
Moving without pressure, over the dead leaves,
In the autumn heat, through the vibrant air,
And the bird called, in response to
The unheard music hidden in the shrubbery,
And the unseen eyebeam crossed, for the roses
Had the look of flowers that are looked at.
There they were as our guests, accepted and accepting.
So we moved, and they, in a formal pattern,
Along the empty alley, into the box circle,
To look down into the drained pool.
Dry the pool, dry concrete, brown edged,
And the pool was filled with water out of sunlight,
And the lotos rose, quietly, quietly,
The surface glittered out of heart of light,
And they were behind us, reflected in the pool.

Then a cloud passed, and the pool was empty.
Go, said the bird, for the leaves were full of children,
Hidden excitedly, containing laughter.
Go, go, go, said the bird: human kind
Cannot bear very much reality.
Time past and time future
What might have been and what has been
Point to one end, which is always present.

T. S. ELIOT

Rites & Conversions

Although we sometimes flaunt our family conventions,
Our good intentions
Mustn't be misconstrued.

Noël Coward

Tresham's Fancy

The whispering houses have gone
Occasionally a stump of them remains
Sterile and hatless, the wind inside their heads,
Sky-heads accosted with shadows.

All stately descendants, hallowed believers ...
The grand masque departed
Frozen in excellent attitudes
As if there was nothing but last parties,

Sinister movements. Shades of the old pretence.
Look to your heads when the virginals begin.

RENNIE PARKER

Lyveden New Bield

Planned as a hunting-lodge by Thomas Tresham,
but left incomplete

Awful and artificial
in its beginnings:
the petrified outcrop
of a mind.
Roofless, floorless:

light is layered
as down a well-
shaft; its shadows
are echoes of walls
within walls – singing

spaces that are
emptiness, defined.
And provisional.
From a mezzanine
in the open-ended

solar it's clear
how his bounds have
drawn in, these past
four centuries:
we read a wood

for his trees,
who was *more forward*
in beginning than
fortunate in finishing
his fabrics: rudiments

of drains withindoors;
outside, a part-cut
frieze, half hieroglyph,
his missing signature,
Tres, like himself

all outline:
the unreachable door,
gold-green light
on the walls; his daughters
at court, his interminable

building – and overall
that expanse of sky
with in suspension
a cupola,
a possible fourth floor.

JANE GRIFFITHS

At Colwick Park

First thing in the morning they went out
to rake over the lawn. The horses
waited quietly in their stalls, snuffling
at wet latches. Birds were already singing
behind the roof; dull blades rusted
in drops of condensation. While others were asleep
they worked, sowing their own bodies in Colwick Park.

Their aprons sweep them round. Rakes to earth,
certain of their footing, they stare
across the field of their flesh
with no apparent emotion. A sharpness comes
to peel away their noses but they counter it

with work: Swish, swish of hewn wood descending.
Recoil of grass, resilient in clouds
of green; the regular clicking of arms.

Clouds can only echo their shapes.
The stubble was dragged clear, the lawns
levelled without anger. Their sullen staring
is what is left when mythologies disappear.

GEORGE SZIRTES

A Banquet at Middleton

What a night in the vale of Tywi. Guests
from London. Paxton's house complete, windows
flame with candlelight. Bat-shadows
scribble on the dusk, a ring of lakes
reflect the house. Music. Murmurs of silk.
They sip their wine from goblets made of ice,
admire the fountain table-centrepiece,
a swan afloat on snow and honeyed milk,
and trapped in an obelisk of glass, live fish
flickering. Piled in frozen pyramids,
ice-apples, peaches, mulberries, figs,
glowing jellies, junkets, creams, a dish
of fine rose-scented butter. Such a stir
it must have caused in deep Carmarthenshire.

GILLIAN CLARKE

The Young Duchess Walks
with Mr Brown To Discuss Improvements

1. The Night Before

It's a scoop, a coup,
could the stable
get her horse ready?
Oh, of course she'll walk,
she longs to be in nature,
and after all, wasn't Mr Brown
her idea? Trees
are so old, magical
almost, she feels giddy
at the very thought
of what he'll create,
but what to wear
to convey exactly
the beauty of her soul?

2. The Walk Begins

She has to confess she's disappointed,
he is really quite ordinary
and that accent – unmanageable,
she can hardly make out a word.
You'd think he'd dress better
and hold back when with quality.
Why, he's hardly looked at her twice.

3. Half Way Through

No really, she's fine,
and yes, delicious
to dream of a temple
up there on the hill.
She can imagine
walking there with friends,
sipping tea, looking
down on the world,
and a Paradian bridge
sounds simply divine.

Oh she'll always get the name
wrong, the next field?
She can't wait.

4. After Five Hours

If she hears the words clump,
horizon or haha again,
she'll scream. The only
consolation is how others
will turn pale with envy.

5. At Dinner That Night

Yes, the villagers may moan
until they see his lake –
she's already planning naval
battles, picnics, and quiet spots
where she'll stand, shadowed,
remembering how he talked
of potential, looking at her
finally as if she was the one
who'd understand
how the costliest things
are worth it, on balance.

6. The Next Day

It was a spiritual experience,
she says, being with Mr Brown,
like mornings in Church
when you have to wake yourself
by singing loudly and
afterwards you can't remember
a word of the sermon,
and yet, you've found yourself
promising to host parties
of orphans.

SARAH SALWAY

County

God save me from the Porkers,
  God save me from their sons,
Their noisy tweedy sisters
  Who follow with the guns,
The old and scheming mother,
  Their futures that she plann'd,
The ghastly younger brother
  Who married into land.

Their shots along the valley
  Draw blood out of the sky,
The wounded pheasants rally
  As hobnailed boots go by.
Where once the rabbit scampered
  The waiting copse is still
As Porker fat and pampered
  Comes puffing up the hill.

'A left and right! Well done, sir!
  They're falling in the road;
And here's your other gun, sir.'
  'Don't talk. You're here to load.'
He grabs his gun, not seeing
  A thing but birds in air,
And blows them out of being
  With self-indulgent stare.

Triumphant after shooting
  He still commands the scene,
His Land Rover comes hooting
  Beaters and dogs between.
Then dinner with a neighbour,
  It doesn't matter which,
Conservative or Labour,
  So long as he is rich.

A *faux-bonhomme* and dull as well,
  All pedigree and purse,
We must admit that, though he's hell,
  His womenfolk are worse.

Bright in their county gin sets
  They tug their ropes of pearls
And smooth their tailored twin-sets
  And drop the names of earls.

Loud talk of meets and marriages
  And tax-evasion's heard
In many first-class carriages
  While servants travel third.
'My dear, I have to spoil them too –
  Or who would do the chores?
Well, here we are at Waterloo,
  I'll drop you at the Stores.'

God save me from the Porkers,
  The pathos of their lives,
The strange example that they set
  To new-rich farmers' wives
Glad to accept their bounty
  And worship from afar,
And think of them as county –
  County is what they are.

JOHN BETJEMAN

Great Edwardian

A cock-pheasant on the steaming muckheap:
Prospero admiring all. Those deep inks,
the bludgeoned, sexual midnight and a pope's

vermillion, are his interiors. He stands,
coat-tails trembling in the breeze, and smokes
and gazes out across the wooded sea.

Mock-Tudor dragonfly, he delays his flit.
Behind him are the lit boxes of his ease,
where guests and sisters sit and wait.

His mind is gaslight. His gaze travels over
the flocked regimental walls, the farm's brickwork:
it seems as if he is about to speak.

The meal is ended. Watching the evening droop,
he hears the clearing of the plates, the tinkle
of a pianola, stubs his *Rey del Mundo*

in a jardinière, and puffs his breast.
A cloud-mass dulls the sheen of his regalia.
He shivers: his island has grown suddenly cold.

TONY WILLIAMS

Metamorphoses

'It takes several hours to get up here.
Now it's all backdrop and photographers.
Top hats and tails and unaccustomed high heels
On the terraces, petticoats caught in the naughty breeze
And smudged lipstick, mascara,
The taxi drivers marking time beneath the trees.
But isn't it fine with the crocus and daffodil banks
And out front the birds in the quincunxes,
Crying 'Leon! Leon!' hoarse with ecstasy?
Look at the view down the avenue,
Yew cut into all shapes, bulls, eagles,
Unicorns and a snake curled round the horizon.'

Do you remember the forest
Noisy and rustling with watchers?
Accounts extant of wolves and bears
Stopping the coaches: in the infamous winter of 1666
Two countesses discovered only by shreds of pink satin
Traced on a clearing. And the cold,
The wind shifting the bride's veil
Till all you could see was a streak of red, her wary eyes?
What was the shadow loping beside her
Into the meticulous courtyard, the shriek
Of feathered women in the night?
This was the first place broken into
When the pales went down, where they fed for the first time
On the meat redemptive, all prepared on a bed of plumage,
The birds from the pleasure garden strung up
By their necks in the bath house.

Down by last year smouldering
On the bonfires, Zeus is on his back,
Dreaming of Io, his member pointing at the smoky sky:
Thinking which bar to spend in
What fantails and leg kicks and proud heads bobbing
In the air full of the many-traitored glance,
Got a drink, mister, under the oily lamplight,
What'll it be, rum and coke? A snap of jaws
In the undergrowth and milky canines;

The spell-bound drinkers longing for a white heifer
Glimpsed beyond the emerald ferns,
A thousand pairs of diamond eyes glittering in the night.

HILARY DAVIES

Care-taking

I keep everything in its place
from the lace wings and moths that flake the sills
to the husk of a mouse outside your door,
(though the cat that caught it is long since dust).

The curtains continue to fade, velvet tattering like antlers,
the walls slough off their paper like snakes.
The rooms look as they must in our absence;
leached of desire, empty as a guest room chair,
this glass vase rimed and flowerless.

As for myself I feel airy and winged like a seed;
it's as if I've already been shed
like my bedside rose in its circle of petals.
(You always said there was nothing of me.)

I make my last round at midnight
checking there's rust in the lock, the bolt's driven home.
I perform my duties as though you were watching,
touching each bar of the window
with hands as clean as the moon.

ESTHER MORGAN

Ripley Eels

That January was a freak-wind.
The low sun kept pricking at the weir's peaty skin
while the clouds chose ice-white
as black had already been taken by the land.
A skate-blade was orphaned
on the bank, and the other one was sleeping
under a thin layer of fate.
A boy, I thought I heard his fingers
on the ice. The bridge shook, tingling
with pleasure, as shadows slithered down the cascade
and hundreds of slimy mouths
funnelled through a tight gap in the fine eel tower
of gritstones from Harrogate.
Eel-man, I want you for supper!
The boy's voice still hadn't broken
and that made my hairs stand. Who was I
to contradict the heir?
                              Now I open the wooden flap
and there is nothing. No agitation,
no swimming bubbles, just a body of lifelessness.
I hate Sundays when the riffraff
in wedlock parade in their cocky trousers
and cleavage-dresses. I loathe the walkers
more than the picnickers as I'm allergic to polyester.
Poor eel-less Castle! Every day I die
a double death, a dead man in dead eels, or vice versa.
My dear little wet bony souls.
I'll swim to the mouth of the Nidd Head Spring
squeezing what's left of my personality
through wet grass wet sand upstream downstream
from Nidd to Ouse to Humber
dissolving my guts in saltwater, enlarging
my eyes, changing their pigments to the dim blue sea
and turning what's left of my body
silvery for the long safe passage
to what's left of the wide Sargasso Sea.
Then, I'll rest and spawn
as the moon counter-shades the midnight sun
and I metabolise transparently
like glass that isn't glass.

KIT FAN

Wycoller Hall

Such long ago see-saw of fortunes
Such toiling of sword-edge and saddle
So much dispossession repossession
Such juggling of Bishops and Kings
So many crucial oaths
So much outward blood and inward joy

So much forgetting of cries
So much determination so much money
So many tons of stone
So many oaks and sawyers and dust
So much energy staring at slant rain
Collapsing into the hill

Such spreading of farms so many tenants
So many couriers so much reckoning
Such coming and going of horses so many horses
Such study of dynasties and tithes
Such studied intermixture of bloods
Such tennis of heraldic emblems

So many generations of leaves
Such flitting of Queens so much re-arming
Such splitting of oak such tread of scripture
Such vigilance of portraits
So much repairing of roofs
Such steely clash of young voices
And old voices, so many feasts
So much merriment between lit faces
So much argument of deeds and holdings

So many years of wedded satisfaction
So many departures, solemn departures
Excited departures, dutiful departures
Such sudden returns, dreaded returns
Such joyful returns, so many returns
Such perpetual returning, so many hooves

So many hopes, so much laughter
So many births
So much sudden punishment by God
So much bitter logic of God
So much sword-length of God
So much blood, such speech-hardening
So many hooves

So much relaxing of memory
So many visitors, so many sunny breakfasts
So much noise of children so many coaches
So much news so many new gowns

So many funerals
So much weeping, so many decisions
So many mornings at the mirror
So much effort
So many years of rain-smoke dimming the hill
Such shrinkage of lands
So many lonely winters of ailment
Hearing the trees and the flood river

So many hours of prayer
So much worship of the old house

So much stubborn history in the old dark house
So much seasoning of old darkening stone
So much safety inside the dark stone
Of the old house, so many lit evenings
So many footfalls listening to themselves
Through the echoing beauty of the old house
Such furious hooves such hatred
Such screams
So many documents

Such vintage of pain

Drained finally to the dregs
Tumbled stones and a dry emptiness

The cup shattered

TED HUGHES

The Changeling

The child, one evening, looks
Into the sudden bloom
Of sunset chimney and roof,
And his reddened printed page
Seems to afford him proof
That he is of another age,
A changeling whisked from the grace
And the ceremonious kiss
Of a noble time and place.
He turns to the darkening room,
The garret grate, the books,
And backed by the bright sky,
He whispers into the gloom:
'What is here in my book is true.
I was changed at my birth. I am I,
And was never born for you.'

Later, in love, beneath
A lamp in a fading street,
Late lit in the summer dusk,
He watches, and waits, and fails.
Expected, hurrying feet
Approach, are strange, pass,
Die away on the paving-stones,
And silence again prevails.
He waits, and cannot believe
In the street's emptiness:
'Since I was given breath,
I was surely born to live.
Why am I tied to a death?'

On a still later day,
A soldier at his post,
He stands in a freezing dawn.
The garret, the lamp, come back,
Pass, salute, return
To a mind on sentry-go.
The scalding tears fall
And frost on the cold bone.
In the ending night alone,

He mouths a silent call
Into the still-born day:
'My life, my life, my life,
Beyond the barrack-wall,
Where are you drifting away?'

Through love and soldierhood
He passes along his track,
Unfinding the sought good;
So that his soul would,
If you could see it, be bent
To a strange anguished shape.
Until in the fall of peace
His days at last relent,
The soldier's tasks cease,
Love takes him by his hand,
And the child to exile bred
Comes to his native land.

And comes, at last, to stand
On his scented evening lawn
Under his flowering limes,
Where dim in the dusk and high,
His mansion is proudly set,
And the single light burns
In the room where his sweet young wife
Waits in his ancient bed.
The stable clock chimes.
And he to his house draws near,
And on the threshold turns,
With a silent glance to convey
Up to his summer sky,
Where his first pale stars appear:
'All this is false. And I
Am an interloper here.'

HENRY REED

A Property of the National Trust

We brought up the rear, the army recruiter and I.
Ghostly bulwarks of white cattle stood their ground.
In the sensible shoes I'd borrowed,
I picked my way through a no man's land

of pasture spiked with poppies.
Where chimney swifts banked and dove,
no gnat was safe in the twilight of England.
On wild mustard a gaseous ground-mist hung.

On the continent, what passed for peace
late in that century threatened to hold,
though somewhere far off. Neighbors still warred
in the old ways, house to house.

What was fifty years to a war?
Nothing to the great gardener,
who loved a beech tree most of all.
He could make England look natural

just by moving a stream, building a hill.
It was 1772. Nothing would change
but he changed it, who wouldn't see the beeches grown.
The manmade lakes overrun with reeds,

the little ruin more ruined than ever –
we'd take the folly first, the man beside me said,
in the crisp voice of retired officer,
Sunday painter, church organist.

All that summer he was bored.

DEBORA GREGER

Great Good House

Horace et al

Even when imagined as the place of a caring lord
who sits to eat with his tenants and forgives their rents
in the bad season – when you, the invited guest,
having rattled over a long Jacobean road

settle in a warm corner and compose for your patron
a Horatian tribute to comfort, food, and drink,
to his lands which serve by delivering their fruits
into his hand; his maids fair to gaze upon

but chaste, his men obedient and strong, his herds
offering their flesh in a spirit of generosity
as good beasts should – still though, it's obvious
that it's not like that, the idea is only words

spoken to please. So the visitor passing here
who just drops in, waving a Heritage Trust
membership card, might suffer the third-degree
from a surly keeper, for notices make it clear

that the well-praised grounds and important architecture
are not to be viewed, the House a Private School,
or a Business Centre, or retreat for Meditation,
or the country home of an agèd rock star

who fishes the ponds for carp. The bought and sold
place has reduced itself to a couple of barely
habitable rooms. Its owner without an heir
cowers by a phutting gas fire with a portly old

cocker spaniel, *like a snail*, as someone found,
in the corner of his tremendous shell, the lord
of photographs, dead gaps among the rooftiles,
and a wealth of centuries gurgling round and round

to vanish with Nursery bath-time down the drain.
The fire that levelled the place could be seen for miles.
Time to be off. Past the lines of dead greenhouses
to the station, along the main road shiny with rain.

MICHAEL VINCE

Corpus Christi

This is the only decaying nineteenth-century house with a stable block
Left among the ranks of square boxes with small gardens covered with grass
And with central heating, a shower, a colour TV, and two-car garage,
And a mortgage high enough to preclude the price of a literary evening class.

In the stable block, which lies well behind the stone pillared portico,
There is no heating, and a jagged hole in the faded flowered wallpaper.
Since some well-heeled family lived out their lives secluded in this house
Leading out their horses on to the uneven mossy bricks we pick our way across
Every Wednesday at eight, it was a receiving place for children in care,
And now a tarted-up Adult Education Centre with plastic chairs in the main hall.

Some places carry their past with them, and this place is one of those.
The tears that were shed the first lonely night here, seep slowly through
The old traditional ballads we are reading now, cruel mothers so far back
They were not read about but told and re-told, or chanted and sung,
The dead returning with the birch bark on their hats, the children returning
From some bedsit in Wandsworth, or some grimy institutional hostel room.

Ballads are full of the babies born on the wrong side of the blanket,
As many of these must have been, led up these stairs, the unfamiliar name
Of stable block as incomprehensible as the kindly, over-worked staff
Who sent them to bed without a comforting packet of chips, or herded them
Out into the vast gardens to play and chant those rhymes which have such links
With the ballads we earnestly listen to on a faulty tape-recorder tonight,
The violent cryptic stories so like the horror comics the bold ones smuggled
In, not understanding Beatrix Potter, or Arthur Ransome with his special children.

These children were special too. Dead father. Sick mother. McCrimon is gone,
Is gone, he will never come back, he will never come back, he is gone;
Quavering in Gaelic, the singer's cracked old voice uses her notes like a wail.
Corpus Christi I think I shall choose for next week's chilly session,
Feeling a wounde that is always bledyng as they lie upon their beds,
With comics under their pillowes and nits in their little heds.
Their hearts are surely turned to ston, Corpus Christi wretyn thereon.

ELIZABETH BARTLETT

Family Seat

Clouds make me look as though I disapprove
Of everyone. You know that grim, grey face
Of limestone cut by famine workmen. Love
Is never allowed to show it rules the place.

But love I took from a ruling family,
And gave them back a wealth of lovely things:
As a trout river talking with propriety
Through cockshoot woods, bailiffed by underlings.

Their silver knives adored their crested forks.
Blue-veiny hands, like yours, kept my clocks wound
On endless landings: others did good works
Like typing Braille. High walls surround my land.

They've all been buried in their name-proud vaults.
Paraplegics live here now, and love my faults.

RICHARD MURPHY

Revesby

The ballroom is kept shuttered. No one has the key.
Roll-eyed carvings guard the stairs – what's the password? –
mirrors echo in the hall, mahogany and vast.
No Ballgames on the Parterre. I told on them, so I'm a spy.

When the gang's coming after me, I scramble
into the straggly box hedge, and watch them searching.
The knot-garden's tangled, a cat's-cradle gone wrong.
My parents say you must learn to make new friends.

Stone ladies in the garden bare their breasts and bottoms
through the bones of a pergola like a broken tomb.
They show off hooks from elbows, orange scabs.
I need a cap-gun, I said, to defend myself.

Once, I hid inside an empty fountain,
staring at the green thing in the middle and willing it to gush.
Dried moss scratched my arms. A Vulcan screamed, so low
it made the twisted chimneys faint. I could have touched it.

No, I never hear *The Blue Danube,* the carriages at dawn.
There's no such thing as ghosts. The others will be waiting
on the backstairs with their skipping-ropes and helmets
to escort me to the basement, where the rats run free.

ANNE BERKELEY

Flensby Hall Day Spa

They patter from myriad hatchbacks to sit in steam,
to rub oils in, to sluice off Moroccan muds
and come out looking the same, but feeling good
or at least not the same. A few accepting men
have joined their quiet wives for Special Days,
but teatime finds them waiting up in the gallery
where crisp skylights show off the Victorian chimneys,
the fat iron guttering embossed with dates.
And down in the pool women's heads bob past
at tiny speeds, all stern and solitary;
and farther off, in the large mosaicked Jacuzzi,
a sultry twenty-something climbs away
from the bald jolly woman full of knots and cancers
between treatments, between friends, here to feel better.

RORY WATERMAN

At a Country-House Hotel

The air is sad, but then we laugh,
Sitting apart on the dry grey lawn ...
Three from the other world, while
A woman from this one aimlessly wanders,
Widowed eyes on the grass between trees,
Gracious and ancient Berkshire trees,
And another sits reading a genteel novel.
These and the colonel with his wife
Are all.

It has come to this, this world
Once many-voiced and green with order;
The meadows, wells, the flowery walks,
The cottages and grovy parkland, the
Splendour, peace, and sage injustice.

This.
Silence.
The colonel comes from the kitchen door,
Walking obliquely with lowered eyes.

History is this rictus,
This rictus on the colonel's face
As he clears away our tea-things
Praying to God we've left no tip.

JOHN FOWLES

Ridge-Foot House

The dignified gate and driveway through the leafy garden
past the greenhouse to this moneyed stone house by the Mill
whose chimney fell when the Great War broke out

becomes a big white Olympia with marble floors
from Italy. Now faces of Frankenstein and Dracula
dream-play science, technology and capitalism,

while, behind all this, I kick my shoes
along the stone-kicking road to Christ Church
where the indissoluble ménage

of economics, suffering, necessity and force
was never christened, nor their divorce.

HERBERT LOMAS

The Space

in memory of Richard Beaumond

Not quite the meadhall, the ballroom at Walcot Hall
where we used to meet, car-sharing poets
with cling-filmed plates for the communal lunch,
but we were glad of the space, the window seats
where we could sit *in parenthesis*, the *solvitur
ambulando* around the lake that took us past those
other solitaries, the fishermen hunched over their rods,
even the bus shelter at the end of the drive
where Michael would wait for a poem to pull in
and take him on board.

Born in the village and dancing with the Bedlams
in blackface, as once you would have been wise to
under the eyes of the gentry, it must have seemed
a glimpse of commonwealth to bring us here,
Richard, the opening of a space words could cross
and re-cross, finding forms as light and as durable
as the ark woven of rushes for the Midsummer
Rejoicing. Here's to the energy we sent through
the room, mind swinging off mind
as in Strip-the-Willow.

ROGER GARFITT

Name-Tag

Every sock and collar has a name-tag.
I have a name, a surname, and a tartan rug
with tassels. What else? A zip-up
pigskin letter-writing case that's pitted
where the bristles have been scorched away.
Once a week we write neat letters home with
our marks and team scores which the master reads.
Mornings, we get a tick for shitting
after the prefect has inspected it.
Through the keyhole old MacMillan
is sitting on his single bed
and talking to the service revolver
he uses with blanks to start the races.
Our toes are fat red bulbs from chilblains.
Already one skin has rubbed away, another grown
harder than the first, a kind of pigskin.
We must never sneak or blub or suck up.
We wear steel studs that spark. Scoured lugs
stick out from crew cuts as we learn by heart
the Latin for pitching camp and waging war
and the psalm where I am made
to lie down in green pastures and a table
is prepared for me and my enemies.
The tables are mopped with swab rags,
the dustbins tipped among the ferns
and bamboo of the watergarden
for this was once a country house
and we are lucky to enjoy the fine grounds
which we see through the barred windows
or on Sunday walks trying to keep up
with the master who ran the marathon.
In the wooden locker by the metal bed
I have a chipped enamel mug,
a toothbrush, a comb, a nailbrush and two shoebrushes
with which, with time, I could scrub away
my shoes, my nails, my hair, my teeth –
given time enough, the buildings, the pitches,
the gate's ironwork with its clawing lion
and all we've learnt till nothing's left
but the Blasted Oak I carved my name on
and perhaps the derelict pavilion.

JAMIE McKENDRICK

A Huntingdonshire Nocturne

Kimbolton Castle

Wind slices at the sashes and the double doors, it lashes
across the cricket pitch, it challenges the right of obedient
classical pillars and portico, with their aristocratic air

of calm, to loiter as they have for so many hundred years,
as if the old Duke hadn't fallen at the final
African debt, as if all the King's boots

hadn't kicked the parquet in their war effort, before
the castle was sold to fill with boys and their skittle-alley
noise learning about the Rhine, Gibraltar, Ulster ...

As all the millennium's nines come up in a last fling
of showers, who is it cowers there at the marble fire,
beneath the self-denying, appeasing gaze of that Montagu,

that smiling regulator, who has an idea what Cromwell
is up to in Drogheda, who knows that only a length away
Aragon withered, the English rose, but who cannot say

what shadows are there before him, or why this late wind
should so chill with its lottery numbers his gilt frame?

JOHN GREENING

The Children and Sir Nameless

Sir Nameless, once of Athelhall, declared:
'These wretched children romping in my park
Trample the herbage till the soil is bared,
And yap and yell from early morn till dark!
Go keep them harnessed to their set routines:
Thank God I've none to hasten my decay;
For green remembrance there are better means
Than offspring, who but wish their sires away.'

Sir Nameless of that mansion said anon:
'To be perpetuate for my mightiness
Sculpture must image me when I am gone.'
– He forthwith summoned carvers there express
To shape a figure stretching seven-odd feet
(For he was tall) in alabaster stone,
With shield, and crest, and casque, and sword complete:
When done a statelier work was never known.

Three hundred years hied; Church-restorers came,
And, no one of his lineage being traced,
They thought an effigy so large in frame
Best fitted for the floor. There it was placed,
Under the seats for schoolchildren. And they
Kicked out his name, and hobnailed off his nose;
And, as they yawn through sermon-time, they say,
'Who was this old stone man beneath our toes?'

THOMAS HARDY

October in Clowes Park

The day dispossessed of light. At four o'clock
in the afternoon, a sulphurous, manufactured
twilight, smudging the scummed lake's far side,
leant on the park. Sounds, muffled –
as if the lolling muck clogged them at the source –
crawled to the ear. A skyed ball thudded
to ground, a swan leathered its wings by the island.
I stood and watched a water-hen arrow
shutting silver across the sooty mat
of the lake's surface – an earl's lake,
though these fifty years the corporation's.
And what is left of the extensive estate
(a few acres of scruffy, flat land
framing this wet sore in the minds of property agents)
a public park. All else is built on.
Through swags of trees poked the bare backsides
of encircling villas, gardening-sheds:
a ring of light making the park dimmer.
Boys and men shouldering long rods –
all licensed fishers, by their open way –
scuffled the cinders past me, heading for home;
but I stayed on – the dispossessed day
held me, turned me towards the ruined Hall.
Pulsing in that yellow, luminous, murk
(a trick of the eye), the bits of broken pillar
built into banks, the last upright wall,
the stalactite-hung split shells of stables,
seemed likely to find a voice – such pent-in grief
and anger! – or perhaps to explode silently
with force greater than any known to progress,
wiping the district, town, kingdom, age,
to darkness far deeper than that which fluffed
now at the neat new urinal's outline,
and heaved and beat behind it in the ruins.
Like a thud in the head, suddenly become memory,
stillness was dumb around me. Scrambling up
a heap of refuse I grabbed at crystalled brick.
Flakes fell from my hand – a gruff tinkle –
no knowledge there of what brought the Hall low,
or concern either. Neither did I care.

Irrecoverably dead, slumped in rank weed
and billowy grass, it mouldered from here to now,
connoting nothing but where my anger stood
and grief enough to pull the sagging smoke
down from the sky, a silent, lethal, swaddling
over the garden I played in as a child,
and over those children – laughter in the branches –
shaking the pear-tree's last sour fruit to ground.

TONY CONNOR

Newstead Abbey

Birds on the lake; a distant waterfall:
Surrounded by its lawns, a vandyke shawl
Of woods, against the washed-in sky of March,
The abbey with its broken wall and arch,
Its scoured and yellow look, has power still
To move.
           The Nottingham Corporation will
At the converted stable block provide
Postcards and teas, and in the house a guide.

Impossible to doubt that he foresaw
His dwelling's destiny, the social law
Which now ropes off his manuscripts and bed;
That pathos and joke were clearly in his head
When for the sentimental lookers-over
He reared the conspicuous monument to Rover,
Designed the too-heroic helmets for
His tripped-up entry in the Grecian war,
Made the monks' mortuary a swimming bath,
Loved these dim women.
               Lout, girl, polymath,
Stare at the puzzling relics of a life:
Grapplings with action, blind turning to a wife.

In bed he could gaze out across the scene
Where now the trees are heavy but not green
With Spring, and see perhaps the rowing boat,
The little broad-beamed *Maid of Athens,* float
At her rope's end, past the blue toilet jug,
The tumbler of magnesia.
            And the bug
That impregnated then this habitation

And kept it quick despite the abdication
Of all it served, of that for which it was planned,
I know too well but really understand
No better than the guide.
                              'The table that you see
Is where the poet Byron wrote his poetry'.

ROY FULLER

Rest on the Hunt

Riders cascade down the valley in the
wrong direction. Here the chase is over
and the dogs relax, chewing, wading
in the ditch and rolling about. The horses
twist their heads uncomfortably. They
are not at ease. The brush has been
detached, examined and is now hung
from the saddle. No one looks at it.
The master seeks further game and waits
for pursuers to wheel his way. How sharp
is this air: the explosion into death
has left a tang. They savour it
and remain stock still, bitten by the acid
into a climax from which all movement would be decay.

GEORGE SZIRTES

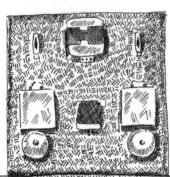

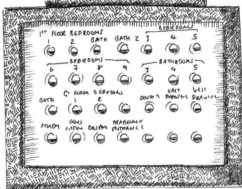

1ST FLOOR BEDROOMS   BEDROOMS
1   2   BATH   BATH 2   3   4   5

BEDROOMS   BATHROOMS
6   7   8   9   3   4   5

G. FLOOR BEDROOMS   EAST   WEST
BATH   1   2   DINING DRAWING DRAWING

STUDY   GUNS   BELLOWS TRADESMEN
        SITTING   ENTRANCE

Fixtures & Fittings

if the Van Dycks have to go
And we pawn the Bechstein Grand ...

Noël Coward

The National Trust

A building on this site existed in
The previous century:
                    records begin
Before the first earl bought the monastery
And so became an earl:
                    Philip his son
Who bought the Tintorettos:
                    Philip's son
Was Richard whose son Philip whose son John
And Henry, without issue:
                    John's son Ned
Who went to sea, was found and told and died
On the voyage home:
                    a flint arrow head
Found in New Holland:
                    the elder sister Fay
Married a diamond merchant in Bombay.
Her son was Krishna, who'd have been eighth earl
If he had known, existed and survived,
But didn't, and so wasn't:
                    the ninth earl,
Who sold the Tintorettos:
                    this is the library –
Five thousand books in corsets:
                    the long gallery
In which they walked in winter:
                    voices and feet
Disturb the centuries:
                    pot pourri hangs
Among the silences:
                    heels click, skirts swing:
– Who failed to marry, who succeeded to
A neighbour's title, whose Poussin is for sale –
Twenty-eight lengths, one mile:
                    pot pourri clings
Within the nostrils like a spider's web:
Earl hangs by varnished earl:
                    I turn, look out.

The air's prised open by impending rain:
The dazzle on the grass, the chiselled clouds,
The white submissive cottages: I turn
Back to the earls and to their paying guests.
Two folio volumes, *Monasteries of the East*,
Sketchbook in the Levant, privately printed,
By Robert Curzon, Philip's brother, known
As Levant Curzon:
                        the Prince of Parma
Sat at this table, took one mouthful, said
'Sell me your cook, Signora.'
                        Lady Emily,
Renowned blue-stocking, did this family tree,
Beginning with Cro-Magnon:
                        the clock that stopped
As the eleventh earl bid seven clubs
Has never been rewound; the Rembrandt bought
Out of his winnings is not genuine.

This is the purple bedroom: the gorilla
That the tenth earl brought back from Africa
Lived here among the dangling wallpaper.
Terrified housemaids darted through the door
Carrying apples, threw them in the corner
Among the droppings, fled.
                        His throaty roar,
The listless drumming on his chest, recalled
A youth of pawpaws, oily orange mangoes,
And the shy sunlight in the purple shadows.
One day, he died.
                        Algernon, twelfth earl,
Married a milkmaid: she collected Spode
And made him happy; and outliving him
By forty childless years, at ninety-three
She wandered, blind, down the long gallery,
Sniffing pot pourri, tapping:
                        'When I die
The house dies too.'

                              A gentleman from Kansas,
          Wallace J. Curzon, junior, we're told,
          Now claims the title:
                              the sixth earl, in gold
          And purple mantle, thought to be by Rubens.

          Krishna, or Ned, or Wallace Curzon: if
          You had succeeded, could you ease your life
          Among these moments and these monuments?
          Could you, could I, or could the paying guests?
          Could you have eaten all those syllabubs,
          Gambled your winnings on the ace of clubs,
          Led all those milkmaids to the high, draped bed,
          Drawn those vast curtains when your mother died,
          Paced the long gallery for centuries,
          Looked through the rain at the persistent trees,
          Looked up; a quiet nod at Uncle John
          By Kneller, sniffed the spidery scent; paced on?

                                        LAURENCE LERNER

Parson's Castle, Birr, Ireland

A passage from the verse novel *Lara*

Chintz, carpets, mahogany, marquetry,
porcelain, damask, bronzes, curtains, chinoiserie,

brass fittings, flagstone floors, ormolu mounts,
rosewood, black-lacquer, Persian rugs,

a sofa veneered with rosewood, plinths inlaid
with stylised arabesques with coil-sprung seats

for comfort; a walnut commode; a red marble-topped
table on a carved frieze above a central column

with spiral fluting surrounded by sphinxes;
a floor-length mirror with a carved softwood frame;

enormous stained-glass windows; ten bed chambers,
a drawing-room, breakfast room, dining-room,

games room, smoking room, garden room, terrace
room, ballroom, library, a medieval tower, ice house,

kitchen garden, lake, box hedges, fernery, fountain,
waterfall, trout pond, deer park, gazebos,

a beech-lined drive, and, in the steaming, belching
bowels of the castle, the cavernous kitchen

where Emma spends her every waking moment,
and the moist cellar next door, where she sleeps.

BERNARDINE EVARISTO

Swarthmoor Hall, Cumbria

Found Poem

two vizard masks
for my sister Rachel
and for my selfe

a wooden writing box

a bed made of lignum vitae
the heaviest wood in the world

eighteen yards
of blacke and sky-coulered ribbin

two scarlet petticoats
to be carried to Kendal

new petticoats
of blacke and of dove couler

wooden crib
with butterfly-motif quilt

painted clover-box
for carriage of ye clover,
grasse seeds of Lancashire

crib with six knobs
for cat netting

shotte to keep crowes
off the wheate

sword chest
painted the green
of Lady Jane Grey's eyes

PENELOPE SHUTTLE

Enýpnion

A bee in the library
Of elm books and oak books,
Holly shelves,
Ivy shelves,
The drowsy-house,
The dreamlike slumber in books;

Polishing the windows
Of the drowsy-house
That open to and fro
One sees out of the leaves;

I open the book and its honey runs over,
The supple binding polished with beeswax,
The dark-veined pages,
The whispering leaves
Inscribed with sentences that hum
In the amber twilight,

A gentleman's library
In which to browse
That is full of Virgil
Who has retired,
Who has finished with all
Heroes larger than beesize.

PETER REDGROVE

53° 09'33.17" N, 0° 25'33.18" W

A lodge-house to an estate, once: the front wall
still ends with one redundant brick gatepost,
its rustic latch clicking only to wind,
and the clean bulk of its limestone cap
shorn of clogs of English ivy, carious and precarious.

There used to be a long metal water-butt
out of bounds, snug to a wall, pungent
with moss and webs, its content a black
lilting mirror when I'd raise the lid
that was wooden and rotten and gave slightly.

And there was a low-slung roof on a breezeblock annexe
with a fat windowsill and convenient external piping
that occasionally broke and had to be mended;
and a cigar-box of old green pennies and shards of pot
from the garden, out of sight in a cracked soffit.

But the side gate remains, a wrought iron cross-hatch
mass-produced in a distant foundry, showing
bends for the feet that are no longer mine,
that kicked off and made it a shrill, dull swing;
and the fence is the matt-green my grandmother painted,
though tarnished now, and in places peeling.

RORY WATERMAN

Late Elizabethan

All ruffs, and furs, and farthingales,
shrouded cadavers on marble tombs,

tall windows with mullions and transoms,
emblazonings of bogus coats of arms –

here I live by candlelight, won't hear the cries
of fishwives, orangewomen, chimney-sweeps.

The street outside's too narrow to receive
coaches or carts. No costermongers call.

My windows are all shut and caulked,
doors padded with flock-bed or with quilt.

Very fine garters I can do without.
I have not dined on pheasants, godwits, lampreys.

I am not of the Queen's Men, or Lord Chamberlain's.
My name is not Orlando Gibbons

but I have heard lute, cithern, and bandora play.
I have seen the pillared porticoes and fluted pilasters.

I have visited the Long Gallery.
In my metopes place what ornaments you may,

for I am already my sarcophagus.
Am obelisk, cartouche, and scrapwork scroll.

ROGER CALDWELL

Cleaning the Candelabrum

While cleaning my old six-branched candelabrum
(Which disconnects in four and twenty parts)
I think how other hands its brass have brightened,
And wonder what was happening in their hearts:
I wonder what they mused about – those ghosts –
In what habitual prosy-morning'd places,
Who furbished these reflections, humming softly
With unperplexed or trouble-trodden faces.

While rubbing up the ring by which one lifts it,
I visualize some Queen Anne country squire
Guiding a guest from dining-room to parlour
Where port and filberts wait them by the fire:
Or – in the later cosmos of Miss Austen –
Two spinsters, wavering shadows on a wall,
Conferring volubly about Napoleon
And what was worn at the Assembly Ball.

Then, thought-reverting to the man who made it
With long-apprenticed unpresuming skill,
When earth was yet unwarned of Electricity
And rush-lights gave essential service still,
I meditate upon mankind's advancement
From flint sparks into million-volted glare
That shows us everything except the future –
And leaves us not much wiser than we were.

Dim lights have had their day; wax candles even
Produce a conscious 'period atmosphere'.
But brass out-twinkles time; my candelabrum
Persists well on towards its three hundredth year,
And has illuminated, one might say,
Much vista'd history, many vanished lives …
Meanwhile for me, outside my open window,
The twilight blackbird flutes, and spring arrives.

SIEGFRIED SASSOON

The Old Bell-board

The old board's not used much: a panel of glass
Up high on the wall, a square of windows
Where the tremblers shake about in their tiny lairs,
Wagging their tongues, red whirling dervishes.
Someone is holding a bell-push down and down,
Threading the house with a cobwebby scrape of sound.
From a numbered room above or below the stairs –
Bedroom One, or Two, or the Breakfast Room –
A lifeline twitches the coverlets askew,
A muscle ticks away at an eyelid's corner.
Who is to fetch and carry, to come and go,
Swishing the air at the twist of a hand or door?
Grandad trims the gas lamp under his breath,
A terrier, cloudy-eyed under rugs of hair,
Is down at his heels; Granny, bobbed with pearls,
Loops her Waterman over her deckled paper;
Evelyn works the kitchen full steam ahead,
Shaving the runner beans to a quick cascade.
The bells can tell you the special smells of things,
The way time picks at the crumbly bones and mortar.
Is it set fair, or storm? They have no lives,
These citizens of a sleepy house and garden:
This doll's house, weather-house, where grown-ups do
The things that a child imagines they have to do.
Their work is a special kind of play and feasting
As they busy away at their sunshine, letters and dust,
Building and filling the ark that I keep in my head.
It rings like the long note held by a rubbing finger
On the rim of a glass, the rim of a memory.
Those tremblers waver and slow, going nowhere,
Coming so lightly to rest, the current warm in the cell.

PETER SCUPHAM

The King's Bed

Tradition holds that on a wet starless night
in 1665 the King slept in this bed, or one quite like it.

He lay his head, or might have, upon a facsimile
of this pillow. And in the morning, that probably

fresh pleasant morning in 1665 or thereabouts,
servants, in befitting manner, brought him the sort

of breakfast popular in those days, dressed him
in the garments that would have been the fashion.

What is known is that he was the monarch
living in those times, and so slept somewhere.

Nearby houses will make their own claims.
By reading this you have brought him to this bed.

PENNY BOXALL

Tapestry

Veins and arteries carry the blood from corner
to corner. The interpretation is easy once you find
the right place to begin. The Duke, on his white
stallion, has killed a knight from the invading
army near the center of the scene. Three of his
own followers lie in a heap at his feet. There are
too many corpses to count. A small stream winds
through the valleys, the rolling hills of the
background, done in a flourish of autumnal color.
In the lower left-hand corner, worked intricately
into the dense undergrowth, is the small signature
of one of the women who worked her life away
on the other side of this scene, in the cold tower
where the tapestry, for centuries, has hung.

WILLIAM VIRGIL DAVIS

The Gunroom

Incandescence of the triggers,
shrewd sideways brightness;
even immobile on their racks,
what certainties in these weapons,
a hundred hands avenging,
blood bursting into tears.
I enter from the outer cold
and breathe warm oil and metal,
the indolence of far-off deaths,
the suffocation that brims from the dreaming barrels.
Speak quietly in here,
we have surrendered.
Here live all the insinuations of aim.
Here the untroubled instruments wait
for the executioners to march in
and take up their perfect partners,
masters of the game.

PENELOPE SHUTTLE

Aspects of a Novel

The house is not locked.
Everyone open the door. The latch is old-fashionedly
stiff and though we are not breaking we're entering.
Uncertainty, cold
as nightlight, follows us into the hall.

We have nothing to go on.
It is very dark until at one end a fire,
the remains of one, unravels the room a little.
Yes, it is home; we are
faced with all the trouble we started from.

The people who lived here so
long ago, were they our family exactly?
or was their fierce kindness built upon difficult
kindling, bad memories to do
with us, with whom we were in the first place?

Our hands make blind-
man gestures along what is left of the panel
for a switch. A bank of them yields one 40-watt
weakling. Grateful, though,
eyes begin to grab at the parcel of shadows.

Charming! A miniature
grandfather clock, four foot yet carved so delicately,
almost tripped us (take care of those tattered curtains
too, they hang by a thread).
But familiar? The effigies hold back, nonplussed.

One thing: at some point
we were rich. The peculiar smell which money
does not have but we find lurking, when money's gone,
everywhere's here.
Later we may coax a story from it.

To the left, a schoolroom:
much needed now but our hypothetical German
governess, Frl. Weber, treated 'like one of the family',
fled from our high jinks.
A Gothic disapproval doused her smile.

The library is wretched.
Louis Seize bindings prop Chippendale amputee
tables; kitchen girls of the last days, working for love,
sealed jam jars with vellum
torn from a coloured atlas of the world

(1712) and we
need bearings, or at least familiars without whom
self-discovery's mere sight-seeing, our daily quest
a boredom opiate –
books *curiosa* like the lavatories'

Edwardian daydream
of two-tone copper ducts and high mahogany
seats giving on bowls archly bordered with peonies.
Dare we think the modern
life sprang whole from minds these rooms gave rise to?

Echoes veto
the notion though much needs to be answered
here, in this house, now. The walls trickle,
a black mildew.
Origins cling to us like sexual pain.

* * *

The house is not locked.
Children open the door. We may generate our own
daylight now and read heraldic doodles
in the beams of dirt
sneaking through chinks their dossier on a world.

Still, it is cold.
There are no voices, no residue of women
who then sorrowing or sweeping or melted by
love brought us back
once and for all where we always were.

Confidence beckons.
Mercy, colossal, a figure from allegory
with the amber flesh of a Titian, deliquescent,
writes her name in dust.
Their mottoes wreathe our heads in ectoplasm.

Be careful. Only
a few eyes, a few chimes of the small grandfather clock
back were we hopeless, transfixed beyond thought of succour
in the empty hall
of a house whose skeleton is gone desire.

How much did happen
since. Arguments, stories that tell the beginning,
throw light on a psyche, only flicker till we know
their structures are
durable prophecies – like a door.

GREY GOWRIE

A Valentine for John and Margaret

Canna House, Valentine's Day, 1978

Warm behind curtains drawn to shut out February's cold,
About to play my embattled card
On the green baize, suddenly tears filled my eyes
To think that there will be a time
When the dear drawing-room of Canna House,
The owl-lamp on the Steinway grand, quartos
Of Schubert, Mozart, Moore's Irish melodies,
The carved funny animals, the barque under glass,
The curious mirrors of carved bones
Made by French prisoners in Edinburgh castle,
Books on birds and minerals, cases of butterflies,
The family miniatures on ivory, piles
Of *The New Yorker*, *Paris-Match*, *The Scotsman*,
The friendly bottles, ash-trays, cigarettes,
The cat-clawed Chippendale and dog-haired cushions, photographs
Of Uist and Barra and of distant friends, all this
Learned happy accumulation, held together
By the presence of John and Margaret Campbell, by little dog
Patchen, successor to Perrita, sister of Cheekie of *The Western Isles*,
By Lobito, Freddie, Semolina and the other cats
Who step as lightly almost as memories
Of Mrs Pink, Kukravat, Thomas Beattie, Reuben, Thoby and their
    friends,
Will be no more. Yet how can what is
Cease to be ever? Where in continuous time
Is moment divided from moment, that we should say
Is, was, will no more be?
What, if not ourselves, is memory
With all the known loved rooms where friends
Have come and gone? If soul
Be memory's place, where shall we look for one another
If not in these dear places still? I think of this
And other rooms and houses and gardens, and all
Cities and houses of the long past, their music and laughter,

And all the happy companionable things that gather
Where life is kind. How
Can all that here and now of then not be for ever?

KATHLEEN RAINE

Knole

Inside the sombre walls the neat quadrangles still are green
As though a light shone on them from a sun, grey-masked, unseen.

And some remoter light leans through the embrasures of the house
And frees the colours of the hangings – crimson, lime and mouse.

The firedogs dangerous weapons, beds tents, rooms an insect's maze,
But nothing burns, loves, spies, through rain- or history-nervous days.

An ancient painted Sackville down the chamber from the frame
Looks over what has lost its meaning yet is still the same.

He stares and will stare pointlessly, stiff in his mint brocades,
Hair reddish, bearded, white of hand, until our living fades.

His face the worried, capable, Elizabethan face,
He stands with the fresh-created ruler's half self-conscious grace.

Of savagery, the codpiece in the fairy's clothes remains;
All else the civilizing new discovery of gain.

Vestigial organs in their jars his stuffs and filigree:
The capital he started now explodes spontaneously.

But still outside, upon the deer-striped lawns, the trees are caught
Spread in the sheltering crystal of the mansion's stored-up thought;

And like those dreams of treasure only stir to accumulate
Their golden leaves in natural rhythms, endless, sad, sedate.

In this calm magic island in tempestuous seas, the plan
Holds yet: the spirits of earth and air still serve the passionate man.

ROY FULLER

Artemis Before a Prospect of Blaxter Hall

Oil on panel, circa 1800. Artist unknown.

The elongated steeplechaser arches
her neck sufficiently to tug a groom
in gaiters to his toes. She wears her plucky
rider like a frivolous panache
of victory. A butterfly
caught stealing colour from the wallpaper
behind her picture as we lift it down
makes use of semaphore to fly away.
Detail sharpens like a change of weather
about the chestnut horse and sick
green deeps of fields and woods. The house
stands back as if in disrepair
or disrepute. A Georgian sash –
left, as we survey it, of the portico –
slides open to invite us to be clever
before the light goes and discover ashes
of a writ cold in a hearth, a bear-skin rug
stained darkly, and a dressing-gown
about the shoulders of a shadow –
in life it seems more cavalier than lucky –
that smiles to see a riding-crop swung high
then takes a razor to remorse
and sends the afterthought of summer, quick
but dying, from the empty room
with little mockeries of lordly shrug
that will not pay the artist or the jockey.

PETER BENNET

Real Estate

for Anne

1

Weary we came to it, weary
With advertisement's weary verbiage
And all those inglenooks, plastic antiquities,
The cocktail bar cottage,
The swimming-pool farmhouse,
The concreted paddocks, the pink mirrors lining
That bathroom suite in the Georgian mansion,
All the stuff that, bought at a steep price,
We could never afford to get rid of, by de-converting.

2

'For sale by auction: The Rectory,
Standing in well-timbered grounds
In this unspoilt village.
A fine period house requiring
Improvement and restoration.
A range of Outbuildings.' Yes.
'A Garage'. Noted.

3

We went. And there it stood,
Plain, white, right,
Austere, but with gables, bow front
('A later addition'), hint
Of indulgence in curves, dips.
Large, but not grand, compact.
Too sure of itself to be showy.
So real, it amazed, overwhelmed you.
So self-sufficient, you wanted it.

4

For sale by auction, at a low reserve,
After Easter, the powerful temptation
Of realness, every inch of the house honest –
With the rendering brutally stripped
Here and there, to reveal
Rot of beams, erosion, cracks
In brick, stone, the sliding,
Minute even now, and slow, slow,
Down into older dampness, of the foundations.

5

Settle there, could you, dare you,
On settlement? Settle ('subject to covenant'),
Bid for a place become
Pure idea of duration, dwelling
Among rook caws up in the black yews,
The taller pines, near graves,
Near enough to feel always
Held there, beyond dislodging –
If the floorboards, only a little aslant,
Hold, if the roof holds, if ...

6

And the gardens, wilderness
Whose high walls keep intact
The pure idea, *hortus conclusus*,
Her who reigned with her lilies
Over wilderness trained, restrained –
Graveyard, no more, true
For bough, blossom, fruit
Gone down into older dampness,
To rise again, fleshed, if ...

7

If not, the dead in their graves,
Near enough, will be heard laughing
At folk who need so much room,
Such an effort of warmed walls,
To make a home for themselves, a peace;
And on their treetops the rooks
Join in, with a raucous guffawing.

8

Let's go, let the place be:
Too real for us to meddle with, pure idea of dwelling.
Not for us will the rooks caw
Or the gardens bear again flowers and fruit;
Not at us will the rooks laugh.
But anywhere, miles from this burial-ground,
The wide-awake dead can tell us a thing or two
About making do with our real estate,
The for ever indifferently furnished, poorly maintained,
Defectively fenced or walled;
About how indifference grows on us, and the chores grow harder.

9

Let's go, and revisit those empty rooms,
Occupy them in dreams that restore without labour
Any house you have lost
Or lacked the means to acquire; improve it, too.
One look and dream takes possession
Of all that the look took in; and will work wonders
With ruins, with rubble, with the bare site,
Instantly will rebuild, instantly raise the dead
For conversation with you, for communion;
And where no root is, no seed,
Break sunbeams for you with the blackness of full-grown pines.

MICHAEL HAMBURGER

Plumbing

A lemon bloomed with frost,
hollowed and filled with sweet snow.
A bowl of ice and Muscat grapes.
Breath on a glass of wine.

Paxton knew these things, and brought from India
his dreams of ice and water engineering,
and from the Mughal gardens his design
of cool reflections and the sound of water.

From his Tower he'd see it all: a garden of streams,
sluices, dams, cascades, and a house on a hill
in a chain of lakes, with reservoirs and ice-ponds,
the healing waters of chalybeate springs.

He piped water to his gate for public use,
to save the rural poor from filth and fevers,
a hundred years ahead of his time devised,
a water system for Carmarthen.

Cisterns, pipes, drains, faucets, closets,
water flowed through his house. Above the springs
with their medicinal powers, he built a bath-house
in a garden, that they might take the waters,

herbal aromas, minerals and steam,
bring colour back to dear Maria's cheek,
cooling the fevers as they basked
in water's opulence.

GILLIAN CLARKE

A Charm for Blagdon

No roving shadow of misfortune stain
The shadows that across your windows pass
In harmless glancing of the wind and rain
Or northern moonlight hurrying on your glass.
Nor fire look out of you with bloodshot eyes
Once, and bequeath a quiet skull to time.
Nor storm nor damp undo you. – I devise
This powerful charm and render it with rhyme.

No cloud of pain across your inward sun
The love that lights you darken or abate,
The light that dark or lit you have of one
Whose love and loveliness I celebrate.
Answer the looking in of sun and rain
With years of beauty looking out again.

LAURENCE WHISTLER

Greenhouses

The sense of unrelatedness that comes
from pale untended greenhouses still haunts
my recent dreams of moonlight. Asylums
for strange hybrids, their limewashed panels taunt
my *a priori* concepts as I pass
their blinds of winter whiteness. Span-roofed shaped
of mid-Victorian ironwork, hazed with glass,
they warp and flake. My nails would like to scrape
at each vague pane, completely clarify
each rectangle and then conceptualise
their picture-written forms to amplify
what the mind means. To detail, recognise
what pillar-plants thrust outwards, fill the gaps:
what cactuses persist, with watery saps.

JOHN GURNEY

The Washstand

In Wilburton Rectory's green bedroom,
once an exemplar of Victorian cleanliness,
now a wood-wormed marker to guests
of a time before wall-mounted sinks.
The washstand's one remaining door hangs
from its hinge, a much-handled thing,
like the cover page of a history chronicle
about to loose itself from its binding.

And what of the common moth in the corner,
little weightless leaf, flatter than its marble
resting place, the dust of its body sealed in sleep?
Or the crane fly, its folded limbs and wings
woven into their tapestry of lifelessness?
In such brokenness, how I'm reminded of beauty.

ELISABETH SENNITT CLOUGH

Mr Gradgrind's Country

There was a dining-room, there was a drawing-room,
There was a billiard-room, there was a morning-room,
There were bedrooms for guests and bedrooms for sons and daughters,
In attic and basement there were ample servants' quarters,
There was a modern bathroom, a strong-room, and a conservatory,
In the days of England's glory.

There were Turkish carpets, there were Axminster carpets,
There were oil paintings of Vesuvius and family portraits,
There were mirrors, ottomans, wash-hand-stands and tantaluses,
There were port, sherry, claret, liqueur, and champagne glasses,
There was a solid brass gong, a grand piano, antlers, decanters, and a
    gentlemen's lavatory,
In the days of England's glory.

There was marqueterie and there was mahogany,
There was a cast of the Dying Gladiator in his agony,
There was the 'Encyclopædia Britannica' in a revolving bookcase,
There were finger-bowls, asparagus-tongs, and inlets of real lace:
They stood in their own grounds and were called Chatsworth, Elgin,
    or Tobermory,
In the days of England's glory.

But now these substantial gentlemen's establishments
Are like a perspective of disused elephants,
And the current Rajahs of industry flash past their wide frontages
Far, far away to the latest things in labour-saving cottages,
Where with Russell lupins, jade ash-trays, some Sealyham terriers,
    and a migratory
Cook they continue the story.

SYLVIA TOWNSEND WARNER

Eighteenth-Century Blocks

for Lynn

I

A billet-doux. The scent of pinewoods.
Gilt pin (to keep a message secret)
pricking the thumb, draws blood.
The garden's so badly lit. Who's gone with whom?

Horns are called on to counterpoint
betrayal that was not betrayal
yet it was.

II

The folly, bent on showing an English
autumn what a Greek temple should be like,
traps the moonlight between its pillars
and shimmers the wrong way up
in a formal lake authentic with ducks.

III

The squire, his foot on a tapestried stool,
drinks green tea and scans the pamphlet. Above,
rococo curlicues of fruit, pods,
ears of corn hang chiselled in limewood.
Perhaps (la, sir) some creditor
is lurking behind that Indian screen.
Milady's fixing patches on
but there's surely time for at least one
hand of cards before the masquerade

It's good sometimes to feign to be
what we aren't –
a highwayman, an abigail,
a shepherdess, a fop.

IV

The shadowy queue of lovers,
garlanded, frivolous,
chatter bitter nothings
paying scant attention
to that distant island
wrapped in its haze of gold.

Maybe they don't believe in such a place.
At any rate there are far too many
to be embarking on that fragile craft

HARRY GUEST

The Laird's Lug

The Highland-granite walls are three feet thick.
The windows, shut against the gritty wind,
still squint at lonely plains of castle lawn.
Here, high as a beanstalk, we strain to hear
full-bellied lowing from a hidden herd,
or muffled shufflings from a floor below.

In halls above the frigid gallery,
we traipse past portraits of the olden dead;
through libraries of the books they would have read,
or maybe did not read. (The vellum Histories
look dry as dust.) In a squat white room
of undetermined age, a corner holds

an unexpected hiding place: a chink
of light betrays a time-old paranoia.
A wooden step leads into whitewashed hush,
a trapdoor in the boards; and – the mystery –
a rough hole opens, undetected, through
the floor onto the gallery below.

The laird's lug, it is called. I think of him,
his knees bent to the rich dirt of the ground,
his ear pressed, anxious, to the gap, to learn
imagined secrecies, or otherwise:
perhaps to learn – much worse – of eavesdropped
mutiny; to crouch in wide-eyed dark.

PENNY BOXALL

Guidelines

good afternoon and welcome come this way
here on the ground floor im sorry no dogs or prams
to your left the two imposing busts portray
the marquis and his wife they were executed
by bartolini yes they look content maam
as well they might do having instituted
eleven sons each with his monogram

the library contains twelve thousand tomes
mostly unread and thus in fine condition
while the famous tapestry hanging opposite comes
from bruges and shows us cupid as he cheers
two noble lovers on to coy coition
the fireplace of course is adam the chandelier
french one of the ninth earls acquisitions

the sofa here in the drawingroom was a gift
from catherine the great to the fourteenth count
dont miss the stuccoed ceiling here is the lift
installed by the national trust and made in preston
in nineteen thirty five here we dismount
to view the bedrooms continue our ingestion
of useless facts in staggering amounts

this fine fourposter the last heir occupied
a bishop who had it carved with every spire
within the diocese and later died
in italy from a painful stomach gout
to be precise in some poor peasants byre
who wouldnt house a heretic being devout
a turn of the wheel one cannot but admire

the rest you can see for yourselves the original lock
on the sixteenth century chest the silverware
sevres vases mirrors screens and clocks
untouched by hand roped off in holy precincts
dynastic gods preserved in musty air
note the virginal with its quite distinct
keyboard of nails and strings of human hair

our tour ends here for those of you who plan
a second visit dont forget a supply
of matches petrol even grenades if you can
youll find me waiting away from the house and drive
behind damp walls where my family serves and dies
after two hundred years still stubborn enough to survive
kept warm by a dream of flames climbing roofhigh

LAWRENCE SAIL

Stately Home

'*Behold Land-Interest's compound Man & Horse.*'
                                    – Ebenezer Elliott

Those bad old days of 'rapine and of reif!'
Northumberland's peles still seeping with old wars –
this year's lawful lord and last year's thief,
those warring centaurs, scratch their unscabbed sores.

But here, horned koodoo and okapi skulls,
the family's assegais, a Masai shield,
the head of one of Chillingham's white bulls,
this month's *Tatler, Horse & Hound, The Field.*

Churned earth translucent Meissen, dusted Spode
displayed on Sundays for the pence it makes,
paintings of beasts they'd shot at or they'd rode,
cantered grabbed acres on, won local stakes,
once all one man's debatable demesne,
a day's hard ride from Cheviot to sea –

His scion, stretching back to Charlemagne,
stiff-backed, lets us put down 40p.

                                    TONY HARRISON

Water-Gardens

Water looked up through the lawn
Like a half-buried mirror
Left out by the people before.

There were faces in there
We had seen in the hallways
Of octogenarian specialists,

Mortality-vendors consulted
On bronchial matters
In rot-smelling Boulevard mansions.

We stood on their lino
And breathed, and below us
The dark, peopled water

Was leaning and listening.
There on the steps of the cellar,
Black-clad Victorians

Were feeding the river with souls.
They left us their things,
Reefs of blue ware

In the elder-clumps,
Tins full of rust in the shed,
And on the bookshelves

English poets, all gone damp
With good intentions, never read.
Their miles of flooded graves

Were traffic jams of stone
Where patient amphibian angels
Rode them under, slowly.

The voices came back
From sinks and gratings,
The treasure seekers

Gone downstairs, while all the time
In King Death's rainy garden
We were playing out.

SEAN O'BRIEN

Fore-edge Painting

Poetry of the Anti-Jacobin:
A sturdy quarto, whose morocco ribs
Texture the claret dye, the wide strapwork
Of burnished ribbons, looped informally.
Endpapers calm their whirlpools into stasis;
The cobalts, whites and azures of dried oil
Chart shoals and spindrift for an unsailed sea.

And as the Tory Pages crisp and fan,
Shaking a landscape from their cockled gold,
A spectral blush of emerald and ochre
Sharpens to grass: a Humphrey Repton world
Which full-fledged oaks recede to punctuate.
An antique springtime rubs to sober autumn,
Tipped on a cut perimeter of leaves.

A stub of figures on the carriage-drive
Pauses past text and margin, their estate
Proof against any but the revolution
Of these equivocal false dawns and sunsets.
The scene dissolves into that wicked glow
Which bathes our childhood, our elected fictions:
All weathers in arrest, all edges gilt.

PETER SCUPHAM

The Property of the Executors

i.m. G.F.H.

It might have been a wedding, or a wake,
Some sort of celebration, a solemnity:
Or is it just shopping for shopping's sake,
A ritual cupidity?
Arriving through the morning mist, the cars
Inclined these visitors
Towards the great dead house now stripped, the striped marquee
Smothering with canvas and plastic the long lawns
He had kept in order, until his will bent,
And he put the gun to his head, and the whole thing went
Down to this one event.

My neighbour yawns
After four hours of this, the auctioneer
Jollying along each lot by lot by lot.
Yes, I agree with her, it's much too hot,
And my other neighbour reaches below his chair
For a swig at his beer, and the objects are raised in the air
By acolytes who respond to the numbers called
By the man who calls out money-names without fear
Of interruptions because, however appalled
Some of us are at this show,
This is the way such rituals must go.

The tables, the chairs, the mirrors, the carved blackamoor,
Then the pictures ('After' whoever and all),
The big mahogany chest that stood in the hall
Along with the cracked Staffordshire, the pattern fish slice,
The wrought-iron door-stop against the front door,
Silver, and screens, and glass.
All of them have their value, most of them fetch their price.

Then the books are parcelled out. Some singles, some pairs,
Some 'Miscellaneous. Quantity'. Here
Is one signed by all of the children for Mama, then *Paradise
Lost*, red morocco, Victorian, all

Jumbled up as home used to be, some below stairs,
Some elevated like trophies, things you could call
Treasures. But the auctioneer
Hurries on to the 'General Contents', the job lots,
At the end of a long hot day.

I stay, anyway,
To Lot Seven-Eleven, 'A Collection
Of Power and Hand tools, etc.', to see who may
Make a bid for it. But when it comes, late on,
The lot is split: Seven-Eleven A
Is what I look for, now described 'As Is':
A leather gun-case, initialled on its lid;
Inside, its wooden rods, its brass accoutrements,
Its roll of cotton pull-through; but the space
In which the shotgun should have been, not hid
But glaring open, empty, like the face
Of someone who should have been there. No offence
Intended. An emptiness instead.

Lot Seven-Forty goes. That is the end.
Loud quacking county voices void the tent
Bent on returning home to Cley and Wells.
I grope through autumn twilight, smell the smells
Of furnace-wood cut by a man now dead
Whose stuff this was, who maybe never meant
To cause all this, this sale, this wake, but can't transcend
What he has brought about. Whatever he meant.

ANTHONY THWAITE

Loyalties & Divisions

Though the new democracy
May pain the old Aristocracy

Noël Coward

Gardeners

England, Loamshire, 1789
A gardener speaks, in the grounds of a great house, to his Lordship

Gardens, gardens, and we are gardeners ...
Razored hedgerow, flowers, those planted trees
Whose avenues conduct a greater ease
Of shadow to your own and ladies' skins
And tilt this Nature to magnificence
And natural delight. But pardon us,
My Lord, if we reluctantly admit
Our horticulture not the whole of it,
Forgetting, that for you, this elegance
Is not our work, but your far tidier Sense.

Out of humiliation comes that sweet
Humility that does no good. We know
Our coarser artistries will make things grow.
Others design the craftsmanship we fashion
To please your topographical possession.
A small humiliation – Yes, we eat,
Our crops and passions tucked out of the view
Across a shire, the name of which is you,
Where every native creature runs upon
Hills, moors and meadows which your named eyes own.

Our eyes are nameless, generally turned
Towards the earth our fingers sift all day –
Your day, your earth, your eyes, wearing away
Not earth, eyes, days, but scouring, forcing down
What lives in us and which you cannot own.
One of us heard the earth cry out. It spurned
His hands. It threw stones in his face. We found
That man, my Lord, and he was mad. We bound
His hands together and we heard him say –
'Not me! Not me who cries!' We took away

That man – remember, Lord? – and then we turned,
Hearing your steward order us return,
His oaths, and how you treated us with scorn.
They call this grudge. Let me hear you admit

That in the country that's but half of it.
Townsmen will wonder, when your house was burned,
We did not burn your gardens and undo
What likes of us did for the likes of you;
We did not raze this garden that we made,
Although we hanged you somewhere in its shade.

DOUGLAS DUNN

Craxton

Sunlight daubs my eye.
It is spring. A snail oils the sill.
My tulips are in good repair.
A thrush hops fiercely
Up the Everest of a rockery.
All the grass leans one way.

Spring. The breeze travels
Over the pools where the carp bask,
Disturbing them with reflections.
I watch from my desk.
They are as old as I am.
Wherever my daubed eye stares
The blown fountains, the granite
Obelisks of dead gardeners,
Changing, remain the same.

It is the usual time.
A tray clashes at the door.
My man Craxton enters,
Tall in his black coat.
On the tray is the cup
He waits for me to drink.
With a huge dry thumb
He shifts the bowl of ink
Towards me. 'Master, write.'
Now he is not here.
Slowly morning leaves me.
My humped hand idles.
The shadows spread widely
From the bases of the obelisks.
In a flurry of hops the thrush
Chips the humped snail from the sill.
The wind chops down tulips.
What is this weather?
Autumn, and it is evening.

It is the usual time.
My man Craxton enters
He ripples the plush curtains
To with a noise like fire.
His huge dry hand
Bandages mine. He lifts me.
The stairs creak as we climb.

He bathes me, he dresses me
In loose silk clothes.
He bestows me in silence
Between polished sheets.
He leaves me in darkness.
Soon it will happen.
I do not want it.

It is the usual time.
My man Craxton enters.
So quietly I do not hear,
Tall in his black coat,
His huge dry hands.
Carry up to my bed
A folded napkin on a tray,
A soupspoon and a bowl of blood.

DOM MORAES

The Cedars at Highclere

I see him in the distance. The stories he tells them
waft across to me as I trim the lawns beneath his cedars.

He loves cedars: his father asked my father to put them in.
The Egyptians made all their tables and chairs out of cedar,

he told me once, were buried surrounded by it. Now he's
alone on that fancy verandah, reading, or glancing up towards

these living crowns – always some fat volume open beside him.
That's (he'd say) since forty days stuck out in tropical seas

with so little to do, between fighting off pirates
and avoiding hurricanes, he fell prey to the bookworm.

But we know. In the old days he would never have stopped
still long enough to have turned a leaf. If it wasn't the sea,

it was the turf; if it wasn't the latest horseless carriage,
it was some infernal air machine. Faster, always faster, until

Trotman comes running to pluck him out from that blazing wreck
in the Black Forest – head smashed, heart stopped.

And all he wanted to know was had he killed anybody.
Next thing, he is making Highclere a home for war-wounded,

young lads cowering behind this shadow-line: muttering, wide-eyed
ghost battalions. M'lord was never one to let the grass grow.

Today he showed us another of his special photographs – one of
a mummified cat, which wasn't at all well received by his dog –

nor by her Ladyship, for that matter. But then, we all have doubts
about this digging up of times long gone. The papers make jokes

about the thousands he has wasted (with 36,000 acres
here to keep) and to my own thinking, when there's talk of a curse

you think twice. He's already had a good nine lives – chased
by a wild elephant in South Africa (more of an achievement

to have escaped than shot it, he said), then only last week
rushed to the hospital with three quarters of an hour to live.

When he dies, it will be in a way nobody could have foreseen.
'I don't think I've lost my nerve,' he whispered, straight

after that accident. And he won't let anyone wrap him up
in bandages. 'I want to be buried,' he laughs, 'out in the open,

high up on Beacon Hill, then – if you like – ' to us, he calls us
his garden angels – 'plant one of de Havilland's DH9s

above me like a pyramid; and make sure the grave is dug
by a professional archaeologist.' Tomorrow he's off out

to the East again. The last season, he has announced
'If the pharaohs don't bite, the mosquitoes certainly will.'

JOHN GREENING

Conservatism Revisited

*with apologies to Peter Viereck, who had
something quite different in mind*

Is it a great house, opened up now for all
And sundry to gape at exquisite loot
Hoarded over the centuries, lovingly tended
By the skills of its servants, its devotees?
Well, in boardrooms this and that heir will sit
Lest the house perish.
                     But, no, it's a factory
Being emptied now of the men and women
No longer needed, when profit can accrue
Not from willing, unwilling hands but a closed circuit
Of instructions obeyed by automatons;
And money, grown parthenogenetic,
Can breed money from money for money's sake,
Fight money with money for money's sake.

What it conserves are its own machinations
Till, confounded by electronics too intricate
For atrophied brains and imaginations,
The controllers blow up the system. Its fall,
Demolishing houses, will level the great with the small.

MICHAEL HAMBURGER

Bone China

I want to leave something behind
like the maid who cracked one night
the length of her heart,
who crept shaking down the staircase
to where the service shone on the dresser,
plates pale as a row of moons.

She stacked them in her arms –
a weight greater than all she owned –
bore their white tower to the kitchen garden
where she stood between the soft fruit beds
and smashed each one against the wall
with a planetary anger.

That dawn she walked out of her story forever,
though her flavour salted the servants' tongues for months,
and clearing the ground a hundred years later
of this self-seeded scrub of ash
I can still piece bits of her together – white and sharp –
as if the earth were teething.

ESTHER MORGAN

Emma

A passage from the verse novel *Lara*

I'm the scullery maid, the skivvy, the flunky
in Mr Mallory's empire – the kitchen.

Up before dawn to scrape ash from the range,
black-lead it, light it, then keep it going all day.

Then it's breakfast for Lord Harrington, his wife
and their two 'flawless beauties' my age, so I'm told.

Kidneys, kedgeree, tongue, ham, cold game pie,
woodcock, bacon, boiled, fried or poached eggs,

mushrooms straight from the dark house, toast –
most of which they waste anyway. (More for me.)

When I arrived years ago the sight of all that food
made me quite sick. (Gout and good riddance to them.)

For dinner it's soup, fish dish, three meat dishes,
a savoury and a dessert all served à *la Russe*

from the sideboard by footmen who are *obsequious*
to their superiors and *condescending* to the likes of me.

I believe in words. I read them, remember them,
load them into my mouth – and fire.

Only way to escape is through marriage.
The local fellows? *Philanderers! Braggadocios!*

I tell them to 'go fuck' themselves too.
Mamó would be so proud of me.

Mr Mallory used to brush against my breasts
until one day I said, 'Leave off my *appendages*, Sir'

in front of Mrs Mallory, the housekeeper, wife.
(Poor man, fancy waking up next to a bulldog?)

Had me sieving rhubarb consommé for hours after that.
Not seen Uncle Lorcan since he brought me here.

He writes at Christmas but Mr Kempster the butler
opens our letters in the pantry, *sullying* them.

Uncle Lorcan says there's a home for me in London.
He's old now, even his children have children,

but Mamó would rise from the dead,
wispy hair stuck about her like a dusty spider's web,

and walk through these thick castle walls, howling.
I might finish at midnight, or dawn, if there's a ball,

I can hear the waltzes and unstoppable merriment.
Before sleep I sit up reading by candlelight.

Pride and Prejudice is my favourite. Enya is a ladies
maid upstairs. She *appropriates* books for me.

BERNARDINE EVARISTO

Mappa Mundi

for Alan Livingstone

In their great houses there were always tables laid,
piled high with simple food and books,
old tables that lay supportive beneath
a drift of nutshells and paper, sharp tools.
Returned from walking behind the byre,
or spreading lant from casks upon the fields,
it was at these boards that they received
the urgent message from the capital,
pushing cheese and almanacks aside
to unroll the hasty map, slopping a harsh red wine
into bowls, spilling it, augmenting the stains.
Later, brooding idly and alone
upon required action they might scan
the worn incisements of their tutored days,
the musical notes whose deep square holes
enlaced a fertile cartography,
in which each emblematic creature rose
above a smoking town, and called aloud
to the beasts at the corners of the world.
It was cold, and there was all of Europe
to decide, and Europe, hooded like a bird,
blinked in its eye-gapes and shifted on its perch.
It was ice. The ink in its beechwood wells
snapped to the black attention of winter,
while fields lay supine in communion clothes
waiting for the word, and a coney limped
to the doorstep of the hall for warmth,
or just to perish there. Tables, shifted nearer
to the blaze, supported the elbows of men
who watched themselves in dreams, in the gases
vapours and *language* of the hearth, for they
etymologised, and watched for others too.
Logs of poplar's yellow wood, the splintered larch,
fed a conflagration which all men scanned
to know their mind or find their visitors:
still many hours away, for example, a grandee in furs
alights from his carriage at a crossroad in the hills
and knows he is regarded, as he bends

to fill the carcass of a fowl with snow,
as well as who regards him. His clear gaze
is lifted for a moment towards a house
he travels to but cannot see, then falls,
as the eyes of his host have also fallen,
back from this fire to an erudite table,
a table spread with the things of the world,
and cut out from the local forest years ago.

PETER DIDSBURY

Stately Home

Those comfortably padded lunatic asylums which are known,
euphemistically, as the stately homes of England. – Virginia Woolf

Patrons paid – and ill –
For poems, music, palaces,
Fountains, parterres and gods and nymphs,
From crops, rents, pigeon-house and mill.

We walk, for a fee, their alleys still.
Bees cruise their linden trees, arrows
Point tastefully to what was only theirs.
The car park is too full.

Pastoral pranks of Jacks with Lady Jill
Are told by beds, and Boucher's
Rosy hangings. On a green morocco
Table lies a golden quill.

Inside their chapel, locked behind a grille,
These first rogues continue condescending,
At ease, in Roman guise. And as before
We others foot the bill.

GEOFFREY GRIGSON

Unexpected Visit

I have nothing to say about this garden.
I do not want to be here, I can't explain
what happened. I merely opened a usual door
and found this. The rain

has just stopped, and the gravel paths are trickling
with water. Stone lions, on each side,
gleam like wet seals, and the green birds
are stiff with dripping pride.

Not my kind of country. The gracious vistas,
the rose-gardens and terraces, are all wrong –
as comfortless as the weather. But here I am.
I cannot tell how long

I have stood gazing at grass too wet to sit on,
under a sky so dull I cannot read
the sundial, staring along the curving walks
and wondering where they lead;

not really hoping, though, to be enlightened.
It must be morning, I think, but there is no
horizon behind the trees, no sun as clock
or compass. I shall go

and find, somewhere among the formal hedges
or hidden behind a trellis, a toolshed. There
I can sit on a box and wait. Whatever happens
may happen anywhere,

and better, perhaps, among the rakes and flowerpots
and sacks of bulbs than under this pallid sky:
having chosen nothing else, I can at least
choose to be warm and dry.

FLEUR ADCOCK

Stanzas on a Visit to Longleat House in Wiltshire, October 1953

To John Farrelly

Dead pomp sneering underground
Glares up at a horned foot of clay
Where the hog of multitude hangs around
Among these tremendous memories
That delegate to our day
The superannuated and damned glories.

A quidnunc with a shopping bag
Stops gossiping with another hag
And where immense conceptions were
Dragged shrieking from their cellars here
The ragged-arsed mechanics squat
Owning what they haven't got.

O rare rain of disinterest
Descend on this fouled public nest
And rout out all vulgarities
That, crowding through its majesties,
Gut to bare shell and bone
The grandeur of the dead and gone.

In car-park, garden and urinal
The free and ignorant, almost
As easy as at a Cup Final
Gawk through the stone-transparent ghost
Of this once noble house, now lost
In the gross error of survival.

'Come,' said my proud and sulking friend,
'Four angels up to Heaven's Gate,
And looking down at Longleat
So far below, shall disappear
The human termite, leaving there
Stones and spectres hand in hand.'

And from that aerial sweep of height
The valley fell through depths of pine
Down through green distances until
From glimmering water rising bright
Longleat, bird's-eyed in sunshine,
Smiled up from its own funeral.

I saw the heroic seizins fade
And hide in laurels of old trees
As brassbands of indignities
Exploded echoes to degrade
The splendours and the miseries
Of that cold illustrious shade.

GEORGE BARKER

Two Versions of Pastoral

Might she have trusted them – the quiet insistence
Of slate-roofed stone below an oak-topped ridge,
A haze of chalk-dust settling in the distance,
Cows in sleeping fields, lambs to the slaughter,
A pattering mill-wheel and a lichen-mottled bridge
      Over green sluggish water?

They who owned the herds, the fields, oaks and water,
Who owned the horses cropping, and their grooms
(Their coupling in the hayloft was as quick
As sudden mice surprised in shuttered rooms,
In a square of sunlight where the dust lies thick)
      Owned the farmer's daughter.

What happened to her in the cellar, in the wood
Where she was planted, means that nothing's any good
Though all England 'has come to terms with its grief' –
Which is a lie as anyone can see who leaves
This land that ceaselessly, unreasonably grieves
      For the fall of a lark or leaf ...

What could it mean to say they loved the place,
Every summer laid out picnic things that shone,
Spread affection for their tenants, neighbours, friends –
Who would have eaten horse-shit rather than lose face –
In the generous shade of cedars, on the lawn
      No booted gardener tends?

The children who disinherit them are gone,
Taking to the City nothing but a name
(What use are their accounts, long-since overdrawn?)
– She haunts the feathery, sun-scoured attic floors
Among the wardrobes, mildewed books and gew-gaws
      No-one will come back to claim.

* * *

Outside Domesday settlements-turned-overspill-towns
The garden centres blossom, the DIY estates,
Bungalows, allotments, and through the gates
Come squadrons of SUVs, crunching up the drive
Of the big house 'nestled in a fold of the Downs';
      And in the year of Our Lord 2005

The regimental colours fade and feed the moths
In the abandoned English country churches,
While forgotten names are fading with the ink
In parish registers and books of searches –
Brides whose wedding-dresses doubled as grave-cloths ...
      Time to take stock, don't you think?

Of the family portraits in the roped-off corridors,
Of the plundered acres and the restless silence
In mile on mile of rape, of the generals and JPs,
The shotgun-cradling imbeciles, double-barrelled bores
And all that England has to show for centuries
      Of robbery with violence;

Of the farmyards where briars and brambles choke
The rubble-heaps, old cars, old bikes, in-fills;
Of the burning stubble and the burnt-out byre,
Of the killing fields, the pheasant-crowded hills
Where white ghosts wander now and black smoke
      Billows from each cow-pyre.

The lads who are left to do battle with the beer
On Friday nights know how their grandads ended,
As they were meant to do – among the shot and shells;
Their wives and girlfriends know what can't be mended
By the High Street parades, the flags and bells,
      The ranks thinner every year.

ALAN JENKINS

Landscape

This autumn park, the sequin glitter of leaves
Upon its withering bosom, the lake a moonstone –
O light mellifluous, glossing the stone-blind mansion,
October light, a godsend to these groves!

These unkempt groves, blind vistas, mark the defeat
Of men who imposed on Nature a private elegance
And died of dropsy. Let still the gay ghosts dance,
They are heartless ones we should wish nor fear to meet.

A ruin now, but here the Folly grinned –
The mad memento that one joker built:
Mocking their reasoned crops, a fabulous guilt
Towered up and cursed them fruitless from the ground.

Light drops, the hush of fallen ash, submission
Of a dying face now muted for the grave:
Through mansion, lake and the lacklustre groves
We see the landscape of their dissolution.

C. DAY LEWIS

At a Warwickshire Mansion

Mad world, mad kings, mad composition – King John

Cycles of ulcers, insomnia, poetry –
Badges of office; wished, detested tensions.
Seeing the parsley-like autumnal trees
Unmoving in the mist, I long to be
The marvellous painter who with art could freeze
Their transitory look: the vast dissensions
Between the human and his world arise
And plead with me to sew the hurt with eyes.

Horn calls on ostinato strings: the birds
Sweep level out of the umbrageous wood.
The sun towards the unconsidered west
Floats red, enormous, still. For these the words
Come pat, but for society possessed
With frontal lobes for evil, rear for good,
They are incongruous as the poisoner's
Remorse or as anaemia in furs.

In the dank garden of the ugly house
A group of leaden statuary perspires;
Moss grows between the ideal rumps and paps
Cast by the dead Victorian; the mouse
Starves behind massive panels; paths relapse
Like moral principles; the surrounding shires
Darken beneath the bombers' crawling wings.
The terrible simplifiers jerk the strings.

But art is never innocent although
It dreams it may be; and the red in caves
Is left by cripples of the happy hunt.
Between the action and the song I know
Too well the sleight of hand which points the blunt,
Compresses, lies. The schizophrenic craves
Magic and mystery, the rest the sane
Reject: what force and audience remain?

The house is dark upon the darkening sky:
I note the blue for which I never shall
Find the equivalent. I have been acting
The poet's role for quite as long as I
Can, at a stretch, without it being exacting:
I must return to less ephemeral
Affairs – to those controlled by love and power;
Builders of realms, their tenants for an hour.

ROY FULLER

Landscape Poem

Like men forced to dig their own graves, my ancestors
planted the hedges that kept them from their land.
The land's enriched by dead servants like a manure.
The landscape was formed by their hands,
as a cook rolls out pastry. Vistas, diced into fields,
garnished and served by footmen and maids,
tended out in the woods by those
who never saw the elegant patterns whole
from drawing-room windows.

Gardeners in the bothies reek
of humiliation like an unpleasant sweat.
Maids in uniforms haunt the lawns.
I sprang from these people. My land. Mine!
Now it grows untidy, but hardly wild –
the trees still haven't dared step out of line.

GLYN HUGHES

The Doll's House

The source of the wealth that built Harewood is historical fact.
There is nothing anyone can do to change the past, however
appalling or regrettable that past might be. What we can do,
however, what we must do, is engage with that legacy and in so
doing stand a chance of having a positive effect on the future.
— David Lascelles

Art is a lie that makes us realise truth.
— Pablo Picasso

Welcome to my house, this stately home
where, below stairs, my father rules as chef:
confecting, out of sugar-flesh and -bone,
décor so fine, your tongue will treble clef
singing its name. Near-sighted and tone-deaf,
I smell-taste-touch; create each replica
in my mind's tongue. My name? Angelica.

This is my world, the world of haute cuisine:
high frosted ceilings, modelled on high art,
reflected in each carpet's rich design;
each bed, each armchair listed à la carte.
Come, fellow connoisseur of taste, let's start
below stairs, where you'll blacken your sweet tooth,
sucking a beauty whittled from harsh truth ...

Mind your step! The stairway's worn and steep,
let your sixth senses merge in the half-light ...
This muted corridor leads to the deep
recesses of the house. Here, to your right,
my father's realm of uncurbed appetite –
private! The whiff of strangers breaks his spell.
Now left, to the dead end. Stop! Can you smell

cinnamon, brown heat in the afternoon
of someone else's summer? This rusty key
unlocks the passage to my tiny room,
stick-cabin, sound-proofed with a symphony
of cinnamon; shrine to olfactory

where I withdraw to paint in cordon bleu,
shape, recreate this house; in miniature.

All art is imitation: I'm a sculptor
of past-imperfect; hungry, I extract
molasses; de- and reconstruct high culture
from base material; blend art and fact
in every glazed and glistening artefact
housed in this doll's house. Stately home of sugar.
Of Demerara cubes secured with nougat.

Look at its hall bedecked with royal icing –
the ceiling's crossbones mirrored in the frieze,
the chimneypiece. The floor is sugar glazing
clear as a frozen lake. My centrepiece
statue of Eve, what a creative feast!
A crisp Pink Lady, sculpted with my teeth,
its toffee glaze filming the flesh beneath.

The music room's my favourite. I make music
by echoing design: the violet-rose
piped ceiling is the carpet's fine mosaic
of granulated violet and rose,
aimed to delight the eye, the tongue, the nose.
Even the tiny chairs are steeped in flavour
delicate as a demisemiquaver.

Taste, if you like, sweet as a mothertongue ...
See how this bedroom echoes my refrain:
the chairs, the secretaire, commode, chaise longue,
four-poster bed, all carved from sugarcane;
even the curtains that adorn its frame,
chiselled from the bark, each lavish fold
drizzled with tiny threads of spun 'white gold'.

The library was hardest. How to forge
each candied volume wafer-thin, each word
burnt sugar. In the midnight hours, I'd gorge
on bubbling syrup, mouth its language; learned
the temperature at which burnt sugar burned,
turned sweet to bitter; inked a tiny passage
that overflowed into a secret passage,

the Middle Passage; made definitive
that muted walkway paved with sugar plate,
its sugar-paper walls hand-painted with
hieroglyphs invisible as sweat
but speaking volumes; leading to the sweet
peardrop of a stairwell down and down
to this same room of aromatic brown

in miniature. Here, connoisseur, I've set
the doll, rough hewn from sugarcane's sweet wood:
her choker, hardboiled sweets as black as jet;
her dress, molasses-rich; her features, hard.
This handcarved doll, with sugar in her blood –
Europe, the Caribbean, Africa;
baptised in sugar, named Angelica,

has built a tiny house in Demerara
sugar grains secured with sugarpaste,
each sculpted room a microscopic mirror
of its old self; and below stairs, she's placed
a blind doll with kaleidoscopic taste,
who boils, bakes, moulds, pipes, chisels, spins and blows
sugar, her art, the only tongue she knows.

PATIENCE AGBABI

The Two of Us

after Laycock

You sat sitting in your country seat
with maidens, servants waiting hand and foot.
You eating swan, crustaceans, starters, seconds, sweet.
You dressed for dinner, worsted, made to measure. Cut:
me darning socks, me lodging at the gate,
me stewing turnips, beet, one spud,
a badger bone. Turf squealing in the grate –
no coal, no wood.

No good. You in your splendour: leather,
rhinestone, ermine, snakeskin, satin, silk,
a felt hat finished with a dodo feather.
Someone's seen you swimming lengths in gold-top milk.
Me parched, me in a donkey jacket,
brewing tea from sawdust mashed in cuckoo spit,
me waiting for the peaks to melt, the rain to racket
on the metal roof, the sky to split,

and you on-stream, piped-up, plugged-in, you worth a mint
and tighter than a turtle's snatch.
Me making light of making do with peat and flint
for heat, a glow-worm for a reading lamp. No match.
The valleys where the game is, where the maize is –
yours. I've got this plot just six foot long
by three foot wide, for greens for now, for daisies
when I'm dead and gone.

You've got the lot, the full set:
chopper, Roller, horse-drawn carriage, microlight, skidoo,
a rosewood yacht, a private jet.
I'm all for saying that you're fucking loaded, you.
And me, I clomp about on foot from field to street;
these clogs I'm shod with, held together now with segs
and fashioned for my father's father's father's feet
they're on their last legs.

Some in the village reckon we're alike, akin:
same neck, same chin. Up close that's what they've found,
some sameness in the skin,
or else they've tapped me on the back and you've turned round.
Same seed, they say, same shoot,
like I'm some cutting taken from the tree,
like I'm some twig related to the root.
But I can't see it, me.

So when it comes to nailing down the lid
if I were you I wouldn't go with nothing.
Pick some goods and chattels, bits and bobs like Tutankhamen did,
and have them planted in the coffin.
Opera glasses, fob-watch, fountain pen, a case of fishing flies,
a silver name-tag necklace full-stopped with a precious stone,
a pair of one pound coins to plug the eyes,
a credit card, a mobile phone,

some sentimental piece of earthenware,
a collar stud, a cufflink and a tiepin,
thirteen things to stand the wear and tear
of seasons underground, and I'll take what I'm standing up in.
That way, on the day they dig us out
they'll know that you were something really fucking fine
and I was nowt.
Keep that in mind,

because the worm won't know your make of bone from mine.

SIMON ARMITAGE

Lord and Lady Romfort

(1) *Villeggiatura (Trio for Bailiff, Housekeeper and Gardener)*

'Prune the roses, plant the lawns with geraniums, shake out the chintzes,
    Re-gild the coronets on the lamp-post,
    Everything must be made ready:
  His Lordship is coming down for the summer months!'

'Open the house, let the air and the sky
    Into the musty old house shut up for the winter:
    The waves roar in at the cushioned rooms,
  Her Ladyship will be coming down for the summer months!'

'Tell the farmers to farm, and the fishermen to be ready,
    Let the lifeboat be on the look-out, the cork strips seen to anew!
  His Lordship will be coming down for the summer months!'

'Re-stuff the mattresses, iron the muslin for the dressing-tables,
    Shave the trees flat at the top for the view:
  Her Ladyship will be coming down for the summer months!'

'Open the windows and let pleasure in,
    Thin the grapes in the vinery, plumpen the peaches,
Tell the band in the Winter Gardens to learn some new tunes:
  His Lordship is coming down for the summer months!'

'Clean the stables, groom the horses, prink the postilions:
    Her Ladyship will be entertaining in the summer;
There will be red massacres of pigeons on the white cliffs,
    And outriders in beaver hats will meet the guests at the station.'

'Crayfield, I don't like the colour you've painted the gates.'
                          'Yes, Lord Romfort.'

'Macnab, I don't like the geraniums where you've planted them.'
                          'No, m'lady.'

'Geraniums should be massed, not spattered like confetti.'
                          'Yes, m'lady.'

'Dawkins, I think the house feels damp.
        Shut all the windows and light all the fires.'

                                                        'Yes, m'lady.'

(2) Golightly

With His Lordship came Golightly,
                Confidential valet,
                Knowing enough secrets
To keep a score of lawyers at work all day for a decade.

Golightly in striped trousers and black coat
Was suave and round and red and white with a slight burr on his tongue.
He had to prop up the image he served as well as to serve it.

In the same way that the Oracle at Delphi
In light of subsequent events could be interpreted,
So, when the image acted without motive, as often, impulsive,
Golightly would afterward put into the action, purpose,
Saying,
        'His Lordship was determined to put his foot down'.

                                        OSBERT SITWELL

The Jacobean Mansion

This is how I wish to remember us:
In the garden of the Jacobean mansion
Watching the ball of heaven turn
Its treasures towards us like berries
And the cool night sweeping us
Up into its arms and all being benediction
Without knowledge of what wound
Would separate us, and both of us at peace.

HILARY DAVIES

At Great Tew

thinking of Cary, Viscount Falkland (1610–43)

'... and would passionately profess that the very agony of the war took his sleep from him and would shortly break his heart. He was weary of the times, he said, but would be out of it ere night.'

i

As he could not heal his country's disease,
he longed for death. Dressing himself cleanly
as one going to a banquet, he drew the flap
and stepped into the tented field. An army
stirred, and small fires through the morning mist
blossomed. A nervous boy
fidgeted fingertips on the war drum.

He stands and gazes. The morning light
gathers like elegance at wrist and neck.
Across an English field he stares
into the mirror of an English field
where small fires blossom.
Between the fields, the dark fume of a hedge,
and a linking gap ...

ii

High summer. The Cotswold stone
returns light, softened. Echoes,
echoes everywhere. The lane
tunnelling green through covertures of scents
leads to a mossed and pitted gate, beyond
which, becalmed now like a photograph,
his house stands, at whose table, before friends,
the wine and meat were sanctified
by ideals of moderation, while the candles
glimmered in Oxfordshire darkness, itself
in an England black with storm.
And the storm rose, and each light failed
one by one. No man survives
alone in blackness, can only grasp

whatever is to hand, and that always
is weapons, the simplicity
of alignment, leading inexorably
to a misty field at dawn
before the battle ...

iii

Hooves
gather to thunder over mist-soft earth.
With light fixed in determined eyes
he kicks blood from his horse and pulls ahead
aimed at the mirrored enemy, that gap
clean in the hedge where image coincides
with image and a hail of lead. Comrades
and foes, stunned, rein back to admire
momently this career of death ...

iv

The picnic crumbles, slips into the grass.
The Sunday paper brightly features
'suicide chic', the hagiography
of exemplary failures:
a poet toppling from a bridge,
an aviator heading out to sea.
The tone of commendation and the staring
ikons of centrality sit well
among advertisements which also fail
to mention price and efficacy ...

v

The Sunday's camera would have caught it well:
that split astonished second when
two hell-bent forces faltered as there lay
between them a small island of one man;
until one side saw in the death
bravery flowering from a certain cause,
the other, panic from a loss of nerve,

and craning forward, screaming, both came on.

BRIAN JONES

In Darley Abbey Park

Avenues of trees, the route of a wall
Nicked with paired initials, the lawn's
Sweep, and steps to a terrace

Slowly disclose an order, blurred symmetries
Leading our casual gaze and pace
Over a verge of latticed shadow

To the mansion some minor noble built
Above a turfed shore: beyond, haze
Flooding the valley, a spreading fleet

Of smokestacks. A board shows the house
Still open, for refreshments. One window
Blazes in a chance of light.

And so we wander through the normal green,
Stretch out by trellises, drink tea,
And try to guess whether an abbey ever tolled

Eternity along this narrow river. A prospect
Ebbs, leaving boys edging down the bank, pebbles flung
Skimming across water, the empty jostling skiffs,

And no name to sanctify our wandering.
Lifting from the grass, our palms
Meet, stained faintly. Continually,

Sunlight spills echoes; a last note
Almost shakes the water. Where will our children
Look for us, strolling through patterns of stone

And grass, names distorted across a park,
The tongue gagged? Smoke scrawls their destinations.
Generations silt the fields. Like ash whirled

Crazily from a blaze, but returning
And through scarcely a breeze, cabbage-butterflies
Pursue random leaf-directed routes.

PAUL WILKINS

Coole and Ballylee, 1931

Under my window-ledge the waters race,
Otters below and moor-hens on the top,
Run for a mile undimmed in Heaven's face
Then darkening through 'dark' Raftery's 'cellar' drop,
Run underground, rise in a rocky place
In Coole demesne, and there to finish up
Spread to a lake and drop into a hole.
What's water but the generated soul?

Upon the border of that lake's a wood
Now all dry sticks under a wintry sun,
And in a copse of beeches there I stood,
For Nature's pulled her tragic buskin on
And all the rant's a mirror of my mood:
At sudden thunder of the mounting swan
I turned about and looked where branches break
The glittering reaches of the flooded lake.

Another emblem there! That stormy white
But seems a concentration of the sky;
And, like the soul, it sails into the sight
And in the morning's gone, no man knows why;
And is so lovely that it sets to right
What knowledge or its lack had set awry,
So arrogantly pure, a child might think
It can be murdered with a spot of ink.

Sound of a stick upon the floor, a sound
From somebody that toils from chair to chair;
Beloved books that famous hands have bound,
Old marble heads, old pictures everywhere;
Great rooms where travelled men and children found
Content or joy; a last inheritor
Where none has reigned that lacked a name and fame
Or out of folly into folly came.

A spot whereon the founders lived and died
Seemed once more dear than life; ancestral trees
Or gardens rich in memory glorified
Marriages, alliances and families,

And every bride's ambition satisfied.
Where fashion or mere fantasy decrees
Man shifts about – all that great glory spent –
Like some poor Arab tribesman and his tent.

We were the last romantics – chose for theme
Traditional sanctity and loveliness;
Whatever's written in what poets name
The book of the people; whatever most can bless
The mind of man or elevate a rhyme;
But all is changed, that high horse riderless,
Though mounted in that saddle Homer rode
Where the swan drifts upon a darkening flood.

W. B. YEATS

Swans

The arc of the driveway is what's left,
where someone built a house and tended a lake
to walk beside, discussing politics
and how a tree moves in the wind. Its music
is a jetty drifting away from the boathouse
whose rolled-shut metal door tricks
visitors into thinking it holds a life raft.

The house drifts beyond its purpose,
is demolished for a car park and picnics
and returns in a special room, small, sturdy,
becoming anonymous as its windows empty,
enormous insects swanning around – they own the place –
occasionally stunning themselves on the glass.

JOHN MCAULIFFE

Woodtown Manor

for Morris Graves

I

Here the delicate dance of silence,
The quick step of the robin,
The sudden skittering rush of the wren:
Minute essences move in and out of creation
Until the skin of soundlessness forms again.

Part order, part wilderness,
Water creates its cadenced illusion
Of glaucous, fluent growth;
Fins raised, as in a waking dream,
Bright fish probe their painted stream.

Imaginary animals harbour here:
The young fox coiled in its covert,
Bright-eyed and mean, the baby bird:
The heron, like a radiant italic,
Illuminating the gospel of the absurd.

And all the menagerie of the living marvellous:
Stone shape of toad,
Flicker of insect life,
Shift of wind-touched grass
As though a beneficent spirit stirred.

II

Twin deities hover in Irish air
Reconciling poles of east and west;
The detached and sensual Indian God,
Franciscan dream of gentleness:
Gravity of Georgian manor
Approves, with classic stare,
Their dual disciplines of tenderness.

JOHN MONTAGUE

A Visit to Castletown House

for Norah Graham

The avenue was green and long, and green
light, pooled under the fernheads; a jade screen
could not let such liquid light in, a sea
at its greenest self could not pretend to be
so emerald. Men had made this landscape
from a mere secreting wood: knuckles bled
and bones broke to make this awning drape
a fitting silk upon its owner's head.

The house was lifted by two pillared wings
out of its bulk of solid chisellings
and flashed across the chestnut-marshalled lawn
a few lit windows on a bullock bawn.
The one-way windows of the empty rooms
reflected meadows, now the haunt
of waterbirds: where hawtrees were in bloom,
and belladonna, a poisonous plant.

A newer gentry in their quaint attire
looked at maps depicting alien shire
and city, town, and fort: they were his seed,
that native who had taken coloured beads
disguised as chandeliers of vulgar glass,
and made a room to suit a tasteless man
– a graceful art come to a sorry pass –
painted like some demented tinker's van.

But the music that was played in there –
that had grace, a nervous grace laid bare,
Tortelier unravelling sonatas
pummelling the instrument that has
the deep luxurious sensual sound,
allowing it no richness, making stars
where moons would be, choosing to expound
music as passionate as guitars.

I went into the calmer, gentler hall
in the wineglassed, chattering interval:

there was the smell of rose and woodsmoke there.
I stepped into the gentler evening air
and saw black figures dancing on the lawn,
Eviction, Droit de Seigneur, Broken Bones,
and heard the crack of ligaments being torn
and smelled the clinging blood upon the stones.

MICHAEL HARTNETT

The Owner Instructs the Master Mason

See that my Howse look to the East
for there riseth the Sunne and that way hung
the sages' star when Christ was born.

Sir, for sure an east wind's rare in our summer shire.
We'll stand square to the dawn.

Let my Howse at night be a Lantern raised
for the lesser folk. Set Glasse
in every side for a Lattice of Light.

Squire, we'll have ten thousand diamond windowpanes
outstare the stars.

Raise high my Halle for lordings to praise
and my servants to please. Make each Chamber talle
and every Hearth wide for the ease of alle.

For stateliness and welcome, sir, your house will stand
a beacon in our land.

Have him believe it's his design, his dream, not mine.
Use courtesy. No need to fawn. This is the art of it.

But some nights when the work's done and I'm trudging
with the team down tracks ghost-deep in moon-flowers,
I look back at my scheme of stone: rising stone on stone
cut free, squared, scabbled, dressed, laid true
by these humming home in the dark – quarrymen, masons,
 brothers –
and the stone is their voice and my honey-gold mark.
Look how I put it:
                    WILLIAM ARNOLD FECIT.

JULIET AYKROYD

A Man

In memory of H. of M.

I

In Casterbridge there stood a noble pile,
Wrought with pilaster, bay, and balustrade
In tactful times when shrewd Eliza swayed.
    On burgher, squire, and clown
It smiled the long street down for near a mile.

II

But evil days beset that domicile;
The stately beauties of its roof and wall
Passed into sordid hands. Condemned to fall
    Were cornice, quoin, and cove,
And all that art had wove in antique style.

III

Among the hired dismantlers entered there
One till the moment of his task untold.
When charged therewith he gazed, and answered bold:
    'Be needy I or no,
I will not help lay low a house so fair!

IV

'Hunger is hard. But since the terms be such –
No wage, or labour stained with the disgrace
Of wrecking what our age cannot replace
    To save its tasteless soul –
I'll do without your dole. Life is not much!'

V

Dismissed with sneers he backed his tools and went,
And wandered workless; for it seemed unwise
To close with one who dared to criticize
    And carp on points of taste:
Rude men should work where placed, and be content.

VI

Years whiled. He aged, sank, sickened; and was not:
And it was said, 'A man intractable
And curst is gone.' None sighed to hear his knell,
   None sought his churchyard-place;
His name, his rugged face, were soon forgot.

VII

The stones of that fair hall lie far and wide,
And but a few recall its ancient mould;
Yet when I pass the spot I long to hold
   As truth what fancy saith:
'His protest lives where deathless things abide!'

THOMAS HARDY

Elizabeth Sweyn, Widow,
at Her Writing Desk in the Hall

For taking a trout out of my water: the cold hill
    water that tumbles white and brown over stones
    to the loch, and loses itself there awhile, and
    then gathers its strands and issues out again,
    tranquil and blue and reed-stained, to the sea,
        I summon you to the Hall.

For making much noise in the bothies and beyond about
    the French and their setting to rights of the
    frame of society (wrenched from its natural
    frame by priest and tyrant): and so casting
    a shadow of doubt and threat and disquiet upon
    this ancient island seat, and sowing mischiefs
    in simple minds,
        I summon you to the Hall.

For arrears of rent. I have had much patience with
    that old perverse one, your mother, who has
    not two farthings to tinkle together when it
    comes to Martinmas and the factor stands in
    the office with his open rent-book and the
    crofters come in, one by one, silver-fingered,
    taking off their bonnets: no, but the same
    bold lady could come back from last Lammastide
    in Kirkwall with a new bonnet and gloves, and
    a dozen white cups and plates with blue scroll-
    work on them: and after cries to Mr Brodie my
    grieve, *What way at all can I pay, and that*
    Stephen of mine never turning tilth, no but
    squandering every sea-sillock-cent in the ale-
    house, morning to night, year-long?
        I summon you to the Hall.

You understand well enough, it's bred in your bone,
    it is as sure rooted in every person in this island
    as the order and priority of stars – one fish
    in seven, and that the best, is to be left at
    the door of the Hall before sunset: and you
    have gone by the door of the Hall every night

this past moon with a string of cod in your
finger to some ignorant red-mouth and sweet-
whisperer in a darkling hill croft; and so
left my five cats hungry.
    I summon you to the Hall.

For continual disrespect, in that when a certain
    person is horse-borne on the island road all
    islanders but one doff bonnets, and crook the
    knee, and cast their eyes down; no, but one
    certain lump of obstinate clay turns his back,
    yea and falls to studying a bird's flight, or
    a flower opening, or a raindrop in a pool:
    for explanation of such and other practisings and slightings
        I summon you to the Hall.

For that all summonses hitherto, delivered by sundry:
    as, the factor Mr Walter, the grieve John-
    William Brodie, Hilda the lass from the
    butter-house here, Ikey the tinker who passes
    word about the crofts in consideration of a
    sup of whisky, Mr Gilfillan the new minister,
    the Hall dog Major (who so delicately carries
    letters in his teeth), since all and every
    summons from here has been a summons to a
    stone, I intend to come with this myself,
    unfaltering from Hall to hovel, six black
    words on a white sheet,
        I summon you to the Hall
For a hundred reasons I cannot think of now, man,
        I summon you to the Hall.

You have hair like spillings of sunlight and the
    distant words of your mouth laughing among
    fishermen are a disturbance to me and (I know
    it) when you walk from your mother's door of
    mornings to the boat *Cloud-racer* the island
    seems to be yours then, and not this foolish
    widowed soon-to-wither woman's; and if I do
    not speak soon, some little slut from the hill
    or the shore will have you to kirk and to bed
    and to bairn-making; and what is authority in
    a place if a yoke cannot be put on a serf, a

mere mingling of brief dust and spume; no
hard yoke either, but a sweet yoke of ease
and privilege; that being undeniably so?
    I ...

    *

Mrs Sweyn, the young widow, left off her writing
here, she smiled, she tore her letter into small
pieces and let them fall and flutter from her
hand into the coal-fire in the study.

GEORGE MACKAY BROWN

Ruins of a Great House

though our longest sun sets at right declensions and
makes but winter arches, it cannot be long before we
lie down in darkness, and have our light in ashes ...
                              – Browne, *Urn Burial*

Stones only, the *disjecta membra* of this Great House,
Whose mothlike girls are mixed with candledust,
Remain to file the lizard's dragonish claws;
The mouths of those gate cherubs streaked with stain.
Axle and coachwheel silted under the muck
Of cattle droppings.

                          Three crows flap for the trees
And settle, creaking the eucalyptus boughs.
A smell of dead limes quickens in the nose
The leprosy of Empire.

                          'Farewell, green fields'
                          'Farewell, ye happy groves!'

Marble as Greece, like Faulkner's South in stone,
Deciduous beauty prospered and is gone;
But where the lawn breaks in a rash of trees
A spade below dead leaves will ring the bone
Of some dead animal or human thing
Fallen from evil days, from evil times.

It seems that the original crops were limes
Grown in the silt that clogs the river's skirt;
The imperious rakes are gone, their bright girls gone,
The river flows, obliterating hurt.
I climbed a wall with the grill ironwork
Of exiled craftsmen, protecting that great house
From guilt, perhaps, but not from the worm's rent,
Nor from the padded cavalry of the mouse.
And when a wind shook in the limes I heard
What Kipling heard; the death of a great empire, the abuse
Of ignorance by Bible and by sword.

A green lawn, broken by low walls of stone
Dipped to the rivulet, and pacing, I thought next
Of men like Hawkins, Walter Raleigh, Drake,
Ancestral murderers and poets, more perplexed
In memory now by every ulcerous crime.
The world's green age then was a rotting lime
Whose stench became the charnel galleon's text.
The rot remains with us, the men are gone.
But, as dead ash is lifted in a wind,
That fans the blackening ember of the mind,
My eyes burned from the ashen prose of Donne.

Ablaze with rage, I thought
Some slave is rotting in this manorial lake,
And still the coal of my compassion fought:
That Albion too, was once
A colony like ours, 'a piece of the continent, a part of the main'
Nook-shotten, rook o'er blown, deranged
By foaming channels, and the vain expense
Of bitter faction.

        All in compassion ends
So differently from what the heart arranged:
'as well as if a manor of thy friend's ...'

DEREK WALCOTT

The Landscape Gardeners

Brutal shuddering machines, yellow, bite into given earth.
Only rich Whigs, commanding labour,
Once had earth shifted, making lakes, and said
– And it was true – 'We are improving Nature.'

GEOFFREY GRIGSON

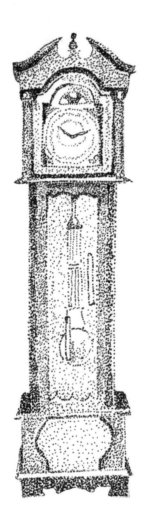

Arrivals & Departures

... those homes serene and stately
Which only lately
Seem to have run to seed!

Noël Coward

Death of King George V

'New King arrives in his capital by air ...'
– Daily Newspaper

Spirits of well-shot woodcock, partridge, snipe
  Flutter and bear him up the Norfolk sky:
In that red house in a red mahogany book-case
  The stamp collection waits with mounts long dry.

The big blue eyes are shut which saw wrong clothing
  And favourite fields and coverts from a horse;
Old men in country houses hear clocks ticking
  Over thick carpets with a deadened force;

Old men who never cheated, never doubted,
  Communicated monthly, sit and stare
At the new suburb stretched beyond the run-way
  Where a young man lands hatless from the air.

JOHN BETJEMAN

Downe: The Extreme Verge of the World

They're dreaming of a garden like the ones they knew
as children. They've searched the railway routes
so he can talk science in London and come back home
for dinner. They've lost a house in Woking –

now it's Kent. A gloomy day. Bolts of blue
from a chilly north-east wind. Sixteen miles –
two hours by train. Fat hedgerows, skeined with paper trails
of wild white clematis, and ancient wooded hills.

Step out. It feels remote. An old flint church:
St Mary's, Downe. A yew, a walnut tree with bark
like silver hair. Villagers smile from open doors.
The butcher, baker, post office. The villa they've come to see.

'Ugly,' she says. 'A desolate air.' The garden, though,
makes up for it. Old trees – purple magnolia, a quince,
a medlar, Spanish chestnut. A goodish hay-meadow.
In September they'll move in. A child will be born,

and buried in the family plot he'll pick at the west door
of this flint church. Through briar rose haws, twisting petioles
of clematis will scribble these hedges like the pencil
of a ferocious toddler with glowing, ochre-coloured wire.

RUTH PADEL

Fall Weekend at Milgate (3)

Milgate kept standing for four centuries,
good landlord alternating with derelict.
Most fell between. We're landlords for the weekend,
and watch October go balmy. Midday heat
draws poison from the Jacobean brick,
and invites the wilderness to our doorstep:
moles, nettles, last Sunday news, last summer's toys,
bread, cheeses, jars of honey, a felled elm
stacked like construction in the kitchen garden.
The warm day brings out wasps to share our luck,
suckers for sweets, pilots of evolution;
dozens drop in the beercans, clamber, buzz,
debating like us whether to stay and drown,
or, by losing legs and wings, take flight.

ROBERT LOWELL

The Mansion

The house stands as it always has,
Its windows tall above the lake
And grass cut almost to the yellow root.

Along the drive a whitelimed kerb
Follows a perfect crescent,
As if stone, like air or water, moved in waves.

My steps dissolve in gardens where
The acid rhododendron thrives,
Its flowers pink and white as naked dolls.

It always was a selfish tree,
Devouring the light, growing
Glossy and alone, the strong inheritor.

At the door they take my card
And a name in silver italics
Grants entry where I never thought to pass.

These hands laid gently on my arm
Disturb an earlier trespasser,
That child under the yew hedge

Who watched the long cars slide through his village
And women shaped like candleflames
Moving over the lawns.

Above his head the berries swelled
As soft as wax around each nucleus,
The black nugget of poison that would grow.

ROBERT MINHINNICK

A Stately Exterior

The tenant absent (Scutcheon Hall is let
To Transatlantic opulence by a lord
Whose peerage pedigree adorns Debrett
With ancestries armorial and historic),
Discreetly I arrive to pace the sward
And ruminate, in unperturbed accord,
With mind appropriately metaphoric.

First let me praise the augustly planned approach
Whose vista, narrowing from wide walls of yew,
Needs nothing but a Queen Anne Period coach
(Plus absence of humanities like dew)
To give the prospect semblance of a print
In elegant autumnal aquatint.
Next let my gaze communicate its paean
Brainward and glorify the Jacobean
Rose-brickwork backed by dense arboreal green –
The faded pink façade, that nectarine
Of pre-taxation Rent-roll style-stability
Planned for an impermutable nobility.

So far, so good. But wherefore its existence
In these dispalaced days? What mortals dare
House their domestic problems in so fair
A setting? ... Silence ... Then from foliaged distance
Some Tennysonian ring-dove calmly coos;
A gardener clicks quick shears beyond the yews;
Red Admirals and Painted Ladies bask
And float along the dahlia-brightened border;
Sunshine performs its horticultural task;
And ripened figs harbour the wasp-marauder.

SIEGFRIED SASSOON

An East Wind

My lady looks across the frozen lake
And regards the future of her desolation.
Who now will keep snowy walks
Or bring expiring plumes of punctual horses
To the elevation of her door?
Love will not keep pin-toed swans
Awkwardly questioning the nature of ice
And knowing this, my lady regards
The stature of the kylins
Keeping the furthest rim of the lake
And is no longer sure of their expression.
Where once she saw twin guardian laughter,
She now thinks she sees
Petrification of an immanent roar
And wrings the cold jewels and bones of her hands.

Aloof from snuffling canine ancestry,
The kylins stare across the lake
In stony resolution at weather and departures.
Now the leonine features predominate
And the heavy paws pin down their spheres
While they regard my lady's dwindling estate.
And they do nothing more than this,
Or care what mad songs she hums to winter's instruments,
Or what history she mouths to infirm reflections
Caught in frosty spandrels of high windows.

FREDA DOWNIE

Effacements

The steady cedars levelling the shade
Bend in the waters of each diamond pane.
Furred cusp and sill: other effacements made
Where the armorial glass in bronze and grain
    Stiffens a lily on the clouded sun.
    The lozenge hatchments of the porch floor run

Far out to grass. The grave Palladians
Have gone to seed, long genealogies
Dissolve beneath their wet and gentry stones;
The leaves lie shaken from the family trees.
    As kneeling putti, children from the Hall
    Are playing marbles on the mildewed wall.

The letters and the memoirs knew His will;
All Spring contracted to the one hushed room.
White swelling grew, he passed the cup, lay still;
To the bed's foot she saw the dark spades come.
    They made such vanishings their deodands;
    The earth records what the earth understands.

Queen's May beneath his firstborn's coffin lid:
A lock of hair reserved, a brief prayer said.
'Each lifeless hand extended by his side
Clasped thy fresh blossoms when his bloom was fled.'
    Pain wrote in copperplate one epigraph,
    Then sealed the album's crimson cenotaph.

Behind locked doors, an audience of hymnals.
Tablet and effigy rehearse their lines
To cold light falling in a cold chancel.
Grammarians at their Roman slates decline
    Each proper noun. Bells close on a plain song.
    All speak here with an adult, eheu tongue.

But those frail mounds, brushed low by ancient rain,
Their markers undiscerned in the half-light …?
The last of day ghosts out a window; stains
The scarred porch wall, whose rough and honeyed weight
    Glows from the shade: stones so intangible
    A child might slip between them, bones and all.

PETER SCUPHAM

The Woods

Two years we spent
down there, in a quaint
outbuilding bright with recent paint.

A green retreat,
secluded and sedate,
part of a once great estate,

it watched our old
banger as it growled
with guests and groceries through heat and cold,

and heard you tocsin
mealtimes with a spoon
while I sat typing in the sun.

Above the yard
an old clock had expired
the night Lenin arrived in Petrograd.

Hapsburgs and Romanovs
had removed their gloves
in the drawing-rooms and alcoves

of the manor house;
but these illustrious
ghosts never imposed on us.

Enough that the pond
steamed, the apples ripened,
the chestnuts on the gravel opened.

Ragwort and hemlock,
cinquefoil and ladysmock
throve in the shadows at the back;

beneath the trees
foxgloves and wood anemones
looked up with tearful metamorphic eyes.

We woke the rooks
on narrow, winding walks
familiar from the story books,

or visited
a disused garden shed
where gas masks from the war decayed;

and we knew peace
splintering the thin ice
on the bathtub drinking trough for cows.

But how could we
survive indefinitely
so far from the city and the sea?

Finding, at last,
too creamy for our taste
the fat profusion of that feast,

we carried on
to chaos and confusion,
our birthright and our proper portion.

Another light
than ours convenes the mute
attention of those woods tonight –

while we, released
from that pale paradise,
confront the darkness in another place.

DEREK MAHON

In Memory of
Eva Gore-Booth and Con Markiewicz

The light of evening, Lissadell,
Great windows open to the south,
Two girls in silk kimonos, both
Beautiful, one a gazelle.
But a raving autumn shears
Blossom from the summer's wreath;
The older is condemned to death,
Pardoned, drags out lonely years
Conspiring among the ignorant.
I know not what the younger dreams –
Some vague Utopia – and she seems,
When withered old and skeleton-gaunt,
An image of such politics.
Many a time I think to seek
One or the other out and speak
Of that old Georgian mansion, mix
Pictures of the mind, recall
That table and the talk of youth,
Two girls in silk kimonos, both
Beautiful, one a gazelle.

Dear shadows, now you know it all,
All the folly of a fight
With a common wrong or right.
The innocent and the beautiful
Have no enemy but time;
Arise and bid me strike a match
And strike another till time catch;
Should the conflagration climb,
Run till all the sages know.
We the great gazebo built,
They convicted us of guilt;
Bid me strike a match and blow.

October 1927

W. B. YEATS

Lissadell

Last year we went to Lissadell.
The sun shone over Sligo Bay
And life was good and all was well.

The bear, the books, the dinner-bell,
An air of dignified decay.
Last year we went to Lissadell.

This year the owners had to sell –
It calls to mind a Chekhov play.
Once life was good and all was well.

The house is now an empty shell,
The contents auctioned, shipped away.
Last year we went to Lissadell

And found it magical. 'We fell
In love with it', we sometimes say
When life is good and all is well.

The light of evening. A gazelle.
It seemed unchanged since Yeats's day.
Last year we went to Lissadell
And life was good and all was well.

WENDY COPE

Final Movement

Believing his mother was named for the passionate countess
he comes to the dispossessed country-house looking for signs.
The last of the family wander the cold mausoleum
surrounded by tangible relics of headier times –
a ship in a bottle, the ghost at the turn of the staircase,
a piano from Leipzig untuned since the days of the rising.

Hands grown calloused from nights in the brickworks and decades
in people's collectives now reach for the dominant seventh
playing populist anthems in praise of the last revolution
on ill-tempered strings. In the pale evanescence of evening
he is thinking of Eva in Salford, of Constance in prison;
as, deaf to his musings, their nieces are tuning to Danzig.

CAHAL DALLAT

Order to View

It was a big house, bleak;
Grass on the drive;
We had been there before
But memory, weak in front of
A blistered door, could find
Nothing alive now;
The shrubbery dripped, a crypt
Of leafmould dreams; a tarnished
Arrow over an empty stable
Shifted a little in the tenuous wind,

And wishes were unable
To rise; on the garden wall
The pear trees had come loose
From rotten loops; one wish,
A rainbow bubble, rose,
Faltered, broke in the dull
Air – What was the use?
The bell-pull would not pull
And the whole place, one might
Have supposed, was deadly ill:
The world was closed,

And remained closed until
A sudden angry tree
Shook itself like a setter
Flouncing out of a pond
And beyond the sombre line
Of limes a cavalcade
Of clouds rose like a shout of
Defiance. Near at hand
Somewhere in a loose-box
A horse neighed
And all the curtains flew out of
The windows; the world was open.

LOUIS MacNEICE

Manor House

Do not reject this fading house
And say its beauty suits a decadent taste.
Much is dying here, but to miss the swan-song
Keeps nothing alive, blasphemes against the moment.

Do not reject this dying house.
It is as lovely over the field of thistles
And crowded round by too-heavy trees
As one a traveller came to years ago
And found the lawns lit with Lent lilies,
The sundial unbroken telling an old time
At the heart of the weedless garden,
And the boys gone squirrel-hunting in the woods.

RUTH BIDGOOD

The Conjuror's Trick

Maybe like this: sunburnt hands
brown as earth, stroking the neck
of his horse, sweat and mud flicking
high in air, cantering into the courtyard,

his mind as unbolted as the servants' kitchen,
where he arranges pots and pans as forests,
skims off foam from his tankard
for a lake, ale spilling over the oak table

until later, upstairs, he unrolls
vellum plans, takes a silky lady
to the window. *You must always,*
he urges, *embrace even disorder*
with necessary order. Arms stretched

in the offer of so many possibilities:
here the sound of rushing water
under a sphinx-lined bridge,
there there there, spaces between trees,
full stops in a constant conversation.

I will give you, he whispers to her hand,
fresh green silence, and it's this
she holds on to, the rush of air
as he rides away and the very land
she walks on is transformed forever.

SARAH SALWAY

The Lakes at Blenheim

High branches drowse and the leaves press
against the dazzle of the sky
through water-vapours and greenness,
and plunge them into fire and light.

Only a sturdy sycamore
planted for shade and not for light:
for its companionable roar
in winter when the wind is high,

but now the tree's far higher than
the stone lodge: now the stream in spate
under the bridge's tiny span
hurls its green water in the lake.

These things are ducal, negligent,
a thousand geese swim on the lake,
and none of it was ever meant
to halt the obscure machine of fate.

The great leaf-banks of chestnut poise,
and will drop soon with little noise.
Mud-shallows. Birds are water-voiced,
boats blazing white, like Russian toys.

PETER LEVI

Somewhere

In all those rooms, no light
Unfiltered by the trees.
Only the broken spears
Of sunlight through smudged glass:
And windows dimmed with webs.

Across the road, thin sheep
And a church behind its yews.
Weeds to a crumbled wall
And an undergrowth of grass
Great roots of beech lay bare.

Indoors, the musty smell
Of old wood drying through
And forgotten food left out.
Sour milk in open cups.
Dead bread along a board.

There are many beds unmade
In that exotic house.
The remains of passengers
Whose lives have fallen in
And thrown them out to the sky.

In the attics, time has knelt
And driven holes through jars.
The scum of paint in tins
Tells of a former care
That blistered in the halls.

A foot of green slime swills
In the cellar by the stairs.
Brick arches built for wine
Are in water to their knees
And toads now croak for port.

Here, on the barren floors,
The vapid slap of soles
Remainders gaiety
To the drone of testy flies.
Even the cat's foot slurs

In unfurnished corridors
And the hinges of the doors
Creak with a hidden weight.
There is black, unmanaged soot
On the ostrich of each grate.

Whoever used these rooms
Has abandoned them to the air.
Air, and the stink of rats.
But outside, the long gallery
Of chestnuts rustles leaves

And the garden gives away
What the mansion chose to lose,
A sense of grand repose.
The stately lines of pride
From a rectitude of prayer

Are simplified to the shape
Of a summer's afternoon
Where growth is an elegance
And people come to read
In the shadow of old trees.

Walking, and loving these,
In the gentle wind and the heat,
May be all that remains to aid
Or obliterate the decay.
It seems so, this summer's day.

GEORGE MacBETH

The Laurel Axe

Autumn resumes the land, ruffles the woods
with smoky wings, entangles them. Trees shine
out from their leaves, rocks mildew to moss-green;
the avenues are spread with brittle floods.

Platonic England, house of solitudes,
rests in its laurels and its injured stone,
replete with complex fortunes that are gone,
beset by dynasties of moods and clouds.

It stands, as though at ease with its own world,
the mannerly extortions, languid praise,
all that devotion long since bought and sold,

the rooms of cedar and soft-thudding baize,
tremulous boudoirs where the crystals kissed
in cabinets of amethyst and frost.

GEOFFREY HILL

Letter of Notice to the Country House

You will not last. Can't you see the swans circling
in the pond as if it were a drain? I know, I know,
you're centuries in the making – Tudor courtyard,
Georgian façades, Gothic vaulting, a long-established
heronry. But one day the final carriage will drive away,

and already the servants are closing up a wing, stillness
creeping like a vine through the hallway. So consider this
your warning: your lawn parties of claret cup punch,
your fish knives and oyster forks, your cream soup spoons –
all of it's doomed. That after-dinner hour

when your drawing room rustles with gossip? It will go up
in cigar smoke. Your foxhunts through autumn woods
will be scratched from the books, your yew trees felled,
the maids' beds tucked like eggs among your attic eaves
ruined. After years of disuse, rain growing holes

in your roof, even your ghost will give up the ghost,
only sparrows to haunt your widow's walk. Listen
carefully. You will be devastated, like every solid thing.
Can you hear the croquet mallet's smack in the grass?
That's the wrecking ball knocking on your door.

CORINNA McCLANAHAN SCHROEDER

A Kind of Jericho

from *A History of Dunraven*

Down in the fruit-garden the children
Were smelling the currant bushes.
'Poultices,' said Annie. 'Tomcats,' smirked the boys,
'Or outside privy after Miss Pritchard
Has come out, smoothing her apron.'
'I'm glad I'm not a bee,' shrieked Annie, tearing off,
Back to the packing cases, the impossibility of it all.

Every day for a month the square green van
With the gold lettering had edged down
The cliff road, past the gate-house, and then up
The castle ascent. The driver carried
A bottle of tea; his young men had basin-cuts
And talked about the palaver, the malarkey.
No complaints though. This was serious work.

They dropped a mirror, nothing fancy, in the courtyard.
Its abacus of icicles lay
Uncleared all week. That said it all.
Milord was upping sticks, putting lot-numbers
On the centuries. In the laundry-rooms,
As big as any estate farmhouse, they were
Coppering the winding-sheets of Dunraven.

Impossible to say now who got what.
The sets of blue Nantgarw were knocked down
To a hundred collectors. There are thatched
Vale pubs where the silver heads of ibex
Frame the video screens. And when the blizzard
Ceased, everything from the catalogue,
Down to the last cracked po, had disappeared.

Yet this was only treachery's prelude.
What remained was the castle, quoined
On a promontory above an ocean
Chalked by porpoises, hostage to leisure.

A team of quarrymen were hired, who placed
Their dynamite under weight-bearing walls,
Consulted for days on the angles of collapse.

A mile away the crowds could feel the tremor
In their knees, saw a flower of spray
Conceal the house. And when it lifted
There was a hole in the world.
There were some who picked for years over
The moraines of plaster the explosions built.
And some who have cursed a plague-plot.

ROBERT MINHINNICK

The Old Squire

Squire England has grown old:
Too stiff to ride to hounds,
Too blind to shoot his coverts,
He takes up his great stick
And potters about the grounds.

The meadows and the pond,
The fig-tree on the south wall,
The plantation of young spruces,
The yew hedge twelve foot thick –
He stares at them all;

And grumbling as he goes,
He stops here and there
To spud up a dandelion.
His mind is full of doubt,
For a stranger is his heir.

House, meadows, walks and trees,
Although his sight be dim
He sees them very plainly;
He prays that none may flout
The things so dear to him.

SYLVIA TOWNSEND WARNER

The Chaos

*From the papers of Sir Magnus Manifold, the 13th Earl,
who died without heirs, 1832.*

Estate? It is my world! God knows, I've paid,
and not only gold, for my 'sequestered grot',
my waterfall, my lake, my lovers'-knot
of paths, my Chaos: carts of quaint rocks laid
in artful confusion, for my children to parade
Romantic notions. So they did, before
one went to childbed, and the rest to war.
I live in one wing with a valet and a maid.

Leeches and lawyers bleed me. Every border
falls to rout with weeds. Rank creepers braid
the stonework. Poets scribble their cod's-rot
about the place's 'melancholy sweet disorder',
damn their eyes! Even the Chaos is decayed.
I knew its ways once, but I have forgot.

PHILIP GROSS

The Library

The fire was never lit. Cold, her body
was alert to words, her pores open to knowledge.
Sealed off from the rest of the house, padded
with paper and board, the only sound was the turning
of the page, a whisper, her shallow breath.

Gone. The books scattered to far corners,
cities a thousand miles away, strange
against paperbacks with rainbow covers,
they still carry the scent of deerskin and beeswax,
mildew – travellers from an antique land.

The model ship that used to drift the dark oak desk
is lost, never to reach the new world,
never to return home. She would touch
its windless sails, wonder at how they could make
everything so small. A planet reduced.

TAMAR YOSELOFF

The Break-up of a Library
in an Anglo-Irish House in Wexford: 1964

If you arrive by a side road
opening out and ending in a gate
made from an alphabet of iron animals

and start up an elm-lined avenue
leading to the house
you will enter and see

books for sale by the window,
sleeved in leather
holding in treatises on reason.

As you leave say to yourself
the word *habitat:*
a natural home or environment

of an animal or plant –
then watch the elms march towards
the day they will lose theirs

with the metal animals who have never,
no matter what sun rose or set,
had one and reflect

the end of empire is and will always be
not sedition nor the whisper
of conspiracy but that

slipper chair in the hallway
that has lost the name
no one will call it by again.

EAVAN BOLAND

The Old Workman

'Why are you so bent down before your time,
Old mason? Many have not left their prime
So far behind at your age, and can still
   Stand full upright at will.'

He pointed to the mansion-front hard by,
And to the stones of the quoin against the sky;
'Those upper blocks,' he said, 'that there you see,
   It was that ruined me.'

There stood in the air up to the parapet
Crowning the corner height, the stones as set
By him – ashlar whereon the gales might drum
   For centuries to come.

'I carried them up,' he said, 'by a ladder there;
The last was as big a load as I could bear;
But on I heaved; and something in my back
   Moved, as 'twere with a crack.

'So I got crookt. I never lost that sprain;
And those who live there, walled from wind and rain
By freestone that I lifted, do not know
   That my life's ache came so.

'They don't know me, or even know my name,
But good I think it, somehow, all the same
To have kept 'em safe from harm, and right and tight,
   Though it has broke me quite.

'Yes; that I fixed it firm up there I am proud,
Facing the hail and snow and sun and cloud,
And to stand storms for ages, beating round
   When I lie underground.'

THOMAS HARDY

After Mr Mayhew's Visit

So now the Victorians are all in heaven,
Miss Routledge and the young conservatives
chatting with the vicar, visiting again
the home for incurables who never die.

The old damp soaks through the wallpaper,
there's servant trouble, the cook
fighting drunk at the sherry, and Edith
coughing and consumptive, fainting away.

Only this time it never ends: the master
continually remarking how the weather bites cold,
the brandy flask stands empty, and the poor
are pushing to the windows like the fog.

KEN SMITH

A Sad Story

Places are made of hearsay and story.
There's talk in these trees of five young servant girls
found dead in their beds one winter morning,
choked, they say, by the fumes of a blocked chimney.
That dawn the house woke to cold ash, no curl
of smoke from thirty hearths burning.
The silence of the dead instead of chatter
and quick feet running on the stairs,
fuel for the fires and jugs of scalding water,
slop buckets, sculleries awash, clatter
of crockery on slate, the chink of silver.
People of no account, poor farmers' daughters.
No names. No documents. No graves. Instead
just talk of a tragedy, five young girls dead.

GILLIAN CLARKE

Orielton Empty

There has been burning, identifiable still
    Behind composure when the shuttered front
Opens its thirteen eyes. I have no leave to count,
    Nor should, as one whom the house knows well.
But to myself this due: the dusk face welcomes me, leads
    Into conversation, asks for scrutiny.
So if I say 'The corner urn needs
    Looking to. Where the guttering drops a new
Course welded in would help', nothing is out
    Of courtesy but the homegoing sun.

Many of the trees are copper, one
    A beech, a Japanese maple another, and the covenanting
Bastions of wood declare a ring
    Burning the reds and yellows into centuries.
The lake is reedy, indistinct with flies:
    Durgi and Soda, gundogs of the Rosebery age,
In this red evening whimper, the cortège
    Halting again at their graverails. Rhododendrons drink
Gapingly like mangrove roots from the nearer bank.
    Of the whole circle there is no one left to thank
For the windbreak, for the island hopes
    Of the heart, for the sickle that blunts and stops.

Up the ride, at the wood's end, is a tower fickle
    With grasses. Kestrels nest where a beldame and her pack
Gamed all her guineas away in a round
    Of parties to dawnlight, foxes going to ground
Before her and the wood shut close at her back.
    A night and a night and only the owl for cock.

The scar has widened, weeping over fire and century,
Reds and yellows falling, by and by
Sodden and historied in leaf and frail.
Outside the circle the sea winds scut and kill.

ROLAND MATHIAS

Interior at Petworth: From Turner

Lord Egremont speaks

It was a way of punishing the house, setting it ablaze
in ruddy, golden flames; smoke
in billows up the front stairs; walls
cringing like leaves.
I say, I am afraid
in my own house. Do not believe
I started this, it was
that man, who was to portray the park alone, mind you,
but then became
enamored of the music room.
And now what have we: floods
of fire rolling from room to room, furniture wrecked
in seethe, my wife
Lady Amelia turned
wraith, God knows what fish
and drowning slaves cast up in the tide
along with pocket Bibles, snuffboxes, antimacassars, the
familiar bric-a-brac of the well-kept house.
Where are Edward, Lavinia, Jane? Why
is no one crying, 'Fire! Fire!'? Am I
alone?
            The man has no sense of proportion.
He had himself lashed to the mast, once, it is said,
on a steamboat off the harbor mouth
in full blizzard: sailors blinded by snow, the boat
crippled, led by the lead, they damn near died to a man, and he –
he was observing 'the light at sea', he said.
The painting? 'Soapsuds and whitewash',
the critics described it so.

But here, in our house, it is catastrophe
of flame, not weather, he loosed.
He is a man
in love with last things, clearly,
the last things, but
never understood the first, it seems to me,
and certainly not the genial *medias res*
of decorous, daily life.

What tea-times we've known in these chambers, what sonatinas,
lieder of an evening, whist,
Emmeline embroidering, the hounds calm at the hearth, now all
dissolved.
            Perhaps there are no flames.
A bloody haze arises, it could be
my own eyes that fail.
I hear nothing, but fear
the upstairs rooms, cramped rooms
I have not entered in ages, only remember
the draughts, creakings, grime in closet corners,
windows too tight to lean from, the smell
of antique damp. And now, who knows
what acts unroll
on narrow beds, on floorboards warped askew?
As steam is rising, rising? As heat
buoys the house up into an atmosphere
all of its own creation?
Who are
the participants? Where has Amelia gone?
Why, in this furnace, can I hear no sound,
or feel my own skin begin to peel?

ROSANNA WARREN

View

At the sea's edge, near Bray
In County Wicklow,
From a lonely
Field for dumping rubbish,
Water and air seemed shining, pearly,
Still. No sound.
Gulls rode the gentlest swell
Of this small estuary.

Nearby in Rocky Valley
Among small concrete homes
Fenced round with wire,
One could smell
Bracken and a few sheep, and see
Both copper domes of Powerscourt
Rising over the haze, far off.
Domes and domesticity, entire
As stallions, but now
Burnt to the ground.

SHEILA WINGFIELD

St Botolph's

from *Chevening*

Through the graveyard filled with change-ringing,
in through the south door, hinges singing.
Powdery light from lancet windows
in the estate family's chantry
baptised you, the cobwebs unnerved;

enough light for the colonel (retd)
to take you all in, so when you transgressed –
running fingers along the white marble
and alabaster tombs –
he turned his good eye blind.

What did you expect your touch to find –
papier-mâché?
The tombs lie real as death's day,
rearing in all our futures,
except England's.

They died in childbirth and of the plague,
they died in their beds and on the veldt,
on Salient and Somme,
and here, as lit candles, live on.
At the door you leave a dollar donation.

ROBERT SELBY

The Ornamental Water

Limned in the lake the rosy portraiture
Of the great house on the rise through reed and bough
Seems still to announce that times are as they were,
Though no bright group descends the terrace now;
The boat mud-foundered, the dry sluice allow
There's no youth coming home with joy this year,
The arbour's rankness hopes for no sweet vow
Sighed out as once within its shelter dear.

Weed-woven the shallowing pool, once pleasure's pride,
Returns to ancient use, the cattle's drink;
The fallen oak-leaves and pale bubbles glide
Over their clear-kept haven at the brink;
The bubbles make sharp stars run over the bed
Of silver sand, brave meteors – sudden-dead.

EDMUND BLUNDEN

Dreams & Secrets

The State Apartments keep their
Historical renown

Noël Coward

The Belvedere

The space between the tall plantation firs
lets light into the forest. Here one meets
an interim experience, pain deferred,
a darkness matched by brightness. Goldcrests peet.
Needles mat the ground like calico.
One hesitates, and feels some distant throe,
but not primordial terror. Each green ride
leads in towards the centre. Certainly
this is no place for cultic sacrifice,
with offerings hung from individual trees.

I walk towards the red-brick belvedere.
A turret on a sand-hill eminence,
it also has an intermediate air,
half fortress, half an amorous residence
for summer assignations. One discerns
the rails around its sides, the winter ferns
that burst in through the windows. Through their frames
one sees a future ruin. At the back
are headstones made of concrete, with the names
of late-Victorian horses, mossed and cracked.

Inside lies the attraction. Here I stand,
a latter-day da Vinci in the way
I scan the flakes and blotches, as my hand
picks slowly at the shapes of grey decay
that stain the grey gazebo. On each wall
infirmities, like clouds, or leprous scrawls,
absorb the thin graffiti, overrun
love's temporal initials. Here the mould
awaits its transformation. For a sun
to flood in past the mullions. Turn all gold.

JOHN GURNEY

The Duke's Pagoda

Tomorrow I will order stones
Beside a lake that is the shape
Of all desire, the lengthened ace
Unshadowed by its border,
No rose to break the perfect rim
Or water falls from wall to wall
To veil the cupolas and still
The single carp. And there
In tiers of rose and grey will rise
A wedding of Greece and China
From which the landscape seems to fall
As stair by stair turns round.
And nothing could be finer than
The way the walks direct the eye
To each of the six corners,
While from the topmost balcony
Showing like trumpets through the trees
The towers of Amboise will be seen
In the still hours of grey and green.

It stands in peace where once were nests.
Lights flicker in avenues
Where I can walk about, and then
About again, towards the stones.
It will suffice to turn my thoughts
Upwards, though at the pinnacle
Where can I look but down? And down
Again, and down the turning stairs
Must at the end of perfect days
Walk. The hills are lit
Beyond the window slits that turn,
Movement in stillness like a love
For everything unknown, and I
Still exiled with a summer frown,
The evening birds against my ear
Secure in leafy thrones,
All sullen beauty may be charmed
By the mysterious blood of building.
Tomorrow I will order stones.

JOHN FULLER

Youth Revisited

The hastening cloud grows thin; the sun's pale disc
Swells, haloes, then bursts out and warms the stone,
Pitching the yew's black tent on brilliant green.
A dozen years have gone since last I saw
This tiny church set on the parkland's edge
Between the glistening hunters and the cattle,
A Sunday exercise for week-end guests,
And I approach it conscious that emotion
Ought to be suffered, as indeed it is.
Did I live here and was I happy then?
A war more innocent, an age of man
Removed, my poems thick with formal doom
And baseless faith in humans. Years that now
Pass with the clarity of hours then
Record the degeneration of the nerves
And the world situation, make a golden
Time from that decade of infirm belief.

I am half glad to find the place has marked
Dramatically my absence. All the roof
Has gone, grass flutters on the broken stone,
A notice says *These walls are dangerous.*
Through unglazed windows marble monuments
Are glimpsed like modest spinsters in their baths.
Bombs or neglect, informants are not sure:
In any case the church will now decay
With other luxuries. The horses are
Not here, no doubt the mansion house beyond
The lake is requisitioned by the state,
And furrows creep across the pleasure ground.

I wonder if my son completely fails
To grasp my halting reconstruction of
My youth. Here, where we brought him in our arms
Was neat then, facing time with fortitude.
The statues in the gloom stood for their moral,
The wicked viscount's smoke rose from the house,
The evils of the epoch had not quite
Made rational the artist's accidie.

And yet, the clock moved on another twelve,
He would have something still to put to his son.
The jet planes slither overhead, a frog
Throbs in the dust half-way across the road,
Over two fields a saw scrapes like a bird.
Creatures, machines and men live yet among
The partial, touching ruins of their world.

ROY FULLER

Night-Scented Stock

White, white in the milky night
The moon danced over a tree.
'Wouldn't it be lovely to swim in the lake!'
Someone whispered to me.

'Oh, do – do – do!' cooed someone else,
And clasped her hands to her chin.
'I should so love to see the white bodies –
All the white bodies jump in!'

The big dark house hid secretly
Behind the magnolia and the spreading pear-tree,
But there was a sound of music – music rippled and ran
Like a lady laughing behind her fan,
Laughing and mocking and running away ...
'Come into the garden – it's as light as day!'

'I can't dance to that Hungarian stuff,
The rhythm in it is not passionate enough,'
Said somebody. 'I absolutely refuse ...'
But he took off his socks and his shoes
And round he spun. 'It's like Hungarian fruit dishes
Hard and bright – a mechanical blue!'
His white feet flicked in the grass like fishes ...
Someone cried: 'I want to dance, too!'

But one with a queer Russian ballet head
Curled up on a blue wooden bench instead.
And another, shadowy – shadowy and tall –
Walked in the shadow of the dark house wall,
Someone beside her. It shone in the gloom,
His round grey hat, like a wet mushroom.

'Don't you think perhaps ...' piped someone's flute ...
'How sweet the flowers smell!' I heard the other say –
Somebody picked a wet, wet pink
Smelled it and threw it away.

'Is the moon a virgin or is she a harlot?'
Asked somebody. Nobody would tell.

The faces and hands moved in a pattern
As the music rose and fell,
In a dancing, mysterious, moon-bright pattern
Like flowers nodding under the sea ...

The music stopped and there was nothing left of them
But the moon dancing over the tree.

KATHERINE MANSFIELD

Oxnead Hall, Norfolk

Byrd composed here –
the dead rise
through the underair
on their sugarlift etching;

in the still-room
rose petals are drying
for the wedding
of the daughter of the house;

windows open simultaneously –
polyphony,
the sudden alembics
distilling Corpus Christi

and the bridegroom
who will play her body
without looking
at the music.

PAULINE STAINER

The Dwelling-Place

Deep in a forest where the kestrel screamed,
  Beside a lake of water, clear as glass,
The time-worn windows of a stone house gleamed
    Named only 'Alas'.

Yet happy as the wild birds in the glades
  Of that green forest, thridding the still air
With low continued heedless serenades,
    Its heedless people were.

The throbbing chords of violin and lute,
  The lustre of lean tapers in dark eyes,
Fair colours, beauteous flowers, faint-bloomed fruit
    Made earth seem Paradise

To them that dwelt within this lonely house:
  Like children of the gods in lasting peace,
They ate, sang, danced, as if each day's carouse
    Need never pause, nor cease.

Some to the hunt would wend, with hound and horn,
  And clash of silver, beauty, bravery, pride,
Heeding not one who on white horse upborne
    With soundless hoofs did ride.

Dreamers there were who watched the hours away
  Beside a fountain's foam. And in the sweet
Of phantom evening, 'neath the night-bird's lay,
    Did loved with loved-one meet.

All, all were children, for, the long day done,
  They barred the heavy door against lightfoot fear;
And few words spake though one known face was gone,
    Yet still seemed hovering near.

They heaped the bright fire higher; poured dark wine;
  And in long revelry dazed the questioning eye;
Curtained three-fold the heart-dismaying shine
    Of midnight streaming by.

They shut the dark out from the painted wall,
 With candles dared the shadow at the door,
Sang down the faint reiterated call
  Of those who came no more.

Yet clear above that portal plain was writ,
 Confronting each at length alone to pass
Out of its beauty into night star-lit,
  That worn 'Alas!'

                          WALTER DE LA MARE

Erddig

Clwyd, North Wales

The coal seam ran under
the old house
and as the new face

of revolution pushed
itself forward
the walls began to sag,

the slag accumulating
in the prospect between
sash and valley

where the black shifts
beyond the dovecote
went peacefully wheeling

out of sight. One night,
the Master found himself
an imaginary room

to dream-commemorate,
at an unblacked grate
in clinker rhymes,

times that no longer
rose up to his summoning
bell, dumb waiters

who had followed the call
of the pithead minarets,
descending, to crawl

to a darker richer birth
beneath the butler's pantry,
the footman's bed.

JOHN GREENING

Osterley Park: Summertide Trees

for John Greening

lime trees in flower   they make you cups of holy tea
the Oriental plane   *Platanus orientalis*
shuffling along on its many three-hundred-year-old elbows

under such a tree sat Hippocrates   teaching medicine in its shade

in our deckchairs we are tiny   only trees are big at Osterley
green wolf-lords   leaf-thanes ruling over crows and parakeets
here's the genial Cork Oak   an official Great Tree of London

venerable *Quercus suber*   *a real corker* says local press
Cedars of Lebanon   needling the sky   death-defying yews
that plane tree still wriggling along the North Lawn

oxen joy of summer   is what the Osterley trees know
rain-humming   to the bees buzzing the big shot's garden
still gossiping about Lady Child after all these years

PENELOPE SHUTTLE

Tapestry Moths

for Vicky Allen

I know a curious moth, that haunts old buildings,
A tapestry moth, I saw it at Hardwick Hall,
'More glass than wall' full of great tapestries laddering
And bleaching in the white light from long windows.
I saw this moth when inspecting one of the cloth pictures
Of a man offering a basket of fresh fruit through a portal
To a ghost with other baskets of lobsters and pheasants nearby
When I was amazed to see some plumage of one of the birds
Suddenly quiver and fly out of the basket
Leaving a bald patch on the tapestry, breaking up as it flew away.
A claw shifted. The ghost's nose escaped. I realised

It was the tapestry moths that ate the colours like the light
Limping over the hangings, voracious cameras,
And reproduced across their wings the great scenes they consumed
Carrying the conceptions of artists away to hang in the woods
Or carried off never to be joined again or packed into microscopic eggs
Or to flutter like fragments of old arguments through the unused kitchens
Settling on pans and wishing they could eat the glowing copper

The lamb-faced moth with shining amber wool dust-dabbing the pane
Flocks of them shirted with tiny fleece and picture wings
The same humble mask flaming in the candle or on the glass bulb
Scorched unwinking, dust-puff, disassembled; a sudden flash among the hangings
Like a window catching the sun, it is a flock of moths golden from eating
The gold braid of the dress uniforms, it is the rank of the family's admirals
Taking wing, they rise

Out of horny amphorae, pliable maggots, wingless they champ
The meadows of fresh salad, the green glowing pilasters
Set with flowing pipes and lines like circuits in green jelly
Later they set in blind moulds all whelked and horny
While the moth-soup inside makes itself lamb-faced in
The inner theatre with its fringed curtains, the long-dressed
Moth with new blank wings struggling over tapestry, drenched with its own
    birth juices

Tapestry enters the owls, the pipistrelles, winged tapestry
That flies from the Hall in the night to the street lamps,
The great unpicturing wings of the nightfeeders on moths
Mute their white cinders ... and a man,
Selecting a melon from his mellow garden under a far hill, eats,
Wakes in the night to a dream of one offering fresh fruit,
Lobsters and pheasants through a green fluted portal to a ghost.

PETER REDGROVE

Greenhallows

All the omens were good, the air smelt of success.
The sun soared over the defeated mist.
I had broken no shoelace, shaved without mishap.
My toga swung handsomely.
The train bounded between the silver roofs.
A girl in muslin with a skipping-rope
Waved from a courtyard. The wires saluted me.
'Greenhallows' – pretty name. Reading between
The careful lines in the personal column
I visualised a sort of chauffeur-secretary
Reliable and relied on as I moved
Expertly among the week-end guests,
Good birth my passport, travel my education.
I thought of the starry-eyed, the exiles,
The handkerchiefs along the quay –
And now for me no more
The accordion in the sailors' café,
The olive-islands grey with anguish, blurred.
I smoothed my clothes
And straightened my new chaplet of acanthus.

Lawn-green are the halls in that superb mansion,
Sea-green the carpet sweeping up the stair
To where you hear in fancy
From nile-green bathrooms siren voices sing.
Somewhere amidst porcelain and laughter
You imagine the guests
Heavy-lipped, high-cheeked, beautiful,
Listening with their eyes.

To those on the sun-roof
Boys with indifferent classic brows carry soft drinks.
Out in the garden pensive waters play,
In the house music from hidden strings.
Remote dynamos make power and light.
Birds of foreign plumage, coppery, dark,
Circle about the electric chandeliers.

I was left long alone, wondering
Whether it was really morning or evening,

Whether the servants had lied about the time,
How it was the murals were of my design
And why the signatures in the visitors' book –
Senators', athletes', film-stars' (even some
Of yours, my friends) – were all in my own writing!
As I entered, why had I felt distinctly
As if someone had just replaced
The ornaments by others of my choice?
Then what was it they had said in the village
About 'attempts' and 'interference'? Was that the reason
For the debris imperfectly concealed
Under a tarpaulin by the garage?
Why the fire in August? Why
The unmistakable odour of disinfectant?

A door clicks. Discreet feet
Ripple the sea-green floor.
'Mr Presumption? My name is Wheels.
Her ladyship will be down directly. In the meantime – '
As I hand over my reference from the priest
I see it is marked with fingerprints of sweat.
My ears hum. A sound of sawing, then
An angel-voice, thin-souled like the wind
Threading a colonnade of icicles –
Mine! a record made at choir-school years ago.
'I'm not quite well – I ought to catch the next train back.'
'Train? But there's no station – '
Lies! 'We had it moved
On account of the noise.' Falsehood! deceit!
The green walls swim apart, the floor rocks,
All revolves. Blackness ... and then
A cool hand, something to drink, white and bitter.
My eyes open and see
The stone smile of a queen
The bust of Minerva on a public building
The Lady of Greenhallows.

My friends, pity me. You have been there
You have all been to Greenhallows in your time.
Yes, though you tore your diaries and re-tore them
And watched the fragments shrivel, you remember.
I need not tell you how I ran,
My chaplet fallen, my toga disarranged.

I noticed the door was marked 'Out Patients'
And a man in a white coat raged and flapped.
The green vistas that deluded, you have seen them
And heard the mocking music that pursued me.
We shall keep, my friends, among us
This unshared secret, the shame and the elation.
One day shall we make, perhaps together,
A journey without omens and mistrust the weather?

JAMES REEVES

The English Sweats

Laid out in the field
is a Doomsday town
depopulated by sudor anglicus.

And up on the hill
past the rectory
the heir looks up his marriage in *Debrett*'s:

the year that he learnt
the bark of muntjac
mating or birthing from the scream of a child;

to tell the marquee
and the caterers' van
from the unmarked car and the white tent rising.

Sometimes in his dreams
his father's spirit
caught by the creeping terror of the 'new build',

shows him a pistol
kept in the desk drawer
to plug his Château Pétrus with dum-dum rounds

or his grandfather
still coming for him
on a transport ship from the pas-de-Calais,

wrists bound saltire-wise
to the ensign pole,
ankles drumming their tattoo on the transom.

JAMES BROOKES

Meteor

I was the brushstroke of light
above your orchard.

I was what the muntjacs found
at daybreak, and dragged turf over.

Then I was a spasm underground.
Roots sucked at my wellspring.

When your wife, still mourning
her firstborn, stepped out

among the apple-rows,
I was what watched

from the eye of a clipped branch,
from the eye on the arse of an apple.

I was the comet blood
in your cider keg, I was the sweat

which boiled off your drunk stupor.
I felt your wife press her face

in that pillow to taste me.
And I was the catch in her throat,

your lost estate, the inheritance
shared between no one and no one.

JOHN CLEGG

Three Riddles

1

My first is in sun but not in moon,
My second a crossroads at the end of the line,
My third is a perfectly circular walk,
The rest just him and me,
And my whole is full of unworthies.

(Stowe)

2

Start at the beginning, the very beginning,
Then move to someone close, very close,
It's the letter on an unfortunate's hat,
Now a French lady, then a mispronounced he,
And last a question to make up my first.

After a pause, let's make it happy, our finish,
To rhyme with what I'll do to this riddle now,
Before it reaches your sweet hands, sealed with a kiss.

(Audley End)

3

Walk with me to the top of the hill,
Where we'll look out over a cloudless sky,
To where a proud English Lord has his home.

(Highclere Castle)

SARAH SALWAY

Architectural Masks

I

There is a house with ivied walls,
And mullioned windows worn and old,
And the long dwellers in those halls
Have souls that know but sordid calls,
    And daily dote on gold.

II

In blazing brick and plated show
Not far away a 'villa' gleams,
And here a family few may know,
With book and pencil, viol and bow,
    Lead inner lives of dreams.

III

The philosophic passers say,
'See that old mansion mossed and fair,
Poetic souls therein are they:
And O that gaudy box! Away,
    You vulgar people there.'

THOMAS HARDY

Up at the House

So sorry if I have offended you
by that poem up at the big house
sorry eaten at the edges is discovered
behind the gun cabinet, a small intense thing
requiring all their powers of detection.

I just put down the first thing that come
to me beyond the formal garden
a birch wood of nervy pathways is seen
striking out across the field line,
thin limbs fired by an unexpected sun.

If it isn't the poem that has upset you,
what has that poem which is
so hungry, that cabinet so curious about
what's locked away and who is who,
the power of fire and motives gone astray.

You glare at me as if I'd committed
a murder. Please burn this together
with all records of whatever's happening.
On no account leave it to smoulder
or hold it near to your body or ear,
the most dangerous thing in the house.

JANE DRAYCOTT

Send for Lord Timothy

The Squire is in his library. He is rather worried.
Lady Constance has been found stabbed in the locked Blue Room,
    clutching in her hand
A fragment of an Egyptian papyrus. His degenerate half-brother
Is on his way back from New South Wales.
And what was the butler, Glubb,
Doing in the neolithic stone-circle
Up there on the hill, known to the local rustics
From time immemorial as the Nine Lillywhite Boys?
The Vicar is curiously learned
In Renaissance toxicology. A greenish Hottentot,
Armed with a knobkerry, is concealed in the laurel bushes.

Mother Mary Tiresias is in her parlour.
She is rather worried. Sister Mary Josephus
Has been found suffocated in the scriptorium,
Clutching in her hand a somewhat unspeakable
Central American fetish. Why was the little novice,
Sister Agnes, suddenly struck speechless
Walking in the herbarium? The chaplain, Fr O'Goose
Is almost too profoundly read
In the darker aspects of fourth-century neo-Platonism.
An Eskimo, armed with a harpoon
Is lurking in the organ loft.

The Warden of St Phenol's is in his study.
He is rather worried. Professor Ostracoderm
Has been found strangled on one of the Gothic turrets,
Clutching in his hand a patchouli-scented
Lady's chiffon handkerchief.
The brilliant undergraduate they unjustly sent down
Has transmitted an obscure message in Greek elegiacs
All the way from Tashkent. Whom was the Domestic Bursar
Planning to meet in that evil smelling
Riverside tavern? Why was the Senior Fellow,
Old Doctor Mousebracket, locked in among the incunabula?
An aboriginal Philippino pygmy,
Armed with a blow-pipe and poisoned darts, is hiding behind
The statue of Pallas Athene.

A dark cloud of suspicion broods over all. But even now
Lord Timothy Pratincole (the chinless wonder
With a brain like Leonardo's) or Chief Inspector Palefox
(Although a policeman, patently a gentleman,
And with a First in Greats) or that eccentric scholar,
Monsignor Monstrance, alights from the chuffing train,
Has booked a room at the local hostelry
(*The Dragon of Wantley*) and is chatting up Mine Host,
Entirely democratically, noting down
Local rumours and folklore.

Now read on. The murderer will be unmasked,
The cloud of guilt dispersed, the church clock stuck at three,
And the year always
Nineteen twenty or thirty something,
Honey for tea, and nothing
Will ever really happen again.

JOHN HEATH-STUBBS

The Body in the Library

It always starts with a dead girl
                                    somewhere in the picture:
Lukewarm and pretty, in an organdy crinoline,
One arm sticking out from under a credenza.

There is a foreigner with dark hair and a secret
Who says *Eet ees not me!* when he is questioned;
A shady dressmaker who's missing a finger;
A doctor struck off for fiddling with his patients;

Another girl, in a bedroom (the second victim),
Dolling herself up in French scent and mascara.
Pretty lips and curls smile back at her from the mirror.
She has a date with the killer. She just doesn't know it.

The detective follows the clues. He is a metaphor
Like the girl in the library, like the guilty pistol,
Like the dressmaker's friend with a fatal knack
For murdering women, like the end of a story

Or its aftermath: the part that doesn't get written,
Four years later, when the case has been closed
And the bodies have been forgotten – how the dead
We have failed to keep remembering are alone.

JANE YEH

The Owl Writes a Detective Story

A stately home where doves, in dovecotes, coo –
fields where calm cattle stand and gently moo,
trim lawns where croquet is the thing to do.
This is the ship, the house party's the crew:
Lord Feudal, hunter of the lion and gnu,
whose walls display the heads of not a few,
Her Ladyship, once Ida Fortescue,
who, like his Lordship very highborn too
surveys the world with a disdainful moue.
Their son – most active with a billiard cue –
Lord Lazy (stays in bed till half past two).
A Balkan Count called Popolesceru
(an ex-Dictator waiting for a coup).
Ann Fenn, most English, modest, straight and true,
a very pretty girl without a sou.
Adrian Finkelstein, a clever Jew.
Tempest Bellairs, a beauty such as you
would only find in books like this (she'd sue
if I displayed her to the public view –
enough to say men stick to her like glue).
John Huntingdon, who's only there to woo
(a fact, except for her, the whole house knew)
Ann Fenn. And, last, the witty Cambridge Blue,
the Honourable Algy Playfair, who
shines in detection. His clear 'View halloo!'
puts murderers into a frightful stew.

But now the plot unfolds! What *déjà vu*!
There! In the snow! – The clear print of a shoe!
Tempest is late for her next rendezvous,
Lord Feudal's blood spreads wide – red, sticky goo
on stiff white shirtfront – Lazy's billet-doux
has missed Ann Fenn, and Popolesceru
has left – without a whisper of adieu
or saying goodbye, typical *mauvais gout*!
Adrian Finkelstein, give him his due,
behaves quite well. Excitement is taboo
in this emotionless landowner's zoo.
Algy, with calm that one could misconstrue

(handling with nonchalance bits of vertu)
knows who the murderer is. He has a clue.

But who? But who? Who, who, who, who, who, who?

GAVIN EWART

The Uninvited

We did not care muchly who, in the murder,
we turned out to be, providing whoever
used to inhabit the white chalk figure
frozenly pawing the blood-stained sofa
was not one of us but a different dier.

Dazzled colonel, distracted lover,
meddling couple of the library whisper,
cook unpoisoned or ponderous super,
sleuth, inheritor, innocent, actual
killer detected or undetected – it

didn't matter, but not that ended
individual manning the hour
he died in, as we would all one *dies*
man one hour, one mo, one jiffy.
Let us be Anybody other than Body!

But then we'd go on with the game all summer:
the three allowed queries on the hot verandah,
the fib in the gazebo, the starlit rumour,
the twitching curtain and the dim unhelpful
gardener's boy: it would all be explicable

soon in the lounge, and we didn't mind waiting.
No, what we minded was the hairless stranger
who wasn't invited and wouldn't answer
and had no secrets or skeletons either,
and got up later than us, then later

than even the bodies, and never turned in,
or blamed or suspected or guessed the outcome
but always was exiting, vanishing, going,
seen on the lawn – then there were more of them
massing, unarmed, parting when followed,

combing the country but not for a weapon
or corpse or clue, then halting and singing
unknown thunderous hymns to a leader
new on us all at our country party he'd
caught in the act of an act of murder.

GLYN MAXWELL

Greenway House

for J

Every night you read yourself to sleep
with an Agatha Christie –
the broken spines and ghastly covers
hang over our bed, the green head
with its bulging eye, the pestle
and mortar, some tablets, a rope.
It's an odd kind of lullaby.

But now your dream has brought us
to Greenway itself, where the paths
climb and intertwine like fugal
plot arrangements (the Boat House,
the Battery) above the estuary
as it darts a half-glimpsed
solution through distracting trees.

And you can sleep easy, *Dead
Man's Folly* slipping from
your fingers, the ferry sailing
across to the other side where
they know all the answers,
the victims laid out for inspection,
everyone gathered in the library.

JOHN GREENING

The Hidden

English summer, rolling down,
ornamental lake,
and the manor, richly brown,
basking like a snake.

Temple, pergola and park:
now the stage is set.
Soon some saucy, cycling clerk
swims into the net.

All he sees, the youth admires:
smooth lawns, tree-lined ways.
Most of all, his tourist fires
burn to try the Maze.

In he plunges cheerily,
never looking back.
Two hours later, weary, he
finds a cul-de-sac.

Shrubbery begins to part.
Through the box and yew,
what was present from the start
shuffles into view.

VICKI RAYMOND

The Blickling Hall Poem

Tranquillity is only a style, whose glyph
is struck at a moment's rest,
phrasing the violence into pattern.
We found the secret garden, banked
in by trees, away from the order
of the *parterre*. We watched the wind
rocking the treetops, though the air
was still on our faces as we kissed
in the tiny summerhouse. You cannot stop
for long in this miniature world, closed
in by beech-hedges, as in the order
of a poem. A solitary sundial,
surrounded by lawn and brick-path,
centres it. It has no motto;
has only, perhaps, the slanting daylight
cut on a shadow's fin, and moving
across its still surface.

ROBERT SHEPPARD

Furlongs

after Eric Ravilious

There's no-one lounging on the curly iron bed or
poking cyclamen into pots in the endless greenhouse.
In the dining room no-one chose the wallpaper
and no-one put a bunch of scrawny flowers in the jug.
By the river no-one stands to feed the ducks.
A criss-cross hill receives an interruption
in the form of a fence-post leaning the wrong way;
no-one comes to set it straight.
Things are what they seem: the sea is like the sea;
the waterwheel is careful pencil.
A train looks up at a long white horse.
The horse looks back; the train is gone.

KATHARINE TOWERS

from *Shugborough Eclogues*

This is the gem you cut, Thomas Anson,
from emerald forest and sheer water
lightflooded on a still spring day like diamond,
a white house rounded like a cabochon
curved to its shadowed setting, and a garden
that melts to woods and fields, a truce
with wilderness. Arcadia has no time
but its own season, spring –
when all things are possible.
And this was your Arcadia: a phrase
from some Greek poet, Theocritus perhaps
with his 'full threshing-floor' and 'canopy
of green leaves'; Virgil's line about 'cold springs,
woodlands and soft meadows' –
words like a seed-crystal dropped
into the saturate solution
that was your mind, blend of philosophy,
ideal politics and peace.
Good farming, a republic
of shepherds and their friends,
temples half-hidden in the forest groves,
Reason in awe of Nature's majesty
a tranquil Zodiac overarching farms
lamplit at evening, lullaby'd by sheep,
and watched all night by the observant stars.

GREVEL LINDOP

Lines on a Tudor Mansion

Slim sunburnt girls adorn
Lawns browsed by fawn and doe
Through three long centuries this house
Has mellowed in and known
Only the seasonal fulfilment
And the commemorated generations.

But *we* know
Samson dead
And Delilah dirtying her hair
In the dust of the fallen
Faiths.

We know
Violence terrible and degrading,
Beauty disfigured,
And the coward cruel brute
Shaping us in his image.

So, grey assured house, surviving change,
For all your cypresses and waving white
Potato rows and clustered irises, no more
Than woodpecker or mouse do we desire
Your burnished peace and all your storied past.

We are of Life,
Teeming and musical
Perfect and instant
As the soft silk flash of the swifts
Which do not care for the houses of the wealthy,
But have instead their own instinctive life,
The flight and rhythm of the blood.

Wherefore we leave no monumental homes,
No marble cenotaphs inscribed with names.
Only the fleeting sunlight in the forest,
And dragonflies' blue flicker on quiet pools
Will perpetuate our vision

Who die young.

ALUN LEWIS

Felbrigg

Families have no beginning, but can end
Though 350 armigerous years
Brighten the vellum. But life may descend
Obliquely, and a score of Norfolk squires
Are summed up here into a fresh dimension
That can progenerate outside the reach
Of county gossip and outlive the plantation
Of those long woods of Spanish chestnut and beech.
For a while over his arable and pasture
The rooks come idling home. The piled clouds grow
And fade this late October afternoon.
Here in his great library, ill and slow,
He leans between his lamp and the young moon,
Become the elements of more than nature.

MICHAEL RIVIÈRE

Ha-Ha

The Archduke has laid his lap dogs in the grave.
      There's a fine how-do-you-do
underneath the terrace where a sundial moved
last night, backwards. Now the new giant housemaid
has spread the heat out upon the lawns to dry.
See how it steams: the children are quite lost in it.

     Too late they have discovered dislocation.
      Take care! Over their shoulders
eyes glare down upon them from the attic panes.
Some thing shakes the branches in no breath of wind,
dead sparrows lie around the dried-up fountain:
time for the garden to be packed and put away.

     The park is stiff with error: whose parasol's
      askew among the rushes?
Noon or midnight both are sure and terrible,
half-light confuses. The ditch is a bad place,
they have been informed. Keep Out? Impossible!
Their steps compelled, they find it full of what comes true.

     As tilted trees insist on what is stared at,
      must not be seen again,
the house has crept so quietly up behind
breath fills their eyes: their leap is cataleptic.
On the far side the open ground up-ends them
to put on show all they have fled. Where nothing's there.

GLEN CAVALIERO

Saltatorium

O drear, O dreary dreary dirge for this deer
that hath stallèd in a ditch all anitch with fear,
and how it twitch, how it fidget and flinch
its formerly fine fetlock, fends off the dog howls,
fends off the fender of the four-by-four Ford,
fleeing its flightpath, shit trails like smoke trails
like entrails. Haven't you though, haven't you
sometimes in a sensitive somewhat sensory
rush hour of solemnity sensed its shadow?
This is no laughing matter, this is no ha-ha
wall at the Hameau de la Reine as grass grazes
garden, and your gaze graces a deer-leap into space.
This is its history, its ditch down, your disown.
Buckshot. *For 2 miles*, forever. Fallow migration.

LISA KELLY

The Manor

What a prize prick he's made of himself,
trudging a dozen furlongs across the plain

to the widowed heiress's country estate
just to be turned away at the lodge, to stare

from the wrong side of the locked gates.
The plan – admit it – was to worm his way in:

to start as a lowly gofer and drudge, then rise
from gardener to footman to keeper of hawks –

her hooded merlin steady on his wrist –
to suddenly making his way upstairs after dark,

now soaping her breasts in the roll-top bath
with its clawed gold feet, now laying a trail

of soft fruit from her pillow to his, his tongue
now coaxing the shy nasturtium flower of love.

Here he is in the dream, gilt-framed, a gent
in her late husband's best brown suit,

the loyal Schnauzer gazing up at his eyes.
And here's the true him tramping the verge,

frayed collar and cuffs, brambles for hair,
the toes of his boots mouthing like grounded fish.

A pride of lions roams the walled parkland
between this dogsbody life and the next.

SIMON ARMITAGE

Ancestral Houses

from *Meditations in Time of Civil War*

Surely among a rich man's flowering lawns,
Amid the rustle of his planted hills,
Life overflows without ambitious pains;
And rains down life until the basin spills,
And mounts more dizzy high the more it rains
As though to choose whatever shape it wills
And never stoop to a mechanical
Or servile shape, at others' beck and call.

Mere dreams, mere dreams! Yet Homer had not sung
Had he not found it certain beyond dreams
That out of life's own self-delight had sprung
The abounding glittering jet; though now it seems
As if some marvellous empty sea-shell flung
Out of the obscure dark of the rich streams,
And not a fountain, were the symbol which
Shadows the inherited glory of the rich.

Some violent bitter man, some powerful man
Called architect and artist in, that they,
Bitter and violent men, might rear in stone
The sweetness that all longed for night and day,
The gentleness none there had ever known;
But when the master's buried mice can play.
And maybe the great-grandson of that house,
For all its bronze and marble, 's but a mouse.

O what if gardens where the peacock strays
With delicate feet upon old terraces,
Or else all Juno from an urn displays
Before the indifferent garden deities;
O what if levelled lawns and gravelled ways
Where slippered Contemplation finds his ease
And Childhood a delight for every sense,
But take our greatness with our violence?

What if the glory of escutcheoned doors,
And buildings that a haughtier age designed,
The pacing to and fro on polished floors
Amid great chambers and long galleries, lined
With famous portraits of our ancestors;
What if those things the greatest of mankind
Consider most to magnify, or to bless,
But take our greatness with our bitterness?

W. B. YEATS

England

I have come to stand at your border
in the darkness where invisible things suffer
& the golden windows of the last estate
cast proprietary glances on the earth.
Where the bailiff parks up with his sandwich
& the burnt-out car is mercifully at rest.
Hermosa, let me try a final
octave turning south into a wind that stubbornly
flitters through torn pennants of sacking,
purrs in the steel tubes of the gate;
that drives each ponderous & docile cloud
slowly out across the State that is only
an image of the body inviolate,
the nation that extends through all time & space.

TOBY MARTINEZ DE LAS RIVAS

Outsiders

The Stately Homes of England
We proudly represent,
We only keep them up for
Americans to rent

Noël Coward

Avington: The Avenue at Dawn

A leaf sways gently on a web.
Herons reveal the hidden river
slowly where they fly.
Mist creeps over the barley.
Time to get up, stiffbacked
from our damp sleeping bags,
where we have trespassed.
Time for the avenue to show
where we are, on a carriage drive
of nettles and grass,
that leads back through memories
of landscaped order: wheels
brushing the trimmed foliage
and the master at the centre
of his park, where the limes
near death are wild giants
now; and abruptly ends
at a gateway crumbling
in undergrowth. Across the lane
a new entrance, young limes
sweeping to the big house.
Here a lonely grey horse
careers across a field,
and quivering in front of us,
stares at the strangers.

JEREMY HOOKER

Knebworth Park

A cave of air softens,
hovers over our heads.
We've waited all year for this:
the March lull, the park
almost tourist free.

Put your ear
to this unsaddled soil,
sound out the mating-calls
of otters, rabbits, voles;
hear horses' hoofbeats
pound nearer-far.

I have made an altar of calm
among these ageing oaks,
lines of stiff-backed trees.

Our walk circles the ancient house,
grounds set off by daffodils.
A five-year-old sings a nursery rhyme,
wanting to pat sheep. Their beady eyes
distract, promising only puzzles.

We call ourselves comfortable explorers,
notice a wine-glass left among the ferns.
A squirrel skids into wintry hiding.
As the light fades, we study
each other's faces
for signs of sun.

KATHERINE GALLAGHER

The Landowner

Rambler, direct your care
   To this magnificent gift.
Dare, rambler, to make durable those views.

— More trust, believe, more debit. —

Lest the day come to see all trust is up,
Learn to speak newly over nature; build
Fresh castles for your chances to enjoy.
   Make chiffchaffs pay to find a way
Within, from a world not edified since Eden.

Hear in the song not only expressive bird,
But a history in your tongue, to beat the bounds.
As a child skims the ways of ideal gardens,
   So can you then,   so have you those
Adventures to go on with, grounds
Possible to their keepers; – outworks, follies.

ALEX WONG

Open Gardens Scheme

Teas are served in the library.
I watch the tablecloth, its snowy
flowerprint, consume you at your sleeve.
Outside, the gardens swarm: men
and women emerging from the soil
catch fire and form while others slither
into the beds like snakes of molten glass,
shutting the little doors behind them in the lawn.

You say the bookcase is a secret door.
If ever lost in thought or contemplation
you slip too far into the cloth or wallpaper
like Narcissus into his pool, please
beware. I do not want to lose you,
run with arms outstretched toward a cloud
of vapour, trying to embrace you
long after you've turned into a tree.

Let's put an end to disappearing,
reappearing as a constellation, cold
and distant, a frightened stag at bay.
Come out from behind that half-closed
door so I can see you clearly
amid the fire, the blizzard in this room.

JANE DRAYCOTT

Open Day at Stancombe Park

The man who takes our coins on the gravel track
is perched with a polythene box upon his knees;
another, strolling, hands behind his back,
keeps one eye on a comical Great Dane
that trots among the geometric trees

made for a stage set: all part of the plot
pretending this is just another scheme
to raise funds for the Red Cross, a spot
where ladies who like claiming, naming things
take tea and cuttings, strawberries and cream.

But what mind dreamed these twisting boulevards?
How can we prove the well-repeated tale
that a love-sot built this folly only yards
from his betrothed bed? For still the house keeps
a blind silence; there are no guides for sale.

From those windows, no union might be guessed:
all routes submerged in a junction-box of brick
where girls emerge from tunnels, looking perplexed,
and couples ask 'is this where we came in?',
unwitting victims of a twilight trick.

Is it a whale's rib, or distressed wood
that shocks us as we round a sudden bend?
The rest is a threadbare maze from childhood,
half recollected, a crazy pilgrimage
of which the outset is forgotten, the end

never quite believed in. Recurring figures snake
above our heads or beyond a gurgling stream
that slides from oblong holes to a distant lake
where fat goldfish, like scattered mosaics,
nose through lily-pads, in some other dream –

drowned souls perhaps, or ancient overlords
saved by knowing the right path from the wrong,
who stepped as we do now, over quaking boards
to a leaky boat and summer-house, where, lost
and loth to rebegin, we long to belong.

DAVID ASHBEE

Open to the Public

What would they think, those writers, those artists,
If they could return home now to hang
All-seeing windows with their flimsy lengths,
Or shuffle through stiffened rooms with the curious?

Sweet recognitions. Hopeless protestations.
The chair still presiding over unworn carpets of light,
The clock holding one hand across its dead-beat heart;
And the watercolours, drawn from other rooms.

But those instruments, out of tune with time,
Letters unfolded, poems blinded by glass,
Nether garments displayed – and punctual intruders,
Unfamiliar and unloved, haunting every room.

FREDA DOWNIE

In the Grounds

Yorkshire, 1975

Barbarians in a garden, softness does
Approve of who we are as it does those
Who when we speak proclaim us barbarous
And say we have no business with the rose.

Gently the grass waves, and its green applauds
The justice, not of progress, but of growth.
We walk as people on the paths of gods
And in our minds we harmonize them both.

Disclosures of these grounds – a river view,
Two Irish wolfhounds watching on a lawn;
A spinster with her sewing stares at you,
And begs you leave her pretty world alone.

More books than prejudice in our young minds ...
We could not harm her, would not, would prefer
A noise less military and more kind
Than our boots make across her wide *parterre*.

We are intransigent, at odds with them.
They see our rabble-dreams as new contempt
For England's art of house and leaf. Condemn
Our clumsiness – you do not know, how, unkempt

And coarse, we hurt a truth with truth, still true
To who we are: barbarians, whose chins
Drool with ale-stinking hair, whose horses chew
Turf owned by watching, frightened mandarins,

Their surly nephews lounging at each gate,
Afraid we'll steal their family's treasured things,
Then hawk them – pictures, furniture and plate –
Round the encampments of our saddle-kings.

DOUGLAS DUNN

Our Weird Regiment

How the rich impress us
with what they own
displaying family photos
on the piano lid

as if no different
to those of us who shuffle
through elaborate rooms
or glance aside

through the leaded glass
into formal gardens
where cabbage
potato and mint perhaps

chive and marjoram
are elegantly deployed
to be admired
not cooked or eaten

our guide explains
the farmlands purchased
to the churchyard wall
and then beyond it

each mound ploughed
and levelled in accord
with his lordship's
goose-feathered whims

yet a scattering of bones
has assembled itself
in a heap by the gate
now beyond the gate

our weird regiment
lurches into the road
a swaying of skulls
and whitened knucklebones

MARTYN CRUCEFIX

Haydn, in a Neo-Gothic Mansion
of the National Trust

Rents were collected. Footmen
Crept. In rear quarters
Kitchen tweenies spun.
Small scullions were whipped.

Yes, starvings were grudged
For blisters of the summer
And strained winter backs. And now
In this late evening

Of sweet art, the great hall
Packed, will this wide playful
Mansion – Gothic windows
Lit, below this

Hunters' Moon, fair
Mists arising – be playing,
Yet, its true, its
True melodious part?

GEOFFREY GRIGSON

Britannia

Careful not to soil her dainty Ferragamos,
the grand piano moves discreetly through the herbaceous border,
a sheaf of cuttings in her handbag:
a cardinal, the Queen's gynaecologist, a dozen QCs.

She has come for the music, of course,
but the atmosphere's lovely, such elegant lampshades.
There is always some Government in the garden
where the sheep are kept in their rightful place
safely grazing beyond the ha-ha.

There are twenty-two minutes before curtain up.
The wind is cold, there's a whimper of rain
but the picnic must go on and be such fun:
an open window serves coloratura with paté de foie gras.
Everyone has a rug for their knees, and she reminds us
again of her night at the Albert Hall,
the swallowing blue of a million delphiniums.
We can almost believe in her cloak-pin and shield.

It's not what it was, she says: the vulgar new building,
every year the path to the lily pond more overgrown –
a negotiation of unripened blackberries and birtwistle.
Hemlines are rising; already accountants wash up on the lawn.

Even today, out at sea with Johnny Foreigner,
I hear her triumphant arpeggios over the waves,
the Broadwood's fin patrolling round the violins.

ANNE BERKELEY

Staying with Friends

The lawn of marital unhappiness,
the big house and the ha-ha,

the scary stabled horse
I knew could kill me with a kick,

would have been grist
to any gossip columnist,

given the fame
that lapped them all,

but we were children,
lost among the bewildering

tall grasses, quarrels, poppies
and adult silences.

LACHLAN MACKINNON

After the Revolution

for Doreen Davie

Any American's likely to entertain
mixed feelings for British monarchy. So I,
transported for a season to British soil,
have more than once been spotted at Sainsbury market
with other middle-aged ladies, shedding tears
– but surreptitious, brief – for swanlike Diana,
and wondering why on earth. Perhaps the children?
Since most of us tread the swamps of maternal passion.

Yet one day squiring my black-eyed second son
to a birthday party flung by a little duchess,
I found myself escorted out of the heated
interior lined with sixteenth-century portraits,
dotted by lamps and comfy brocaded sofas.
The garden roiled with nannies, mums, and hedges
as the maid explained she couldn't offer us tea,
not even in the kitchen. We swept away.

'But why on earth,' my friend asks as we stride
past gilded posts of Buckingham, where the guards
are not, this winter day, disposed to change,
'did you decide to send the boys to Vaulted
Hall? The council schools are free, and good –
or used to be, in my day.' I can't answer,
reviewing the titled ladies, all unconscious,
who caused my tears, saltwater stained with tea.

EMILY GROSHOLZ

Brockham End House

for George and Olga Lawrence

'Lawrence, of virtuous father, virtuous son ...'
Putative ancestor! The proved one's bust
Stands in your hall, a long, grave, bony face
That suits with marble. 'Here lies Henry Lawrence
Who tried to do his duty.' In the long
Unlighted corridor I explore your books,
'Lawrence and Havelock: Heroic Lives.'
Dust gathers here on Sleeman and on Meadows
And on 'The Chronicles of Dustypore'.
Here, on a shelf, an Empire's rise and fall,
And half an hour here from the bus to Bath
The little hills that 'run into your face'
Enclose a steep demesne of woods and pasture
Where the forget-me-not among the nettles,
The tame white rabbit chasing Chinese geese,
The low clouds gathering on the view of Bristol,
The fair and feathery pencilling of tall trees,
Bluebells, primroses, very early cowslips,
Mare's-tails, molehills like stepping-stones in grass,
Moss on the dry-stone dykes, all work together
With the sheep's morning meh, the rooks' cawing,
An unidentified bird on a cherry tree
That sounds like a baby's rattle, strawberries,
Giant strawberry plants, that are to climb up canes,
And fennel rooted up to cook with fish,
Your cider from the cask, your English beef,
Your friend the Everest climber, who throws up
A new-laid egg to prove it will not break
Upon the lawn, and breaks three eggs in turn,
All work together, as I say, to make
Me, a townee, sink back in generations
To when my folk were farmers in Caithness:
Most bleak to this, but the land's feel remains:
London seems far in purgatorial smoke
And it seems heaven up on your high ridge.

G. S. FRASER

Stourhead

Happy New Year to all our ancestors,
The rich ones (you) who made the lake, and me
Who called a remote gardener to his tea.
Mine have all died back and so have yours.

We are the wintry paying sightseers
Whose home is somewhere else and who
Live comfortably on salary and fee
And like this place. Nothing above ground stirs.

Lichen has stopped climbing round the urn.
The mole-hills look extinct. The temples crouch
But will not now scuttle away. A turn

In the path brings us full circle through the plans
Of those improvers, and in the last reach
Shine one still light and seven motionless swans.

PATRICIA BEER

At Burghley House

We walk here
Where each tree and shrub
Is a planned cypher
In Capability Brown's charter;
Where Englishness
And Tudor stone surround us
And pale sun whitens
Our footprints in the grass.
Your questions
Curl with American vowels
As they should after all those years
Since we walked along the Rhine
On a November day
Bright with dread and ashes
When flames had taken
Our holiest places.
Overnight
We had learnt the language
Of terror, but still could walk
Carelessly, as children will,
By that river that shone.

LOTTE KRAMER

The Inherited Estate

to Mike Kitay, an American in Europe

A mansion, string of cottages, a farm,
Before you reach the last black-timbered barn
And set your foot upon the path that leads
Up to the hill where Follies and façades
– Typical products of intelligence
That lacks brute purpose – split, disintegrate,
    And, falling with their own rich weight,
Litter the slopes, a record of expense.

So generations of the reckless dead
Put up the ruins you inherited,
And generations of ganged village boys
Have used as fort and ammunition those
Droppings of fashion you explore today.
What country boys and gentlemen have left
    Now smells of green, the fat dark drift
Where the weed's impulse couples with decay.

Is comfort so impermanently built,
A summer house with blurring fungus spilt
At random on the leaning walls? is time
Only a carved head that you fish from slime,
That winks with muddied eyeball? does the crash
Of failing stonework sound for all desires?
    For, once the dilettante tires,
The ornaments he raises fall in trash.

A calm discrimination marks your hate:
Once you inherited the wide estate
The Follies like the land and farm were yours.
Distance has flattered them, for from the moors
The fronts resembled solid palaces:
And though you are not so trusting to believe
    That all is sound which others leave,
You come not crediting half your bailiff says.

He told you all, an honest labourer.
But had not noticed this, that in the year
When you were born a twist of feckless wind
Brought one small seed and left it on the ground
Between the chance and choice to live or die.
It drew the means of living undeterred,
    Uncurling in the shell it stirred,
To rise, and sway upon your property.

Its art is merely holding to the earth –
But see how confidently, from its birth,
Its branches, lifting above failures, keep
Vigour within the discipline of shape.
Come here, friend, yearly, till you've carved the bark
With all the old virtues, young in fibre, names
    That swell with time and tree, no dreams,
No ornaments, but tallies for your work.

THOM GUNN

Domesday Book

Let nothing be done twice –

When Harold fell
with an arrow in his eye at Hastings,
the bastard Conqueror taxed
everything in his Domesday Book:
ox, cow, swine,
the villages and hundreds
his French clerks tore to shreds
and fed
to berserk hawk and baron.
His calculated devastation,
never improvidently
merciful to the helpless,
made anarchy anachronism
and English a speech for serfs.

England/Scotland/Ireland
had better days –
now the elephantiasis of the great house
is smothered in the beauty of its English garden
changed already to a feathery, fertile waste,
lawns drenched with the gold-red sorrel.
The hectic, seeded rose
climbs a neglected gravel drive
cratered to save the children from delivery vans.
The beef-red bricks and sky-gray stones
are buried in the jungle leaf of June –
wildflowers take root in the kitchen garden.

The dower house goes with the house,
the dowager with her pale, white cup of tea
she inspired with brandy.
Lathom House, Middleton Manor,
New Hall, Silverton,
Brickling with its crinkled windows
and rose-pink gables
are converted to surgeries, polytechnics,
cells of the understaffed asylum
crumbling on the heads of the mad.

The country houses that rolled
like railways are now
more stationary than anthills –
their service gone. Will they fall
under the ax of penal taxes
they first existed to enact ...
too grand for any gallery?
Will the house for pleasure
predecease its predecessor,
the cathedral,
once outshone in art and cost?

Cold chimneystacks and greening statuary
outlive the living garden
parceled to irreversible wilderness
by one untended year –
from something to nothing ...
like King Charles who lost his head
and shared the luck and strange
fibered Puritan violence
of his antagonist, the Protector,
whose carcass
they drew on a hurdle to Tyburn,
hanged and buried under the gallows.

If they have you by the neck, a rope will be found.

Nulle terre sans seigneur.

The old follies, as usual, never return –
the houses still burn
in the golden lowtide steam of Turner.
Only when we start to go,
do we notice the outrageous phallic flare
of the splash flowers that fascinated children.

The reign of the kingfisher was short.

ROBERT LOWELL

Higham Hall

Down past the Himalayan cedar
staring out over Bass Lake to Skiddaw
and round behind fulsome rhododendrons
there's a laburnum tree in full spate,
humming with bees like a synagogue.
It's so pretty I jump back in disbelief
and then approach as though it was a burning bush.
The warden's put its Latin name on a plaque
so you can take your pick between
mind and matter, though the tree's long since
torn up these things with its hands and thrown
them away. Best go with the look-at-me
blossoms, this impossible lantern
sailing over an English lawn
towards the Strawberry Hill Gothic house
(blood on its scutcheon, flowers in its purse)
ardent for summer, happy to ship
you off to native or to foreign parts
just by standing still, breaking out
the one language you never knew you spoke.

WILLIAM SCAMMELL

Inheritance

What I was seeking was a mulberry tree,
  To draw the crinkled edges of its leaves
And catch the serpentine sprawled shape
  The trunk twists into through the years.
It was autumn – too late for berries now.
  And then that lady said to me –
I scarcely knew her – 'I have a mulberry tree.
  The gardener will show you where.' Her stretch
Of Gloucestershire I'd never visited. It lay
  Riverwards beyond the interminable highway,
Among farms and cottages, lost England
  Still communing with itself across the clay
That Saxon ploughs first broke. The house
  Stood on a hill, a buttressed church
Almost in its garden. Now I have been
  And seen, the first thing I recall
Is not the mulberry dome of yellow leaves,
  But the woodland walk beyond it:
When the house was at its height, the guests,
  Shaded by parasols and foliage, would climb
On a zig-zag pathway up the hill
  And in the summit summer-house confront
Over flatland fields that thrived
  Under the salt encroachment of the tide,
A foreshore of two hundred acres.
  The summer-house has gone, a single chair
Stares out at space. As you descend
  You see how that tide of woodland brought an end
To shape and form here, and the ornamental yews
  Must lose themselves to spindly neighbours,
Where a medlar grafted to a thorn
  May well outlast the mulberry tree
If once the undergrowth were cleared.
  Our gardener guide has more for us to see:
The superannuated ice-house, the pond
  Where once the carriages were driven in
To be cleansed of mud. A rootstore
  Remains there still, where root crops
Having been harvested, now lie
  In the cool beneath a roof of earth

Packed tight above a roof of tile,
  And, all around, the half-kempt gardens
Once there were hands enough to tame.
  And, beyond these, the house itself
Stands where a house has always stood
  Throughout centuries. We reach
That chapel of the buttressed church
  Whose memorials confront us, slow our steps
And silently explain too much:
  Three stones, three sons, the war –
That duty done, another must be paid
  To parsimonious England craving coin:
Beyond inheritance, how should the dead
  Argue against a levy on that death
They did not grudge? Inside the walls,
  The mulberry tree has watched it all:
The generations tasting at that tree
  Could scarcely have foreseen this dereliction.
I draw the intricate foliage leaf by leaf
  Under the cloudy seashore in the sky
That echoes the tide beneath it, where
  The estuary waters slowly slide
Lacking all sea-like definition to the sea.

CHARLES TOMLINSON

In the Formal Garden

A peacock feather. And a simple stone
in the herbaceous border like a child's
first tooth, carved *BENJIE*.
EVER FAITHFUL. 1899.

And I've been here before.
A gust of dead leaves brushes by
like bustled skirts. I step aside; I know
my place: the gardener's boy

who crouches by the trellis, there,
to glimpse three lacy Misses flit and chime,
their shuttlecock hung motionless
above their heads, like time.

A spaniel pup flop-lollops at their heels.
Then that dry rustling: Lady M.
stands over me ... Pa wrings his cap and begs:
'He's not a *bad* boy, ma'am.'

She freezes: 'If I ever catch him
looking at my gels again ...' Unmanned,
bowed, slashing weeds, I catch the hush
of silks, and round, my billhook in my hand,

on a pinched proud face, beneath
its silly coronet. Waddling in draggled finery,
the peacock stares. It rattles up its fan
in a shivering hiss. And screams.

The sky is darkening fast. 'Get in,'
Pa calls. 'Daft ha'p'orth.' From the shed
we hear it shriek again. Pa grins,
'Like the voice of the dead!

Damned bird. I'd wring its neck.'
The first drops streak the pane.
Somewhere, a yappity panic breaks and falls
to whimpers: Benjie, left out in the rain ...

PHILIP GROSS

Ickworth

An estate
is too far.
Panoramic,
neat, historical,
unpeopled.

A curve of sandstone,
an arc of lavender,
the sense of green
spreading below the feet:
this scale of things
we might manage.

But look at that bee,
focused on the job
of applying and re-
applying its perfect body
to the mauve universe.

The longer we watch
the more there are
and lavender has black
spots and is moving in
plain sight, though we
hadn't noticed before.

REBECCA WATTS

Knole

The Sackvilles were mostly mad.
This book blames a 'rogue gene' for
that 'slow reclusive despair'
which drove them out of their minds.

Knole was, according to Burke,
'a pleasant habitation ...
a grand repository':
oppressive clutter, more like.

But I remember the park
from winter afternoon runs:
setting off close to the gates,
rapidly losing the pack,

veering away to the right.
Distant scatter of antlers;
leafmould, twigs snapping, creatures
scuttling; not a soul in sight.

Along the wall of the house,
downhill back to the valley:
the runner's stumbling rhythm
leading to poems like this.

NEIL POWELL

J.P.

Trespassing, we were caught like moths
In the headlight trap of the Wolseley.
We glimpsed his face behind the windscreen,
The bright figurine on the car bonnet
Pointing at our guilt. In that world
He was legend, a tiny octogenarian
In panama and summer suit
Poised with secateurs above a rose-stem,
Or tapping with the polished ferrule
Of his cane through the gutter dust.
I remember the inquisitive gleam
Of his eyes, head cocked like a woodmouse,
As he regarded the extent of our crime,
Still the magistrate at the bench,
The jealous landowner. In the mansion-house
We had burgled rooms he never opened,
Broken the seal of the dust. And now,
Awaiting sentence, we shifted resentfully
In that hot stain of light. For Llangewydd's
Square mile of history, its cwms and
Slow decaying farms, the blaze of lawn about
The magistrate's estate, was an inheritance
We claimed. Even then the idea was alive
Within us: we belonged; we continued;
For ours was an instinct that mastered fear
And fired a tribal defiance of that
Black car as we stood our ground,
Staring together into its powerful beam.

ROBERT MINHINNICK

Moonlight

Tomorrow. Drive up without lights. Wait for the all-clear.
Half mile from the road. – No, you can't.
                          Shut it.
No, no one living there. – No, no dogs.
Then quick and up with ladders. Mick's got the gear.

East wing first. Crawler boards. Start at the ridge.
Can't have some silly fucker falling off.
Flashing, gutters, downpipes, hopper heads, the lot.
Then straight back to Jacko's with the load.

Both trucks. – Two, three nights.
                          No clever tricks.
You get paid when I do.
                Don't. Ask.
Used twenties.
             You'll get paid What You're Owed.
Course not, *if it rains*. Fucking daft.
One more word from you and you'll get this in your gob.

Yeah, there's fireplaces too, but that's another job.

ANNE BERKELEY

Breaking

I was a child but might have been any age
when this Sunday arrived and time to kill
but how? By talking? By lounging around?
No, all that was dull. By tagging along
with some others who rattled a stick in my gate
to call me out. (Others, you see, not friends.)

We drifted away through the village, its boundary-
field scraped flat for the plan of a new estate
with things like tent-pegs stuck in, with tapes
which held us up for a while as we traipsed
from room to invisible room, invented stairs,
and plumply sat ourselves down on cushions of air.

A mile beyond that was a proper house
(proper meant diamond panes, half-timbered, intact;
proper meant real) but nowhere I'd seen before.
No wonder. It stood so far from the world
it might have been dropped from a plane, or plucked
(I was thinking of books) straight out of the earth on a wish.

Anyway: someone a lifetime ago had thought
the way it tucked in on that narrow plateau
overlooking the valley was perfect: the village
remote but clear (its windows each night
a miniature Milky Way); the woodland beyond
a line of defence which kept every detail in place.

Who says they were wrong? Nothing we found
said anyone living there went to the bad, or worse –
only that time had run out. In boredom perhaps.
More likely (we fingered the eye-height letter-box
open and gazed down the track of the empty hall)
in death, not that we said so aloud.

But it made us feel free to break in –
with somebody smashing a window-pane,
the rest slip-sliding clean through
amazed at ourselves, as if in one step
from the sill to the bare wooden floor we had left
whatever it was we knew and started to dream.

Pale squares on the walls where pictures had hung;
a hand-shaped burn by the grate where a log
once popped; a zig-zag wallpaper rip at the turn
of the stairs where they angled the furniture out;
a slug gone mad in a basin; a giant turd
and no paper blocking the downstairs bog.

Everywhere something beginning its journey
to nothing – or so we imagined, when one of us
(still in our dream) decided that what had been started
slowly should end in a rush, and dragged indoors
from the garden, the hopeless garden, a pole
he said had been cruelly holding a tree to a wall.

There must have been six or so helping,
young, like I say, and every one keen and fit.
We did the walls first – impossibly hard at a glance
but easy as soon as the first crack appeared:
our fingers squirmed in and tore them clean back
to rib-cage wattle and spars, like flensing a corpse.

Then grates (hard work for not much return).
Then windows (but quietly). Then to the bog
to unfetter that agonised turd. Then stairs.
Lastly the floor-boards, working like painters
carefully in from the corners to meet all together
at once by the narrow front door. Then shut it. Then kick it in.

And then spin away down the valley and off
to our homes before it got late. I told you just now,
they were others, these people, not friends,
and even before we came close to the village
I knew I would never be with them again,
not if that's what I chose. It was what I chose.

Dandering in through the sketched-out estate
I fell back and left them without even saying good-bye.
The tent-peg things were still there, and the tapes,
and the stripped-away earth. I just needed some time
to think about what I had done. I had to be sure
this thing I had helped to create would always be mine.

ANDREW MOTION

The Manor Garden

The fountains are dry and the roses over.
Incense of death. Your day approaches.
The pears fatten like little buddhas.
A blue mist is dragging the lake.

You move through the era of fishes,
The smug centuries of the pig –
Head, toe and finger
Come clear of the shadow. History

Nourishes these broken flutings,
These crowns of acanthus,
And the crow settles her garments.
You inherit white heather, a bee's wing,

Two suicides, the family wolves,
Hours of blackness. Some hard stars
Already yellow the heavens.
The spider on its own string

Crosses the lake. The worms
Quit their usual habitations.
The small birds converge, converge
With their gifts to a difficult borning.

SYLVIA PLATH

The Plain Sense of Things

After the leaves have fallen, we return
To a plain sense of things. It is as if
We had come to an end of the imagination,
Inanimate in an inert savoir.

It is difficult even to choose the adjective
For this blank cold, this sadness without cause.
The great structure has become a minor house.
No turban walks across the lessened floors.

The greenhouse never so badly needed paint.
The chimney is fifty years old and slants to one side.
A fantastic effort has failed, a repetition
In a repetitiousness of men and flies.

Yet the absence of the imagination had
Itself to be imagined. The great pond,
The plain sense of it, without reflections, leaves,
Mud, water like dirty glass, expressing silence

Of a sort, silence of a rat come out to see,
The great pond and its waste of the lilies, all this
Had to be imagined as an inevitable knowledge,
Required, as a necessity requires.

WALLACE STEVENS

Asleep in the Orangery

The gardener and his boy, they found him early,
coiled in a sack from the roots of a bay tree:
asleep in the Orangery like a cat curled.
His hair was feathered rime – more like
a bird that dropped and scuffled there to die
the night the outhouse heating failed.
The tall white panes were scrolled with light
and dripped like chandeliers at the sun's touch.
His eyes were frozen and he clutched
what might have been a pebble or a martyr's bone.
How could a child survive and be so cold?
They woke him slowly at the stove:
ribbed like a rake and close as shears.
The bay tree broke its heart for him that night
and all through February and March shed cardboard tears.

STUART HENSON

To a Stately Home

Drizzle, an oak-lined drive, spectres of sheep.
Electric buggies trundle the infirm
down to that pristine vale you chose to keep

plebeians out of view. Now they form
disorderly queues beneath your portico,
gawp at drapes and family plate, yawn

in front of tarnished oils in gilt that show
your erstwhile owners – tubs of lard on horse
who knew to wield the crop, who let you go

in lieu of tax, but kept a flat, of course,
a tranche of garden, a private gate, the London
house. Tweeded volunteers rehearse

their spiel in dim-lit rooms. You are abandoned
to this leisure world, where those whose kin
would once have scrubbed your marble floors dream on

life *downstairs*. Not for them the sin
of envy. The pleasure's knowing that their betters
had the taste, the loot, the ear of the king

whose pricey chamber remained, despite those letters
of scraping invitation, unused. Autumn
now, the chill end of the season, your shutters

lock in place the dark of a vacant tomb.

DAVID CLARKE

To a Cedar Tree

Do you remember Lebanon?
The stillness and the snows?
The cool cold glare
And a blue sky – pitiless –
Or sometimes grey and heavy with unfallen snow?

In the summers that were of polished brown hills
(But always the stillness – the mountain tops)
Here Solomon's men came to hew and fell the cedars
And the trees were taken to stand
Proudly in the temple of God ...

But they had been nearer to God,
Had lived with God in the hills,
Had whispered to God in the stillness;
They had been proud then and unafraid.

And you, my Cedar tree, in my garden by the Thames,
Brought in a ship and planted in a strange land
Near to the river
With farm lands all around,
Close to the toil and the labour of men,

Stately you grew, your branches wide,
Gracious you stand
With smooth clipped lawn all around you
And an English herbaceous border
Flaunting its bloom on a summer's day.
You are a part of England now:
'Tea will be served on the lawn
Under the Cedar tree.'

But do you remember Lebanon?
Beloved tree – do you remember Lebanon?

AGATHA CHRISTIE

Notes on the Poets and Poems

Fleur Adcock (1934–)
A New Zealand poet who settled in the UK, her many honours include a Cholmondeley Award, an OBE and the Queen's Gold Medal for Poetry. Sir Peter Wentworth was a sixteenth-century Puritan Parliamentarian and the poem (in which he speaks) describes the vanished manor at Lillingstone Lovell, Buckinghamshire.

Patience Agbabi (1965–)
Born in London to Nigerian parents, she is a performer as well as an award-winning writer of drama, poetry, short stories and work for children, often collaborating with fellow writers and musicians. She has been writer in residence at the Brontë cottage, and Canterbury Laureate, a post which led to the Chaucer-inspired *Telling Tales* in 2014. Her poem here was written for Ilkley Literature Festival's 'Allegories of Power' project.

Simon Armitage (1963–)
Even before becoming Oxford Professor of Poetry and Poet Laureate, he was acclaimed, following *Zoom*, his aptly titled debut. His hands-on experience as a probation officer makes him especially sensitive to social divisions. This is as true of 'Those Bastards in Their Mansions' (quoted briefly on p. 16) and 'The Two of Us', which are from his 1990s Faber collections, as it is of 'The Manor' from his 2018 illustrated collection, *Flit*, published by the Yorkshire Sculpture Park.

David Ashbee (1945–)
A retired English teacher who lives in Gloucestershire, he has been closely involved with the Cheltenham Poetry Society. His first collection *Perpetual Waterfalls* appeared from Enitharmon, and *Loss Adjuster* from bluechrome.

W. H. Auden (1907–1973)
Poet, playwright, librettist, translator – he was fluently productive from his youth and his *Poems* (1930) set the tone for the 'Age of Auden'. He remains a powerful presence, the early work in particular 'inexhaustibly original' (Jeremy Noel-Tod). He could probably have written a poem on anything (in any form), but human psychology is at the heart of his best poems. Given the circles he moved in, he would certainly have experienced country house culture.

Juliet Aykroyd (1944–)

Born in India, she is best known as an actress (RSC and several British TV hits such as *Whatever Happened to the Likely Lads?* and *Open All Hours*) but has written poetry and plays for many years. Her plays include *The Long Bones, Darwin and FitzRoy* and *Vanbrugh's Castles*.

George Barker (1913–1991)

He led a remarkable and somewhat unconventional life, leaving school early and dedicating himself to poetry; his output was impressive, as was his love-life. He had close associations with Norfolk, but the poem here is set in Wiltshire. Longleat is now a noted safari park and much more commercialised than Barker can have imagined: he clearly disapproved of both the place and the people visiting.

Elizabeth Bartlett (1924–2008)

Brought up in Kent in a working-class family (her mother had worked as a parlour maid), she emerged in the 1980s following five years of psychoanalysis, which were crucial to her poetic development, as 'Corpus Christi' obliquely suggests. At the end of the poem she weaves in quotations from the Early English 'Corpus Christi Carol'.

Patricia Beer (1919–1999)

Before things changed for the better, she was one of very few English women poets whose names were even mentioned, and her witty, accessible style brought her quite a following. From a Plymouth Brethren family, she made her home in Devon and wrote extensively about the West Country. 'Stourhead' is the first sonnet in her late 'Wessex Calendar', about the Wiltshire gardens and their Palladian mansion.

Peter Bennet (1942–)

A former art teacher (he attended Manchester College of Art & Design), he lives in a remote Northumbrian cottage 'near the Wild Hills o' Wanney' (according to the *Guardian*). His earliest poetry appeared in Jon Silkin's *Stand* when he was 40 and his recent books have been from Bloodaxe. 'Blaxter Hall' is the fictional seat of the Pringle family, a 'home of lost romance' as the poet describes it.

Anne Berkeley

Originally from Ludlow, she edited the magazine *Seam*, featured in a Carcanet Oxford Poets anthology, and performs with the Joy of Six. She also co-edited the work of the late Rebecca Elson in 2018. *The Men from Praga* appeared from Salt in 2009, and was shortlisted for the Seamus Heaney Centre prize. It features several poems about Revesby Abbey, a ruined mansion in Lincolnshire near where she lives.

John Betjeman (1906–1984)

His poems about suburban London brought him a very wide readership. Not only did his lines drop into the language, but he became one of poetry's few celebrities, assisted by his regular television appearances as an architectural enthusiast and by his appointment as Poet Laureate. He took his 'First steps in learning how to be a guest' (*Summoned by Bells*) at Sezincote in Gloucestershire and had close associations with several great country houses, including Pakenham Hall in County Westmeath, Ireland, and Chatsworth, in Derbyshire.

Ruth Bidgood (1922–)

A highly respected Welsh local historian and poet, she read English at Oxford and only began writing poetry in the 1970s after serving as a coder in WW2 and working on *Chambers's Encyclopaedia*. There have been thirteen books of poetry, and recordings of her reading (made when she was approaching 90) can be heard on the Poetry Archive website.

Laurence Binyon (1869–1943)

One of the most quoted (or misquoted) poets in English because of 'For the Fallen', Binyon was also an expert on Oriental art and became Keeper of the Prints and Drawings at the British Museum. Surprisingly enough, he was a friend of Ezra Pound's (who nicknamed him BinBin) and a champion of Isaac Rosenberg. He himself was a stretcher-bearer during the Great War.

Edmund Blunden (1895–1974)

A war poet, man of letters, editor of other poets, and author of books about rural life, at one time he was at the centre of literary life in England: his bibliography runs to 700 pages. Mapledurham, near Reading, is best remembered for its association with Alexander Pope. The sonnet evokes something of the same atmosphere as Blunden's celebrated war sonnet about Vlamertinghe Château.

Eavan Boland (1944–2020)

She was influential well beyond her native Dublin (she taught at Stanford) and she championed women's lives and voices from the start of her career – even when literary culture preferred to regard them as muses. Given her fascination with the traces left by conflict and with the fruitful tensions of domestic life, it is not surprising to find Boland drawn to the country house in this very late poem from her posthumous collection, *The Historians*.

Penny Boxall (1987–)

Winner of the prestigious Edwin Morgan Poetry Award, this Scottish poet has worked at the Ashmolean Museum, Oxford and is currently based at Laurence

Sterne's Shandy Hall on the North York Moors. A 'laird's lug' (lord's ear) is a ventilation hole for eavesdropping (e.g., in Edinburgh Castle).

Alison Brackenbury (1953–)
Very much a poet of rural England, she is originally from Lincolnshire but lives in Gloucestershire. Her most recent collection is *Gallop* (horses are of immense importance to her), which draws on all of her earlier books. Wilton – not far from Salisbury and Stonehenge – was a cultural hub during and after the brief life of Sidney. Many poets are said to have gathered there, including Shakespeare.

James Brookes (1986–)
A teacher and librarian, he was brought up in Sussex (near Shelley's Field Place). He has received an Eric Gregory Award, and his collections include *Spoils* (2018). Clearly influenced by Geoffrey Hill, the historically informed poetry is demanding but lyrical. The English sweating sickness was a mysterious contagious disease of the fifteenth and sixteenth centuries.

George Mackay Brown (1921–1996)
Born in Orkney, which he barely left (he was once in England, briefly), he wrote almost exclusively about that area, its history and mythology, which he saw as 'a microcosm of all the world'. His experience as a writer of fiction and drama shines through in the little known poem here, which also reveals his wry sense of humour, his quiet awareness of social injustice, and his gift for finding the human dimension in any story.

Roger Caldwell (1948–)
He is from St Albans, but has lived in Tehran, Canada and Germany. A philosophical poet with a light touch, he gives few clues to the setting of his evocative poem but has suggested 'the fact that I grew up in Hatfield, Hertfordshire, and visited Hatfield House' must have influenced him.

Charles Causley (1917–2003)
One of the most popular poets of the late twentieth century, noted for his children's poetry (such as the piece included here) which is no less impressive than his other work and which frequently has a Cornish dimension. He spent much of his life in Launceston, where he was a primary school teacher. To visit the town is to find yourself walking familiar lines from his poems. His cottage is now a writers' retreat.

Glen Cavaliero (1927–2019)
Educated at both Oxford and Cambridge, author of various collections since the 1970s, he was also a Church of England clergyman and Fellow Commoner

of St Catherine's College, Cambridge, where he was a member of the English faculty (he has written about rural tradition in the novel). Although Cavaliero's poetry has rather receded from view, he is highly regarded. He died while this anthology was in preparation. His 'Blue Bedfordshire' is undoubtedly Woburn.

Agatha Christie (1890–1976)
Few remember or even realise that the crime writer was a playwright (not only *The Mousetrap*) and a poet. It seemed appropriate to give the last word to one whose name is synonymous with the country house – albeit not in a good way! She owned a glorious property, Greenway, in Devon, but the one in the poem is Winterbrook (Wallingford), her home for forty years, and where she died. In her autobiography she describes how the 'particularly fine cedar tree' originally lay beyond the ha-ha in a field, but she hoped to extend the lawn so they could have tea under it.

David Clarke (1972–)
'Teacher, blogger, researcher, poet', he was born in Lincolnshire, won the Michael Marks Award with his debut pamphlet, and *Arc* appeared from Nine Arches in 2015. His latest, *The Europeans*, could only have been written in the age of Brexit. One critic has suggested that the poem included here (loosely based on Dyrham Park near Bath) 'needs to be broadcast before every re-run of *Downton Abbey*'.

Gillian Clarke (1937–)
She has written (and kept sheep) in west Wales for many years and has been the Welsh 'National Poet', but she has a loyal readership far beyond Offa's Dyke. The banquet poem and 'Plumbing' here are from a sequence, 'The Middleton Poems', which recreates the Regency mansion whose gardens are the basis of the National Botanic Garden of Wales. 'A Sad Story' is from a group of (chiefly) sonnets, 'Nine Green Gardens', inspired by Aberglasne.

John Clegg (1986–)
Although the poem here may seem unrelated to our theme, it does shoot across the territory of the landed gentry – muntjacs (also mentioned by his contemporary, James Brookes) were escapees from Woburn, and that 'lost estate' is significant. The work of this imaginative young Gregory Award winner is often preoccupied with the spirit of place and a certain kind of 'significant soil'. He works for the London Review Bookshop and his first full collection is *Holy Toledo*.

Tony Connor (1930–)
Author of at least nine volumes of poetry (Anvil Press brought out a *Selected* in 2006), he has spent much of his teaching life in America, but he comes from

Manchester. Clowes Park is in nearby Salford and is the site of Broughton Old Hall. In the early nineteenth century, Reverend (and orchid collector) John Clowes developed the area as a site for villas for 'wealthy gentlemen'.

Robert Conquest (1917–2015)
Remembered as a polemicist and for his studies of the USSR, he wrote in many genres, even editing SF anthologies, but was a central poet of 'The Movement', and edited *New Lines*. He became literary editor of the *Spectator*, speech-writer for Mrs Thatcher, and held academic posts in the USA, receiving the Presidential Medal of Freedom. One wonders whether he was drawn to Houghton House by its proximity to the village of Houghton Conquest.

Wendy Cope (1945–)
Originally from Kent, she studied at Oxford and was a primary-school teacher before finding a popular following (even among those who will not usually read poetry) with her parodies and light verse. Since *Making Cocoa for Kingsley Amis*, she has emphasised (it is the title of a later collection) her 'Serious Concerns', though they are often satirical. The villanelle here is typical of her relish for formal games with a literary twist. See W. B. Yeats's poem on p. 243.

Noël Coward (1899–1973)
Wikipedia lists him as almost everything but a poet, yet his lyrics do stand as light verse, carried by their wit even without his music. This anthology could hardly refuse admission to 'The Stately Homes of England', even if they are here presented in fragments and bereft of their infectious melody.

Martyn Crucefix (1956–)
Born in Trowbridge, he lives in London where he teaches. He is a distinguished translator (of Rilke and notably Peter Huchel, for which he received the 2020 Schlegel-Tieck Prize) and an extremely versatile poet who has a very English, unflamboyant take on the curiosities and mysteries of land and landscape. His most recent full collection is *The Lovely Disciplines* (Seren), and some of his new work is an oblique response to Brexit.

Cahal Dallat
A poet, critic, teacher and musician (notably for the Troubadour Coffee-House reading series, run with Anne-Marie Fyfe) he is originally from Co. Antrim, but based now near Yeats's demesne, Bedford Park. Frequently called upon to discuss Irish poetry in the media, his many and various literary projects include a residency at Charles Causley's house, and a Research Fellowship at Austin, Texas.

Elizabeth Daryush (1887–1977)

Daughter of the Poet Laureate, Robert Bridges, she was brought up in the family manor house, Yattendon, then at Boars Hill, Oxford – Chilswell House, which her father designed. John Clegg has speculated that 'Still-Life' is set there in its breakfast room, now part of a conference centre, and points out that the hill is 'thick with poets' (from the lawn Arnold's 'signal elm' would have been visible to the 'young heiress').

Hilary Davies (1954–)

The poetry of Hilary Davies (who has been a teacher and dedicated editor) is spun from spiritual and historical threads. 'Metamorphoses' is 'partly an ironic comment on the underbelly of the "big house", what goes on there, and also what happens when there is social upheaval', she notes. Her Jacobean mansion is Old Gwernyfed Manor (not far from Hay), a hotel she visited with her first husband. She was later married to the poet Sebastian Barker, son of George Barker.

William Virgil Davis (1940–)

Born in Ohio, he studied at Ohio University and the Pittsburgh Theological Seminary and has lived and taught in Austria, Denmark and Wales. He is retired from Baylor University, where he served as Professor of English and Writer-in-Residence. Awards include the Yale Younger Poets prize, the New Criterion Prize, and the Helen C. Smith Memorial Award. *Dismantlements of Silence* appeared in 2015 and his critical books include studies of R. S. Thomas and Robert Bly.

C. Day Lewis (1904–1972)

Anglo-Irish, he was the tail-ender of the 'MacSpaunDay' Thirties group (and father of a well-known film actor). He was an active communist in his younger days before becoming an establishment figure and Poet Laureate. He is buried next to Hardy in Stinsford, Dorset. The location of the tapestries in his poem remains unclear.

Walter de la Mare (1873–1956)

Despite the French name, he was a uniquely English figure, whose poetry conjures a lost dream world of childhood, sometimes with disturbing dissonances. One would not, alas, expect a de la Mare poem to refer to a named location, but the houses they feature will invariably be haunted. Most people will remember his work for classic poems such as 'The Listeners', although he was a memorable short-story writer too.

Peter Didsbury (1946–)
Author of several collections from Bloodaxe (including a *New and Collected*) and recipient of a Cholmondeley Award, he is a poet preoccupied with the past, with the weight of history. Not surprisingly, he became an archaeologist. He is one of several important British poets who live in Hull.

Freda Downie (1929–1993)
A Londoner who lived through the Blitz, she worked in music publishing and found success as a poet late in life, championed by, among others, Geoffrey Grigson and George Szirtes (who edited her *Collected Poems*). She wrote a memoir of her wartime years, *There'll Always Be an England*.

Jane Draycott (1954–)
Her work characteristically evokes the vague evanescent world between waking and sleeping. She has recently translated the medieval poem, 'Pearl'. 'Open Gardens Scheme' could be any small private manor house; 'Up at the House' quotes a note found and exhibited at The Vyne in Hampshire (although 'spookily', she explains, the curatorial team later 'denied all knowledge of any such item').

Douglas Dunn (1942–)
Born in Paisley, near Glasgow, he was initially a librarian, like (and with) Larkin, in Hull. He later became a professor specialising in Scottish literature. His poetry, whose reputation was established with poems that evoke the ordinary lives of 'Terry Street', makes much of social divisions harking back to the Highland Clearances. It has been suggested that the setting of 'In the Grounds' evokes Hull MP Marvell's Appleton House, although that property no longer exists.

T. S. Eliot (1888–1965)
His ancestors emigrated from East Coker, but there are memories of America too. Eliot remarked to John Hayward when discussing these lines from *Four Quartets* that mice '*did* get into our country house in New England, and very pretty little creatures too'. Although East Coker had contained the ancestral home of the Eliots, there was in the poet's day, as he himself said, 'No house there. Said to have been destroyed by fire'. By contrast, Burnt Norton is the name of an actual country house in Gloucestershire.

Bernardine Evaristo (1959–)
Born in Woolwich, London, to an English mother and Nigerian father, she works in many genres and her awards include the Booker Prize (with Margaret Atwood). Barack Obama selected *Girl, Woman, Other* as a favourite novel of 2019. Evaristo consistently champions under-represented writers of colour, and

her own work often concentrates on the African diaspora. The poems here are extracted from *Lara*, one of her verse novels.

Gavin Ewart (1916–1995)
Remembered for some scurrilous light verse and a few genuinely moving poems, he had what the *Times Literary Supplement* called 'a strong gamey talent'. Few could rival his formal ingenuity as demonstrated in the murder mystery parody here. The author has noted (perhaps unnecessarily) that 'This poem was written to be read aloud, and the 'oo' sounds at the ends of the lines should be intoned like the call of an owl'.

Kit Fan (1979–)
A writer of fiction and poetry, he was born in Hong Kong 'when the city was the last British colony' but settled in the UK when he was 21. He currently lives in York. Among other awards, he has won the inaugural Hong Kong University International Poetry Prize. His most recent collection is *As Slow as Possible* (Arc Publications, 2018), and his novel, *Diamond Hill* (Dialogue Books), was published in 2021.

U. A. Fanthorpe (1929–2009)
Late in life, as what she liked to call 'a middle-aged drop-out', Ursula Fanthorpe found an eager audience among those, perhaps, who missed the voice of Betjeman speaking for the common reader. She certainly had a sharp eye for the curiosities of (specifically) English customs and curiosities. The Tudor manor, Owlpen, to which she gives a voice here, is in the Cotswolds; her haunted house remains unidentified.

James Fenton (1949–)
He has been war correspondent, drama critic and Oxford Professor of Poetry (his published lectures are some of the finest writings on modern poetry). As a poet he is hard to classify, although he has a penchant for light verse. He is also an unforgettable performer. Having written some lines for *Les Misérables*, he was able to settle in what Ian McEwan described in the *Telegraph* as a 'scene-of-the-crime house' with 150 acres.

John Fowles (1926–2005)
Among the leading novelists of the last century (*The Magus, The French Lieutenant's Woman*) he originally considered himself a poet, although it may be that he will be best remembered for his fascinating journals, many of which were written at Belmont, his grand house at the top of the hill in Lyme Regis. Fellow poet-novelist, Adam Thorpe, edited a selection of his verse from which the poem here is taken.

G. S. Fraser (1915–1980)

A very influential and highly readable Glaswegian critic, whose taste helped to define an era but whose poetry has rather drifted out of view. His experience of war and his travels in the Middle East were especially formative. Brockham End House, near Bath, was built by the dedicatee's father in 1907 and is now divided into flats, although the park and gardens may be visited.

John Fuller (1937–)

A prolific and formally ingenious poet (son of Roy Fuller), he is an Emeritus Fellow at Magdalen College, Oxford. Apart from his many collections, there is also a notable study of Auden and the intriguing, entertaining *Who is Ozymandias?* about puzzles in poetry. The pagoda in his poem makes a fitting emblem for his own work – playful and eye-catching – but appears to be the product of this Duke's fancy, rather than one that can be climbed (such as Sir William Chambers's at Kew).

Roy Fuller (1912–1991)

Perhaps the only poet to have worked for the Woolwich Building Society, as well as becoming Oxford Professor of Poetry, his best work was recently gathered into a *Selected Poems* by his son, John. Newstead Abbey was Byron's ancestral home (see illustration, p. 140) and Knole (1,000 acres) has been home to many famous figures including Cranmer, Dudley and the Sackvilles.

Katharine Gallagher (1935–)

Australian by birth, she has lived in London for many years, very active in the poetry community around Stevie Smith's old patch, Palmers Green. *Carnival Edge: New and Selected Poems* is a usefully representative volume of her work. Knebworth in Hertfordshire was the home of the writer and politician Sir Edward Bulwer-Lytton, but is now better known for pop concerts and corporate events.

Roger Garfitt (1944–)

Editor, memoirist, inspirational teacher and performer, as a poet he is drawn to rural themes and to related mythologies. His most recent collection is *The Action*, from Carcanet. He has a close association with Madingley Hall in Cambridge. The Walcot Hall of his poem is in Shropshire; the Bedlams are Morris Dancers.

Grey Gowrie (1939–)

Grey Ruthven, 2nd Earl of Gowrie, was a conservative politician (he raised the idea of a National Lottery with Mrs Thatcher, who did not approve) and an important figure in the world of the arts. His own poetry has only achieved recognition in recent years. A friend of Robert Lowell's, he too feels the burden of his name and there is something of the American's manner in the verse.

Robert Graves (1895–1985)

A war poet and popular historical novelist, he had a powerful sense of English traditions and conventions, but 'A Country Mansion' was written as he was settling in Mallorca, so the house might symbolise all he was rejecting. The poem seems to embroider elements from the life of John Parr of Albebury, and the homes of noblemen who befriended him – perhaps nearby Loton Park where there is a painting of him.

John Greening (1954–)

He grew up not far from Robert Adam's Osterley House, and used to go fishing in its park. Although he has worked in Upper Egypt, and taught for many years in a converted stately home (Kimbolton Castle, as described in 'A Huntingdonshire Nocturne'), he and his family have since the 1980s been content in a tiny mid-terrace gamekeeper's cottage on the old Duke of Manchester estate.

Debora Greger (1949–)

A prominent American poet and visual artist, she has received innumerable awards – from the NEA, and both the Guggenheim and Ingram Merrill Foundations – and an Amy Lowell Traveling Scholarship. She spends part of her time in the UK (her partner is the poet and critic William Logan) and often writes about it from fresh perspectives. The poem here was inspired by Wimpole Hall, not far from Cambridge.

Jane Griffiths (1970–)

Brought up in Devon and Holland, she won the Newdigate Prize at Oxford, where she later completed a doctorate on Skelton. She now teaches at Wadham College. Her collections have been published by Bloodaxe since her debut in 2000. Her affection for Old Hall, the house described in her 'haunted' poem, can be seen in her article for *PN Review* 240 in April 2018. The poem about Lyveden dates back to the mid-1990s.

Geoffrey Grigson (1905–1985)

An essayist, editor, art historian, cultural commentator, writer of superb books on English natural history and life in the countryside, including its stately homes (see *Britain Observed*, for example), Grigson was a potent satirist too, as we discover in some of these poems. He lived in Broad Town, Wiltshire, with his wife, the cookery writer Jane Grigson.

Emily Grosholz (1950–)

This professor of philosophy from Philadelphia may well be the only poet ever to have been a member of the Center for Fundamental Theory/Institute for Gravitation and the Cosmos. Yet her poetry is invariably accessible, often reflecting her time in Europe, although the loss of her childhood home seems to haunt her. The poem here is dedicated to Donald Davie's wife and presumably dates from an emotionally disconcerting time when all eyes were on Kensington Palace or Althorp House.

Philip Gross (1952–)
A prolific and exhilaratingly unpredictable, yet self-effacing poet, his collections from Faber and Bloodaxe should really be in every public and personal library (and certainly that of any self-respecting country house). His Quaker leanings are occasionally and increasingly evident. His early collection for young people, *Manifold Manor*, tours an imaginary ruined estate and touches on one of his preoccupations: identity.

Harry Guest (1932–2021)
A teacher, poet and prolific translator, though based in Devon (he died shortly before this anthology was published) he maintained an international outlook and a particular fascination with Japanese culture. The 'blocks' in the poem included here do not refer to any particular house, and Guest pointed out to the editors that his real subject was 'not the places but the pictures'. Nevertheless, they do conjure the Watteauesque complacency of a country estate.

Thom Gunn (1929–2004)
One of the most admired poets of the late twentieth century, born in Gravesend, but resident for much of his life in California. The 'American in Europe' is Gunn's lover, although the poem is from his 1957 collection before he could be open about his relationships. The topic is grist to Gunn's neo-Elizabethan mill: one of his favourite poets was Fulke Greville, who built Warwick Castle.

John Gurney (1935–2000)
Neglected since his premature death, he may come to be remembered for his verse dramas and astonishing long poems (the epic *War* is especially noteworthy). His work combines a rare mystical insight and openness to the paranormal, with an appreciation of everyday suffering. He read English at Oxford and taught in Bedford for much of his life, but he is one of the few poets to have been a fighter pilot. Bedfordshire's Shuttleworth estate featured in these poems has a celebrated aircraft collection.

J. C. Hall (1920–2011)
He was born in Ealing, brought up in Tunbridge Wells. A pacifist, he was nevertheless literary executor for war poet Keith Douglas. Alfoxton ('All the Foxes Den' according to Coleridge) dates from 1710 and is more usually spelt Alfoxden. Wordsworth and Coleridge planned *Lyrical Ballads* and composed

several key poems there. In a footnote, Hall informs those who know 'it is now a hotel' and that it was unoccupied when he visited.

Michael Hamburger (1924–2007)
He was internationally known as translator of Goethe, Hölderlin and other German writers. Another of the poets drawn to East Anglia, he settled with his wife in a Suffolk farmhouse (was it the same property featured in 'Real Estate'?) where he cultivated apples. 'Conservatism Revisited' is the title of a book by the poem's dedicatee.

Thomas Hardy (1840–1928)
He was an architect before he was a poet or novelist, and designed his own dwelling place on the edge of Dorchester: Max Gate. In his work there is often a contrast between the life in the big house and the humble cot.

Tony Harrison (1937–)
A proudly working-class poet from Leeds (its terraced houses are the backdrop to many of his distinctive sixteen-line sonnets), he became a fine classicist, translator, verse dramatist and pioneer of the television poem film. If he seems an unlikely contributor to a book of country house poems, it must be remembered that social division has always been at the heart of his work, most passionately exemplified by his long poem, *V.*

Michael Hartnett (1941–1999)
One of the last century's major Irish writers, he wrote in both English and Irish – a tension that runs throughout his work – and frequently explores the troubled history of Ireland's relationship with England. For a while he was curator of Joyce's tower at Sandycove (he had also been a night telephone operator and lecturer in creative writing), but his personal life was turbulent.

Seamus Heaney (1939–2013)
Unlike Yeats, but like most Irish poets since who have written about country houses, the Irish Nobel Prize winner adopts the point of view of the dispossessed. He was famously unhappy to be in a Penguin anthology of 'British Poetry', but we trust that he would understand why he finds himself here among so many British mansions. A phrase in 'Servant Boy' provides the title to one of his early collections.

John Heath-Stubbs (1918–2006)
Blind from an early age, he made his name with quirky allusive historical pieces, riffs on classical themes (and classical music, about which he was very well informed), and witty narratives such as the one here. He was extremely

prolific: there is a large *Collected Poems* and a recent Carcanet *Selected* edited by one of his younger followers, John Clegg.

Stuart Henson (1954–)

Playwright and Gregory Award-winning poet, he used to teach (alongside one of the present editors) in the old home of the Dukes of Manchester, Kimbolton Castle. His work, best represented by *The Way You Know It* (Shoestring Press, 2018), frequently displays a sympathy for those 'below stairs'. The second poem came to him 'sitting in the Orangery of a big house near Bridlington, waiting to hear Penelope Shuttle read'.

Geoffrey Hill (1932–2016)

He was from Worcestershire and its landscape is recognisable in early books such as *Mercian Hymns* and in the work of his extraordinary late efflorescence. His reputation grew steadily in his last decades after a period when he published very little. Among other honours, he was elected Oxford Professor of Poetry. A prolific poet of knotty, furrowed seriousness, he shows a profound and sometimes baffling appreciation of English tradition and history.

Jeremy Hooker (1941–)

A poet of delicacy and spiritual insight, with a rare appreciation for landscape, he specialises in poems of place, often set on the south coast of England, although he has strong connections with Wales too. Avington Park (see illustration on p. 310) is in Hampshire and was visited by both Charles II and George VI.

Glyn Hughes (1935–2011)

This respected novelist was nevertheless (as the *Guardian* obituary put it) 'a poet in essence'. Born in Altrincham, he was devoted to Yorkshire and his own patch at Mill Bank, near Sowerby Bridge in particular, as 'Landscape Poem' suggests.

Ted Hughes (1930–1998)

For decades he was the UK's best-known poet (and eventually Poet Laureate), with a dedicated readership and a string of successful, unconventional books – from the early nature poems, through cartoonish *Crow* to the late gift of *Birthday Letters*, about Sylvia Plath. He had a passion for (and owned some) big old houses. Sixteenth-century Wycoller Hall in Lancashire, not far from Haworth, now a ruin (see illustration on p. 122), may have been the model for Charlotte Brontë's Ferndean Manor in *Jane Eyre*. Intended as the finale to *Remains of Elmet*, the poem was little known before the *Collected Poems*.

Alan Jenkins (1955–)
He was born in Surrey, and that suburban world is prominent in his collections (as well as in the poem included here), though he never sounds like Betjeman. A stronger influence is Ian Hamilton, whom he has edited. Jenkins studied at Warwick, worked for the *Times Literary Supplement* in London for almost forty years, and has won many major awards – despite which, he was once advised that his most fruitful subject was 'loss'.

Brian Jones (1938–2009)
Born in Islington, educated in Ealing and at Selwyn College, Cambridge, Jones was widely honoured in the 1960s (on television, in *The Sun*), considered as exciting as Heaney. But from the 1980s he was rather left behind – or rolled over, perhaps, by a rock musician of the same name. He had little enthusiasm for publication, but there is now a substantial *New & Selected*. 'That House' is not identified, yet it is perhaps grander than the manor at Great Tew.

P. J. Kavanagh (1931–2015)
Not to be confused with the Irish Kavanagh – who hated the very idea of him – this Sussex Patrick was much preoccupied with English landscapes. Lecturer, columnist, memoirist, actor, broadcaster (his father was a successful radio comedy scriptwriter), he produced a modest collection of gently attentive and frequently grief-stricken poems, direct descendants of Edward Thomas, and occasionally Ivor Gurney, whom he edited.

Lisa Kelly
She describes herself as 'half-Danish, half-deaf', and both play into her poetry (she uses sign language when she performs the title poem of her Carcanet collection, *A Map Towards Fluency*). She has an M.A. in Creative Writing from Lancaster University and works as a journalist, but according to her publisher has been 'actress, life model, Consumer Champion, waitress, sales assistant and envelope stuffer'.

Mimi Khalvati (1944–)
Born in Tehran, she was brought up on the Isle of Wight, and was an actor before turning to poetry and publishing ten collections with Carcanet. She has been a quietly influential figure, co-founding The Poetry School, for example. Her most recent book is a sequence of sonnets. The poem selected for this anthology comes from a much earlier sequence, 'Entries on Light'.

Lotte Kramer (1923–)
Born in Mainz, Germany, she came to the UK as a Jewish refugee with the 'Kindertransport' and her work (represented in her Rockingham Press *New and Collected Poems*) inevitably draws on the trauma of those war years. She lived

for many years in Peterborough and writes much about the Fen landscapes. Burghley House is in Stamford, home of William Cecil.

Laurence Lerner (1925–2016)
Born in Cape Town, he was a university teacher (Heaney was one of his students), a popular critic and very witty poet, although he has been somewhat overlooked in recent decades. He can be heard reading 'The National Trust' from his last collection, *Rembrandt's Mirror* (1987) at the Poetry Archive.

Peter Levi (1931–2000)
An academic, reviewer, biographer (of Milton, most memorably), translator, Oxford Professor of Poetry – but he was also a much-respected poet himself as well as a Jesuit priest, until he renounced those orders in 1974 to marry Deirdre Connolly.

Alun Lewis (1915–1944)
One of the finest poets of WW2, he died by his own hand in what was then known as Burma (Myanmar). This poem was published in 1942, so the mansion concerned may have been near a training camp: Longmoor (Hampshire), Morecambe, Gloucester or Woodbridge. The owner is evidently 'digging for victory' (those potatoes) and it may even have been requisitioned. 'Tudor' has special significance to a Welshman.

Grevel Lindop (1948–)
Born in Liverpool, educated at Oxford, he was until 2001 Professor of Romantic and Early Victorian Studies at Manchester University. Along with several collections from Carcanet, he has written major studies of De Quincey and Charles Williams and a literary guide to the Lake District, and has edited Chatterton's poetry. He has close connections with The Temenos Academy founded by Kathleen Raine.

Herbert Lomas (1924–2011)
Originally from Todmorden, where the house in the poem appears to be located, he came to be thought of as an East Anglian poet, living for many years in Aldeburgh. He was closely associated with Finland, whose poets he translated.

Robert Lowell (1917–1977)
A volatile Bostonian from a family of some celebrity and distinction, he was at one time the undisputed pack leader in American poetry, but he has in recent years been overtaken by his friend Elizabeth Bishop. The late poems here are from his time in England with his third wife, Lady Caroline Blackwood, at her Georgian mansion, Milgate Park, in Kent.

George MacBeth (1932–1992)

A familiar editor-presenter on BBC radio, *The Times* called him 'the single most influential official in the field of British poetry since T. S. Eliot'. He called himself 'a poet who would like to have been an architect' and wrote of a 'sense of aristocracy' in his work. He lived in (and restored) the rectory at Oby and then St Mary's Hall, Wiggenhall St Mary Magdalen, Norfolk.

Lachlan Mackinnon (1956–)

From Aberdeen originally, he was educated at Charterhouse and Christ Church, Oxford. He has published books on French literature and Shakespeare. He taught for some years at Winchester and retired to the Fens where he is married to the poet Wendy Cope. Chatto and, more recently, Faber have published his collections, and he is frequently to be found reviewing in the *Times Literary Supplement*.

Louis MacNeice (1907–1963)

One of the most enduring of the Thirties poets, he worked for the BBC in London, but in 'Soap Suds' is harking back to his childhood in Carrickfergus, recalling his step-uncle's home, Seapark. The house in 'Order to View' is more of a symbol, perhaps, as Robyn Marsack has suggested, 'of derelict England'.

Derek Mahon (1941–2020)

For many readers he was the leading Northern Ireland poet since MacNeice, and like him worked for the BBC in London. He was formally versatile, with translations and work for the theatre to his name. That dexterity owed much to the era he honours in his evocation of Sir Philip Sidney's Penshurst (and repeating Marlowe's famous, much-echoed line). But inevitably there is the shadow of Anglo-Irish relations. 'The Woods' describes the estate surrounding a Victorian house – originally Ford Manor – where he and his wife rented a flat in 1975.

Katharine Mansfield (1888–1923)

A New Zealander, associated with many of the major artists of the early twentieth century, she died young. She is remembered more for her short stories than her poetry, yet the one included here, slight though it is, has a certain charm. It was composed in 1917, but the war seems far off.

Toby Martinez de las Rivas (1978–)

From Somerset originally, he studied history and archaeology at Durham before turning to poetry and winning several awards. He is indeed 'unlike most of his contemporaries' (*New Statesman*) and comparisons with Blake are somehow more apt, although Geoffrey Hill and C. H. Sisson also come to mind. The poem here is from his scorching (and controversial) second Faber collection, *Black Sun*.

John Masefield (1878–1967)
From Ledbury (now home of a celebrated poetry festival), he was considered daringly modern before WW1, and his books sold in the tens of thousands, but is now remembered chiefly as Poet Laureate (for 'Sea Fever' too, and 'Cargoes'). He settled on Boar's Hill, near Oxford, where a number of poets have lived.

Roland Mathias (1915–2007)
Considered one of Wales's most prominent poets and literary critics, he spent much of his life in England, as a headmaster and eventually a full-time writer. He is remembered especially for his editorial work on the *Anglo-Welsh Review*. His poetry often has a religious and rigorously intellectual quality; it frequently focuses on landscape, history, family.

Glyn Maxwell (1962–)
One of the luminaries of the English 'new town', Welwyn Garden City, he is a prolific and much decorated poet, published by Bloodaxe, Faber and now Picador. He is also an actor-playwright, specialising in verse drama. He studied under Derek Walcott at Boston University and spent many years teaching in Amherst and New York.

John McAuliffe (1973–)
From County Kerry, he has taught in Irish universities and directed Ireland's largest poetry festival. He is currently co-director of the Centre for New Writing in Manchester and Associate Publisher at Carcanet. His last Gallery collection, *The Way In*, won the Michael Hartnett Award in 2016. The poem here is part of a sequence which included map references to identify locations: its starting point was Coole Park.

Jamie McKendrick (1955–)
There is an Italianate aspect to his work, and a related interest in the visual arts – but there is something very English too, as typified by the poem selected here about a school converted from an old country house. He has published several collections with OUP and Faber, and received a number of important awards. He was shortlisted for the T. S. Eliot Prize.

Robert Minhinnick (1952–)
This prolific Welsh poet (twice Forward Prize winner, shortlisted for the T. S. Eliot Prize), essayist and environmental activist has several times written about the manor house Cwrt Colmana (now a hotel): 'My grandfather worked as a gardener on the estate and my mother and her sister were also employed there. I was brought up in a house on the edge of the estate … it was great fun to trespass on the grounds. I have always written about what I know and part of what I know is the estate' (*PN Review*).

John Montague (1929–2016)
Born in Brooklyn, raised in Co. Tyrone, living for many years in France, he was an impressively productive lyric poet (a translator and essayist too), but could write acerbic verse on the Troubles. Woodtown Manor is in Rathfarnham (the poem's dedicatee lived there) and dates from *ca.* 1700.

Dom Moraes (1938–2004)
A Mumbai writer, he won the Hawthornden Prize when he was still at Oxford. Widely respected during the 1960s (sharing *Penguin Modern Poets 2* with Kingsley Amis and Peter Porter), he rather disappeared thereafter, though is highly regarded in India. His life, according to *In Cinnamon Shade* (2001), was 'hectic and romantic', as was his poetry ('first Byronic, later more nuanced and hermetic').

Esther Morgan (1970–)
Born in Kidderminster, she read English at Newnham College, Cambridge. *The Silence Living in Houses* emerged after a period as caretaker of Haydown, an Edwardian house in Oxfordshire ('crumbling quietly behind its horse chestnut trees', featuring original furniture, servants' quarters, a back stairs and bell-board, together with 'a big iron bath that seemed to freeze the water as soon as you ran it'. She says she writes of 'family and ancestry, the domestic space, the secrets of hidden lives'.

Andrew Motion (1952–)
Former Poet Laureate, he established the invaluable Poetry Archive, and is an acclaimed biographer (Larkin, Keats). Now living in the USA, he continues to look back to his childhood, to rural settings and overwhelmingly to the loss of his mother (as in the recent *Essex Clay*). The poem here is reminiscent of Graham Greene's story, 'The Destructors'.

Richard Murphy (1927–2018)
From Mayo, his poems about Western Ireland made his name, although much of his childhood was in Sri Lanka; the sonnet here is from a later sequence 'voiced' by certain buildings. His *In Search of Poetry* explains that 'Ballinamore was a formidable house built to dominate a vast estate of poor land acquired by conquest and marriages'. It belonged to his mother's maiden aunts, 'who lived unscathed through the Troubles'.

Sean O'Brien (1952–)
He is a highly regarded, prize-winning Picador poet (something of a formalist) and a noted critic, scourge of the privileged classes. Yet he is capable of considerable tenderness and lyricism in his often bleak or elegiac verse. He is from Hull, so inevitably associated with Larkin and Douglas Dunn.

Ruth Padel (1946–)
Professor of Poetry at King's College London, her own remarkable poems and her newspaper column analysing other people's have combined to make her a familiar name. *Darwin* (Chatto) was a bold experiment in verse biography (she has recently turned to Beethoven). The extract here describes the family's arrival in July 1842 at Down House, Kent, where Charles would work on his theory of evolution. The child is Mary, born that September, who died the next month and is buried in Downe churchyard.

Rennie Parker (1962–)
She lives in the East Midlands in John Clare country and was education officer at his cottage in Helpston. Her poetry is striking for its response to particular places and for a singular appreciation of rural life. She has written a book on the Georgians and has a particular interest in Ivor Gurney. 'Tresham's Fancy' is based on the same Northamptonshire building, Lyveden New Bield, as Jane Griffiths's poem: they both appeared in the same edition of *The Rialto*.

Sylvia Plath (1932–1963)
Had she not committed suicide, the Bostonian would still be a major poet, often drawn to features of landscape or history during her life in the UK. 'The Manor Garden' is the first poem in her first collection, *The Colossus*, and was written in 1959 while at the artists' colony, Yaddo. The estate in Saratoga Springs is identifiable but not named, allowing something from her time in England to infuse the poem.

Peter Porter (1929–2010)
An Australian poet who settled in Britain and became a familiar (witty and illuminating) presence wherever poetry was discussed. His newspaper reviews were especially notable. His poem here is in the voice of a seventeenth-century letter-writer before she became Lady Temple (after a prolonged and secret courtship). Presumably it is set at her home, Chicksands priory, Bedfordshire.

Neil Powell (1948–)
Suffolk-based, he has written biographies of Crabbe, Britten and Roy Fuller, and there have been several Carcanet collections. The opening of 'Knole' (Fuller also has a Knole poem) refers to *Inheritance: The Story of Knole and the Sackvilles* (Robert Sackville-West, Bloomsbury, 2010); the second quotation is from a 1791 letter from Edmund Burke to John Sackville, 3rd Duke of Dorset. The 'Ruined Garden' was at Toys Hill (Sevenoaks, Kent) where Octavia Hill founded the National Trust, and site of the ruined Edwardian Weardale Manor.

Craig Raine (1944–)

Best known for his early 'Martian' poems, which spawned something of a movement in English poetry, he subsequently became poetry editor at Faber and a don at New College, Oxford. He is a poet and essayist who delights in controversy, but, most relevantly for this anthology, also one who appreciates the subtle nuances of the class system.

Kathleen Raine (1908–2003)

A fine love poet, modern mystic and authority on Blake and Yeats. Her *Collected Poems* have recently been reissued, but her autobiographical writings are worth exploring (there were marriages to Hugh Sykes-Davies and Charles Madge, and a complex relationship with Gavin Maxwell). The house featured in her poem is on the Hebridean Isle of Canna, where Dr John Lorne Campbell and Margaret Fay Shawe dedicated their lives to preserving the local customs and language.

John Crowe Ransom (1888–1974)

A poet with deep loyalties to the heritage of the American South, he is now considered one of the twentieth century's most distinguished formalists. He said of himself that he was 'in manners, aristocratic; in religion, ritualistic; in art, traditional.' He is remembered particularly for his landmark study, *The New Criticism* (1941), and his critical works have overshadowed his poetry. 'Romance of a Youngest Daughter' owes something to his beloved Tennessee, but draws on English country house traditions (another poem, 'Philomela' dates back to his time as a Rhodes Scholar in Oxford).

Vicki Raymond (1949–)

An Australian, she spent much of her early life in Tasmania, but this award-winning poet now lives in London, and brings an incomer's clear eye for the old ways. Her first book won the British Airways Commonwealth Poetry Prize. Her second, *Small Arm Practice*, was published by William Heinemann Australia in 1989 and there was a British *Selected* in 1993.

Peter Redgrove (1932–2003)

One of contemporary poetry's most original voices, Peter Redgrove stayed much of his life in Cornwall with Penelope Shuttle, travelling only in imagination. 'Enýpnion' means 'something seen in sleep', but the poem of that title is as much about the 'gentleman's library'. Shuttle suggests it combines various Cornish locations: Trerice Manor's haunted library, Lanhydrock House, which is full of rare books, and the Morrab library in Penzance.

Henry Reed (1914–1986)
Known for one or two distinctive and satirical war poems, and for his work at the BBC, he is a poet of considerable scope (with a real gift for parody – witness his 'Chard Whitlow', after 'Four Quartets').

James Reeves (1909–1978)
Born in Middlesex, he was educated at Stowe and Cambridge, and taught for some years before becoming well known as an editor and for his school anthologies. He was closely associated with Robert Graves. 'Greenhallows' is untypical but all the more remarkable for that – 'as if Ishiguro wrote poetry instead of fiction' (Kevin Gardner).

Anne Ridler (1912–2001)
Forever in the shadow of T. S. Eliot – for whom she worked at Faber and with whom she shared certain spiritual preoccupations – she nevertheless developed a distinctive personal voice as poet, translator, dramatist (and indeed as a singer in the Bach Choir).

Michael Rivière (1919–1997)
Born in Norwich, he had a passion for local history, but worked as a brewer and retired to Dilham Grange, as if 'to leave a hero's mark, a palace, an invention, an example' ('Urbino'). His war experience (in one of the last mounted units) involved twice escaping from a P.O.W. camp before ending up in Colditz. His copy of the *Oxford Book of Sixteenth Century Verse* helped him through: he had it memorised by 1945.

Vita Sackville-West (1892–1962)
Brought up at Knole, she established a celebrated garden (with Harold Nicolson) at Sissinghurst Castle in Kent. Her best-known collection is *The Land* (1926), but she also wrote a country house novel, *The Edwardians* (1930). The poem 'Sissinghurst' is dedicated to her friend Virginia Woolf.

Lawrence Sail (1942–)
A prolific poet and editor, he has lived and taught in Exeter, Devon for many years but contributed significantly to British literary life as festival director and competition judge. A volume of new and selected poems (*Waking Dreams*) appeared in 2010 from Bloodaxe, but did not include our choice: 'Guidelines' (from *Opposite Views* [1974]) is a formal tour de force whose relentless lower case is in itself satirical.

Sarah Salway (1960–)
Poet, novelist and journalist, she has been a Royal Literary Fund Fellow and taught creative writing at the universities of Sussex and Kent. She has written

extensively about English gardens, especially those in Kent where she was Canterbury Laureate in 2012. The poems here are from *Punctuation in the Park*, about Lancelot (Capability) Brown.

Siegfried Sassoon (1886–1967)
The family home of the celebrated anti-war poet and memoirist was the neo-Gothic mansion, Weirleigh (Kent), but he settled in Heytesbury House in 1933. A decade earlier he wrote: 'when I have "settled down" and come into a fortune, I will buy a little manor-house in a good hunting country and keep three or four "nailing good performers", and play on a grand piano in a room full of books, with a window looking on to an old-fashioned garden full of warbling birds and mossy apple trees'.

William Scammell (1939–2000)
A brilliant satirist, parodist and critic, he could also praise heartily when required. His work has never quite received the recognition it deserves. He lived for many years in the Lake District. Higham Hall (*ca.* 1800) is in Cockermouth (Wordsworth's birthplace) and in recent years has been used for adult education.

Corinna McClanahan Schroeder (1985–)
Born in North Carolina and raised in Ohio, she has several qualifications in Creative Writing. She currently lives and teaches near Los Angeles. Her collection, *Inked* (Texas Review Press) is 'full of twisting roads and highways, of inhabited rooms and abandoned houses'. It won the 2014 X. J. Kennedy Prize.

Peter Scupham (1933–)
A former schoolteacher and bookseller, he is a prolific lyric and narrative poet (there is a very substantial *Collected* and some later volumes too). He lives in a beautiful rambling manor house in Norfolk that he and his wife discovered *in extremis* and lovingly resuscitated. This remote spot has over the years become a focal point for poetry and drama – not least for the legendary summer poetry picnic held in its grounds.

Robert Selby (1984–)
Born in Kent, where he still lives, he is a freelance writer who edits the online poetry journal *Wild Court* and has produced an edition of Mick Imlah's prose. The poem included here is part of a Chevening sequence from his first full collection *The Coming-Down Time* (Shoestring, 2020), whose epigraph is Eliot's 'History is now and England'.

Elisabeth Sennitt Clough (1974–)

Born in Ely in the Cambridgeshire Fens, she writes a great deal about this atmospheric region of the UK; but she has spent much of her life abroad, especially in Fresno, California. She has published several collections, including *Sightings* (Pindrop, 2016), and received prestigious awards for her poetry.

Robert Sheppard (1955–)

A professor in Liverpool, he is associated with a poetic movement which produces 'linguistically innovative poetry' and exists somewhat apart from more conventional 'establishment' voices. There have been many collections since 1985 (especially from Shearsman): the major long poem, *Twentieth Century Blues*, appeared gradually over several years and in its entirety in 2008.

Penelope Shuttle (1947–)

Born in Staines, she has long been based in Cornwall, for many years with the late Peter Redgrove. Her book of elegies *Redgrove's Wife* was shortlisted for the T. S. Eliot Prize. She collaborated with John Greening on *Heath*, a book of poems about the area around Heathrow, which includes Osterley. Her early poem about the gunroom was written after one of her regular visits to Lanhydrock House in the early eighties.

Edith Sitwell (1887–1964)

Brought up with her younger brothers at Renishaw Hall, near Scarborough, she is remembered especially for *Façade*, her collaboration with William Walton (involving the megaphone mentioned in Gregory Woods's poem). F. R. Leavis thought the Sitwells belonged to 'the history of publicity rather than that of poetry'.

Osbert Sitwell (1892–1969)

The 'witty controversialist and polemicist of a famous and eccentric family' (Martin Seymour-Smith), but also librettist of Walton's *Belshazzar's Feast*. He succeeded his father as fifth baronet Sitwell in 1943.

Sacheverell Sitwell (1897–1988)

Not remembered much as a (very prolific) poet, but for being a Sitwell, a traveller and art critic. His more than sixty books include well-received studies of baroque art and eighteenth-century composers. The extract from 'Bolsover Castle' included here comes from the very end of his long poem.

Ken Smith (1938–2003)

This most widely travelled of British poets was son of a farmer and shopkeeper. Associated with Jon Silkin and Tony Harrison at Leeds, he showed a similar concern for the social outcast and spent some time as poet in residence in

Wormwood Scrubs prison. The poem here comes from the Whitbread Award-winning *Terra*. Henry Mayhew documented the conditions of the poor in Victorian London.

Stevie Smith (1902–1971)
If country houses have produced eccentrics, so has the house of the muses. Stevie Smith was very much a city person (Hull, then Palmers Green, London) and in the characteristically whimsical satire chosen for this anthology, she delights in the chiming of 'Grange' and 'change'.

Jean Sprackland (1962–)
Originally from Burton-on-Trent, subject of several of her poems, she is an established presence in British poetry, published by Cape, short-listed for major awards, and a professor of creative writing in Manchester. The castle in her poem is, she has said, 'an amalgam of several places'.

Pauline Stainer (1941–)
She has regularly published collections with Bloodaxe since her haunting debut, *The Honeycomb*, in 1989. Her beautifully musical and mystical lyrics can feel like elusive modern tributes to Emily Dickinson. Oxnead Hall was home to the Pastons, remembered for their letters. Now it is a popular wedding venue.

Jon Stallworthy (1935–2014)
He was best known for his writings on Wilfred Owen and the war poets, but he also wrote a fine biography of Louis MacNeice. There are various Elm Ends (from Huntingdon to York) – but the name is evocative, since the English Elm decline in the 1970s severely afflicted many country estates.

Wallace Stevens (1879–1955)
Perhaps the most influential of modern American poets. Late to establish himself as a writer, he spent his life as an executive for an insurance company in Hartford, Connecticut, and for all his European preoccupations he barely left the USA. The diminished 'great structure' in what is one of his last poems might represent poetry itself, much like Yeats's gazebo.

George Szirtes (1948–)
He came to Britain from Budapest in 1956, and is now one of the UK's leading formal poets, as well as one of its wisest, most restrained commentators, with a remarkable range of publications (originally OUP, now Bloodaxe). He is a trained artist: his sensitivity to location and keen eye for design are evident in his poems. He is drawn to pastoral, to 'the delicacy of the ankles of the beautiful enormous horses in Stubbs's paintings and the isolation of the poor blank-faced grooms that attend on them'.

R. S. Thomas (1913–2000)

A Welsh vicar whose brief, intense poems of doubt and vision made him a well-known figure, even tipped for the Nobel Prize. Although he chose to write chiefly in English, there is an ever-present bitterness about English treatment of the Welsh and their language; this is often expressed through specific locations, be it a bright field, a country church, a hovel or a big house.

Anthony Thwaite (1930–2021)

His death was announced as this book was going to press, and the obituaries inevitably pigeon-holed him as the editor of Larkin rather than as a poet in his own right. Yet he was prolific – a substantial *Collected* from Enitharmon – and influential as a critic, anthologist and radio producer, initially working alongside Louis MacNeice. Like George MacBeth (another BBC man, whose poetry Thwaite edited) he lived in Norfolk; but his own work draws on experience of life abroad (Japan, Libya) such as Larkin would have abhorred.

Charles Tomlinson (1927–2015)

Although less than adequately acknowledged in the UK (more so in the USA), he may prove England's most enduring contemporary poet of place and landscape – of the area around his home in Gloucestershire, but also America, Italy and his native Stoke. It is often forgotten that he was an artist, which accounts for the Ruskinesque attention to detail.

Katharine Towers (1961–)

Born in London, living in Derbyshire, she has published two Picador collections which are memorable for their focus on minutiae of the natural world. Furlongs is in Sussex (near Charleston), a hub for artists, much visited by Eric Ravilious when he painted his distinctive visions of the 'long white roads' of the chalk South Downs.

Michael Vince (1947–)

Recipient of a Gregory Award, he has several collections to his name. Having spent many years in Greece, he is now based in Cambridge. He says he is 'interested in the historical and psychological pressure points of living in a particular place, especially where this involves personal identity'.

Derek Walcott (1930–2017)

The Nobel Prize-winner's poetry was often on an epic scale, and it overlaps with his extraordinary dramas. The landscape of his homeland, St Lucia, pervades his verse (as it does his paintings). 'Ruins of a Great House' is evidently set in the West Indies, but the lines are evocative of a privileged Anglo-centric world in which 'no man is an island'.

Sylvia Townsend Warner (1893–1978)
She was a novelist and poet, much influenced by the Powys family. If she shows pastoral tendencies, there is complex musicality too (a musician herself, she prepared the ten volumes of *Tudor Music* for OUP). She joined the Communist Party and was actively political with her partner Valentine Ackland. They settled in Chaldon Herring, Dorset. Her poem alludes to *Hard Times*, but was she thinking of Bounderby rather than Gradgrind?

Rosanna Warren (1953–)
One of the most engaging contemporary American poets, she is daughter of poet Robert Penn Warren and novelist Eleanor Clark. Petworth (owned by the National Trust) is in the South Downs and has a park. Warren provides a note: 'Turner painted a series of paintings for his patron, Lord Egremont, between 1830 and 1837. Some were interiors from Lord Egremont's own house, Petworth. I have taken liberties with the historical character of Lord Egremont'.

Rory Waterman (1981–)
Critic, editor, senior lecturer at Nottingham Trent, author of several Carcanet collections, he is one of the most impressive younger UK poets, interested in Englishness, although he has an Irish background (his father is the poet Andrew Waterman). He was brought up in a lodge to the estate at Nocton Hall, as identified by his map reference title. The spa poem is based on Thoresby Hall in Nottinghamshire.

Rebecca Watts (1983–)
She was born in Suffolk and lives in Cambridge. Her first collection of poetry, *The Met Office Advises Caution* was shortlisted for the Seamus Heaney Centre for Poetry's First Collection Poetry Prize in 2017, and she has a reputation as a (sometimes controversial) essayist. She recently edited a new selection of Elizabeth Jennings's poetry, and there has been a second collection, *Red Gloves*.

Laurence Whistler (1912–2000)
Although in 1935 he received the very first King's Gold Medal for Poetry, he is now better known for his memoirs and glass engraving (notably, commemorative windows for Edward Thomas and Edmund Blunden). The sonnet here was the basis for 'a first attempt at the craft [of engraving]', he has explained, adding that 'the charm was ineffective' since a fire broke out at Blagdon. It did perhaps save the window, however, which had already been removed because of the war.

Paul Wilkins (1951–2007)
He grew up in London but spent much of his life teaching in Northern Ireland, and there is tension in his work between those locations and loyalties, which is one reason why his poem about Darley Abbey is in the 'Loyalties & Divisions' chapter. An Eric Gregory Award winner, he had two collections published by Carcanet.

Tony Williams (1977–)
A university teacher of creative writing, Tony Williams is the author of three poetry collections. He grew up in Derbyshire, a setting reflected in many of his poems. His doctoral thesis includes studies of two distinguished poets of northern England, Sean O'Brien and Peter Didsbury. He also publishes fiction.

Clive Wilmer (1945–)
Poet, critic, journalist, broadcaster and Emeritus Fellow of Sidney Sussex College, Cambridge, he is (importantly) very much a Yorkshireman. A substantial *Collected Poems* has been published by Carcanet. While he does not identify the manor house in his poem, the reference to the M4 motorway is a clue. It is in fact Kelmscott Manor, home of William Morris (whom he has edited).

Sheila Wingfield (1906–1992)
Viscountess Powerscourt lived what her biography calls 'a colourful and complicated life'. Although born in Hampshire, she had strong Irish connections. When her beloved Powerscourt literally 'burnt to the ground', the *Irish Times* called it the country's 'greatest architectural disaster for many years'. Her poetry (which Yeats admired) can be richly concentrated in the manner of Geoffrey Hill, but plainspoken and observant as here.

Kieron Winn (1969–)
He read English at Oxford, where his doctorate was on Herbert Read and T. S. Eliot. His poems appear in magazines such as the *Times Literary Supplement*, *Spectator* and *New Statesman*, and his first collection is *The Mortal Man* (2015). He has been artist in residence at Lady Margaret Hall, Oxford and poet in residence at Rydal Mount, Wordsworth's final home.

Alex Wong (1988–)
A literary scholar, he lives in Cambridge. *Poems without Irony* appeared in 2016. His very musical poetry mixes the classical, the archaeological and the erotic and he likes to stylise the past into a contemporary dream-world, sometimes reminiscent of the Sitwells – or Swinburne, whom he has edited.

Gregory Woods (1953–)
Born in Egypt, he was for fifteen years Chair in Gay and Lesbian Studies at Nottingham Trent University. He is the author of five books of literary and LGBT Studies criticism, along with seven poetry collections in which he demonstrates much formal ingenuity. He is evidently fascinated by country houses and their owners, having made them the focus of several long poems.

David Wright (1920–1994)
Born in South Africa, he settled in Cumbria, becoming a widely respected poet, translator and editor. He was severely deaf, and this feeds into much of his work, including the poem on Canons Ashby. This is an Elizabethan manor house in Northamptonshire with a notable eighteenth-century garden and associated with the Dryden family.

W. B. Yeats (1865–1939)
The Irish master liked to claim that he had no house but friendship, yet he always felt at home with aristocrats and treasured Lady Gregory's (now demolished) mansion at Coole Park. Lissadell near Sligo (open to visitors – including Wendy Cope and Cahal Dallat) was important to him too, and that 'gazebo' is symbolic, perhaps, of poetry itself, as well as nationalism. Both Gore-Booth girls were politically active, but Constance participated in the 1916 Easter Rising and was the first woman elected to the UK House of Commons.

Jane Yeh (1971–)
Although she has lived in the UK since 2002, she was born in New Jersey and studied at Harvard. There have been three Carcanet collections. Critics often seem to reach for the word 'architecture' when describing her poems, which are full of whimsy and *trompe l'oeil*. Typical is her playful treatment of the 'country house murder' conventions in the poem included here.

Tamar Yoseloff (1965–)
Born in the USA, she has been very active on the British poetry scene and was Writer in Residence at Magdalene College, Cambridge, dividing her time (in true pastoral style) between city and country, London and Suffolk. She founded the exemplary poetry press, Hercules Editions. The poem here draws on memories of the house where she grew up in farm country in New Jersey.

Note: Where no dates have been given it is at the request of the author.

Gazetteer of Houses

Aberglasney (G. Clarke) is a Grade II-listed medieval manor situated in the Tywi Valley in Carmarthenshire. Its fabulous gardens, including a yew tunnel, parapet walk, and cloister and walled gardens, were developed in the Elizabethan era. The poet John Dyer ('Grongar Hill') lived there in the 18th century. Restored in the 1990s, the gardens are among the finest in Wales. 24 miles N of Swansea.

Acton Burnell Castle (Parker) is the ruin of a fortified medieval manor house in Shropshire. It was built in the 13th century by the Bishop of Bath and Wells, but all that remains today is a shell maintained by English Heritage. It is believed to be the site of the first English parliament fully to represent the commons. 10 miles SE of Shrewsbury.

Alfoxden House (Hall) was built in the early 18th century. William and Dorothy Wordsworth lived there during their early friendship with Coleridge, prior to their move to the Lake District. A Grade II-listed building, Alfoxden (sometimes spelled 'Alfoxton') has undergone much renovation and for a time was a country hotel. In *The Making of Poetry*, Adam Nicolson notes that Alfoxden 'remains a beautiful and haunting place. The house is now decrepit, and the park broken and ragged' (William Collins, 2019). In the Quantock Hills of Somerset, 45 miles SW of Bristol.

Audley End (Salway) is one of the finest Jacobean houses in England. Though now but a third its original size, it was built as a prodigy house for entertaining the king. Following Vanbrugh's designs, portions of the house were demolished in the 18th century. Robert Adam designed new staterooms, while the parkland was designed by Capability Brown. Now in the care of English Heritage. In Essex, a mile W of Saffron Walden.

Avington Park (Hooker) is a 16th-century house rebuilt in the 17th century and refronted in the Palladian style in the 18th century. In 1847 it was sold to Sir John Shelley, younger brother of the poet Percy Bysshe Shelley. It remains in private hands but house and grounds are occasionally open to the public. In Hampshire's Itchen Valley, 5 miles NE of Winchester.

Ballinamore House (Murphy) stands just outside the town of Kiltimagh in County Mayo. It was built in the late 18th century and was part of an estate granted to the Ormsby family by Queen Elizabeth I. It now serves as a nursing home. 46 miles N of Galway.

Birr Castle (Evaristo) in County Offaly, Ireland, is mostly 17th-century and built in the English style incorporating the gate tower of a 12th-century Anglo-Norman castle. The house was designed by Sir Laurence Parsons, whose descendants, the Earls of Rosse, still occupy the house. It was Gothicised in the 19th century, when the Parsons family also significantly increased their domestic staff. 60 miles SE of Galway.

Blagdon (Whistler) is a mid-18th-century, Grade I-listed house in private ownership. The estate has been in the White Ridley family since 1698; the current Viscount is the science writer, Matt Ridley. Open only on rare occasions, Blagdon's renowned gardens were designed by Sir Edwin Lutyens, father-in-law of the third Viscount. During World War II, the house was converted into a hospital; in 1944, a fire gutted the top floor and stair hall, but most of its treasures were saved. Near Cramlington, Northumberland, 11 miles N of Newcastle upon Tyne.

Blenheim Palace (Levi, Winn) is a splendid Baroque pile designed by John Vanbrugh in the early 18th century and among the most famous and most visited of all country houses. It was a gift from Queen Anne, along with the Duchy of Marlborough, to John Churchill in gratitude for his stunning military victories on the continent in the War of the Spanish Succession. It is the birthplace and ancestral home of Winston Churchill. In Oxfordshire, 12 miles NW of Oxford.

Blickling Hall (Sheppard) is the 15th-century estate in Norfolk where Anne Boleyn was born, antedating the present Jacobean house. The library, which holds the Blickling Homilies, is of great historical and cultural significance. The last private owner, the 11th Marquess of Lothian, passed the property to the National Trust upon his death in 1940. During the war, Blickling was requisitioned for use by the RAF and subsequently had to undergo significant restoration. 14 miles N of Norwich.

Bolsover Castle (S. Sitwell) was founded in the 11th century but fell into ruins in the 14th. In 1612, Sir Charles Cavendish undertook the construction of a *faux* Norman great tower, which rises above the Vale of Scarsdale. Charles I and Henrietta Maria were entertained in lavish staterooms with a masque specially written by Ben Jonson with an elaborate stage setting designed by Inigo Jones. A scheduled ancient monument, Grade I listed, now in the care of English Heritage. In Derbyshire, 6 miles E of Chesterfield.

Brockham End (Fraser) is a Tudor-style house and woodland gardens, conjoining some Roman ruins, on a hilltop near Bath. The house was built in 1907 for Sir Alexander Waldemar Lawrence. In the late 20th century, the upper floor was divided into flats. It borders Pipley Wood, a serene and ancient woodland, preserved and opened to the public by Sir Alexander's son. Approximately 5 miles NW of the centre of Bath.

Burghley (Kramer) is a leading example of the Elizabethan prodigy house. It was built by Sir William Cecil, Lord Treasurer to Queen Elizabeth I, and is still occupied by the Cecil family. The house has extraordinary stone-masonry, interior carvings by Grinling Gibbons, an extensive art collection, and a park landscaped by Capability Brown. Straddles the boundary between Lincolnshire and Cambridgeshire, 2 miles SE of Stamford.

Burnt Norton (Eliot), a 17th-century Cotswold manor house near Chipping Campden, was originally known as Norton House. In 1741 the owner, Sir William Keyt, built an extravagant estate next door for his mistress, a former housemaid; when she abandoned him, he sank into a prolonged bout of drinking, set the new house on fire, and intentionally perished in the blaze. The powerful inferno scorched the near wall of Norton House, giving it its new moniker. Burnt Norton was unoccupied when Eliot visited its derelict gardens in 1934, but it has been recently restored and renovated. In Gloucestershire, 11 miles SW of Stratford-upon-Avon.

Canna House (Raine) was the home of John and Margaret Campbell. It is small, as country houses go, and fairly new; it was built in 1860 by Donald MacNeil, a Hebridean laird, and is now a property of the National Trust of Scotland. On the Isle of Canna, in the Inner Hebrides, a 73-mile drive and ferry ride from Fort William.

Canons Ashby (Wright), built in 1550, was the home of the ancestors of John Dryden, England's first Poet Laureate. His kinswoman, Anne Hutchinson, the Puritan controversialist banished from the Massachusetts Bay Colony, was born there in 1591. The house sits amid splendid gardens, near the remains of a medieval priory church. In Northamptonshire, 12 miles NE of Banbury.

Castle Drogo (Waterman) is a young country house, designed in 1910 by Sir Edwin Lutyens for Julius Drewe, the wealthy founder of Home and Colonial Stores. Drewe's enthusiasm for the project waned when Adrian, his son and heir, was killed at Passchendaele. Drogo was completed in 1930, a year before Julius's own death. In Devon, 15 miles W of Exeter.

Castle Howard (Betjeman), a palatial house in Yorkshire, has gained fame as the setting of Brideshead in film and television adaptations of Evelyn Waugh's country house novel. Construction began in 1699 according to designs by Sir John Vanbrugh, who also designed Blenheim. It remains the home of the Earls of Carlisle. 15 miles NE of York.

Castletown House (Hartnett) is Ireland's oldest and grandest Palladian-style house. Built in the 1720s for William Conolly, Speaker of the Irish House of Commons, Castletown was designed for large-scale political entertaining and of course to showcase the owner's power. The Conolly family lived in the estate until the 1960s. Desmond Guinness's 1967 purchase rescued it from vandalism and decay, and it became the home of the Irish Georgian Society. The house is now in the care of Ireland's Office of Public Works. In County Kildare, 13 miles W of Dublin.

Chevening (Selby), a 17th-century pile just off the London Orbital, sits in 3,000 acres of parkland and woodland. For seven generations the home of the Earls of Stanhope, Chevening was bequeathed to the nation in the 1960s for use as a cabinet minister's residence. The estate church, dedicated to St Botolph, is mostly 16th century built around an Anglo-Saxon core and contains an outstanding collection of monuments. In Kent, 4 miles NW of Sevenoaks.

Chicksands Priory (Porter) was founded in the 12th century as a Gilbertine monastic house. After the Dissolution of the Monasteries, the house passed into the possession of the Osborne family, who held it until it was purchased by the Crown Commissioners in 1936. It was a US Air Force 'listening post' at the time Porter wrote this poem. In Bedfordshire, 30 miles SW of Cambridge.

Chilswell House (Daryush) was designed and built by Daryush's father, Robert Bridges, on Boars Hill, beside Youlbury Woods. Elizabeth lived there from her years as an undergraduate at Somerville College until she was in her 70s. It is now a Carmelite Priory. 5 miles SW of Oxford.

Colwick Hall (Szirtes), in Nottinghamshire, was built around 1775. During the disturbances surrounding the Second Reform Bill in 1831, Colwick was sacked and burned by rioters. After a hundred years of use as a racecourse and public house, it was restored and converted into a hotel. It is a Grade II-listed building. 3 miles SE of Nottingham.

Coole Park (McAuliffe, Yeats) was built in 1770 for Robert Gregory, of County Galway, Ireland. His descendant, the playwright Lady Gregory, wrote here and entertained William Butler Yeats, George Bernard Shaw, Sean

O'Casey, John Millington Synge and many others. The house was wantonly demolished by the Irish government in 1941. The gardens surrounding Coole Park survive as a nature reserve, with a lake and swans which Yeats famously counted every year. 22 miles SE of Galway, Ireland.

Cwrt Colman (Minhinnick) is a former country house, now a hotel known as Court Colman Manor, in the Garw Valley of Wales. The manor was in monastic hands until the Dissolution; the present house was built in 1766 and enlarged in the early 20th century. It remained a private residence until its conversion to a hotel in the 1980s. In Pen-y-Fai, just outside Bridgend, Glamorganshire, 22 miles W of Cardiff.

Darley Abbey Hall (Wilkins) was an ivy-clad Georgian country house in Derbyshire, demolished in 1962 to make way for urban expansion as Derby grew rapidly. It was built by industrialist and mill-owner Thomas Evans, who developed much of the nearby mill village. The historic village and park are about 2 miles N of Derby's city centre.

Ditchley Park (Mathias) is an ancient estate, visited by Elizabeth I and James I, and the birthplace of John Wilmot, the infamous Earl of Rochester. The present house was designed by Gibbs in 1722 for the second Earl of Lichfield. Purchased in 1933 by the Anglo-American MP, Ronald Tree, and used as a secret base for Churchill's political negotiations with the United States, both before and during the war. In Oxfordshire, 9 miles SE of Chipping Norton.

Down House (Padel) was built near the village of Downe, Kent, in the 1770s and in 1842 was purchased by Charles and Emma Darwin. Neither was initially pleased with the place, which Charles's brother Erasmus said should be called 'Down-in-the-Mouth'. It is now a fascinating museum operated by English Heritage. 10 miles NW of Sevenoaks.

Dunraven Castle (Minhinnick) was a manor house on the South Wales coast, built in the 16th century then rebuilt as a castellated hunting lodge in the 19th century. The house itself was demolished in the 1960s, but the gatehouse, walled garden and ice tower survive and are Grade II listed. In Glamorganshire, 23 miles W of Cardiff.

Dyrham Park (D. Clarke) is a Grade I-listed baroque pile in south Gloucestershire with an impressive collection of Dutch masters. The park includes sumptuous gardens, an orangery, an estate church, and a large herd of fallow deer. Now in the care of the National Trust, it was home to the Blathwayt family for 300 years. During World War II, Dyrham housed child evacuees. 9 miles N of Bath.

Eastwell Manor (R. Fuller), originally constructed in the mid-16th century, was rebuilt in a neo-Elizabethan style in the 1790s. It was expanded in the Victorian era and was subsequently home to Prince Alfred; his mother, Queen Victoria, and elder brother, the future King Edward VII, were frequent visitors. Alfred's daughter, Princess Marie (subsequently Queen of Romania), would later recall 'beautiful Eastwell with its great grey house, its magnificent park, ... [and] its garden with the old cedar tree which was our fairy mansion'. It is now a hotel, 4 miles N of Ashford, in Kent.

Erddig (Greening) was built in the late 17th century for the high sheriff of Denbighshire, was expanded in the 18th century, and then passed into the hands of the Yorke family, who owned and occupied the house until 1973, when its reclusive squire ceded the house to the National Trust. The integrity of the house had been severely compromised by mining subsidence, and its survival is something of a miracle. John Harris's *No Voice from the Hall* (John Murray, 1998) contains a lively account of a visit to a critically dilapidated Erddig in the 1950s. Today, it is considered one of the finest country houses in Wales. In Wrexham, 17 miles SW of Chester.

Felbrigg Hall (Rivière) is a 17th-century country house with Jacobean exterior and Georgian interior. Having been in the Wyndham family since 1475, the Felbrigg estate was bequeathed to the National Trust by its final owner, the historian Robert Wyndham Ketton-Cremer. The estate includes a walled Victorian garden and an orangery. In Norfolk, 22 miles N of Norwich.

Ford Manor (Mahon) is a Grade II-listed Victorian country house in Dormansland, Surrey, designed by Robert Kerr. Constructed of Wealdstone, its long, rambling façade is a gallimaufry of architectural oddities; Mark Girouard described it as 'appalling'. Ford Manor hosted many house parties prior to the Great War, when it had close associations with the Astor and Bowes-Lyon families. Requisitioned during both wars, Ford Manor was renamed Greathed Manor after a new Ford Manor was constructed nearby. Now a care home, near the borders of Kent and Sussex, 16 miles W of Tonbridge.

Furlongs (Towers) is probably the most modest of our country homes, and far from stately. Architecturally, it is a 19th-century farmhouse in Sussex; however, through much of the 20th century it functioned as some country houses did, such as Garsington and Charleston, hosting and entertaining artists. It was occupied by painter and sculptress Peggy Angus from 1933 until the early 1990s. 12 miles NE of Brighton.

Gable Court (Reed) in the pretty Dorset village of Yetminster is a Jacobean house with early 20th-century additions, featuring signature gables, rough stone walls, mullioned windows and enchanting landscaped gardens. Also known as Millord House, this Grade II-listed private residence was home to poet Henry Reed from 1949 to 1950 and, according to his editor Jon Stallworthy, was the setting that inspired 'The Changeling'. 6 miles SW of Sherborne.

Garsington Manor (Mansfield), though unnamed in the poem, is surely the house Katherine Mansfield reimagined. A Tudor-era manor, Garsington was completely restored in the 1920s by Lady Ottoline Morrell and her husband Philip Morrell. From 1915 on, Garsington was a literary salon presided over by Lady Ottoline, a haven for writers and intellectuals including D. H. Lawrence, Siegfried Sassoon, Aldous Huxley, Bertrand Russell, E. M. Forster, Virginia Woolf, and of course Mansfield. 6 miles SE of Oxford.

Great Tew (Jones) was a large Cotswolds manor house belonging to Lucius Cary, second Viscount Falkland. In the 1630s, Cary hosted the Great Tew Circle of writers and clerics, an extensive group whose members included Abraham Cowley, Edmund Waller, Sir John Suckling, Jeremy Taylor and Ben Jonson. Cary fought in the Civil War on the Royalist side and was killed at the first Battle of Newbury in 1643. The original Jacobean manor was demolished around 1800, and the Great Tew estate has gone through significant changes since. In Oxfordshire, 9 miles SW of Banbury.

Greenway (Greening) is the beloved Devonshire home of Agatha Christie. The present 18th-century house replaced a much grander Tudor mansion; the gardens were originally landscaped by Humphrey Repton. Christie and her husband, the archaeologist Max Mallowan, bought the estate in 1938 and lived there until their deaths. Greenway appears, thinly disguised, in several of Christie's novels, notably *Dead Man's Folly*. 8 miles SW of Torquay.

Hardwick Hall (Redgrove) is an Elizabethan prodigy house built for Bess of Hardwick, Countess of Shrewsbury. The architect, Robert Smythson, demonstrated new concepts in domestic architecture, such as chimneys in internal walls and numerous and massive windows. The house passed to her descendants, the Dukes of Devonshire, and eventually functioned as hunting retreat and dower house. The last duchess to occupy the hall was committed to preserving Hardwick's textiles. In Derbyshire, 8 miles SE of Chesterfield.

Harewood (Agbabi) is one of the great treasure houses of England and is home to an extraordinary art collection. The current Earl of Harewood has embraced the estate's hidden history and has been uncommonly open about how this family's wealth was founded upon slavery and the West Indian sugar trade. In Yorkshire, 9 miles N of Leeds.

Hatfield (Caldwell) is a Jacobean prodigy house built by Robert Cecil, Earl of Salisbury and Lord High Treasurer to King James I, and remains in the Cecil family to this day. Hatfield's architect, Robert Lyminge, also designed Blickling Hall in Norfolk. Hatfield is noted for its marble hall, a grand oak staircase, and a clock tower attributed to Inigo Jones. In Hertfordshire, 4 miles S of Welwyn Garden City.

Heytesbury (Sassoon) is a former country house in Wiltshire. It was built in the 1780s on 90 acres of parkland for Sir William à Court, Bt. Two hundred years later it was cut off from its adjoining park by the construction of the A36 bypass, and the house is now divided into flats. During Sassoon's occupancy, its many famous visitors included William Walton, Hilaire Belloc, T. E. Lawrence, Edmund Blunden, Geoffrey Keynes and Lady Ottoline Morrell. 22 miles SE of Bath.

Higham Hall (Scammell) is an Elizabethan revival Lake District house built in 1828 by railway pioneer Thomas Hoskins. It commands spectacular views of Bassenthwaite Lake and a range of the Wainwright hills. The estate contains a large stone circle. The hall has seen life as a youth hostel and a boarding school, and it now serves as an independent trust for adult education. In Cumbria, 25 miles SW of Carlisle.

Highclere Castle (Greening, Salway) is an ancient house entirely redesigned in the early 19th-century Jacobean Revival style by Charles Barry, in grounds laid out by Capability Brown. The home of the Earls of Carnarvon is famous today for its use as a film location for *Jeeves and Wooster* and *Downton Abbey*. In Hampshire, 14 miles NW of Basingstoke.

Houghton House (Conquest), not to be confused with Houghton Hall, Sir Robert Walpole's Norfolk estate, is the ruin of a 17th-century Bedfordshire manor now in the care of English Heritage. Reputedly the inspiration for Bunyan's 'House Beautiful', it was built around 1615 for the Dowager Countess of Pembroke. The shell, a mix of Jacobean and Classical styles, still stands, commanding impressive views from its hilltop setting. Situated between the villages of Ampthill and Houghton Conquest, 10 miles S of Bedford.

Ickworth (Watts) is a neoclassical country house in Suffolk, once home to the Marquesses of Bristol. Its unusual design, based on a central rotunda, was called 'an overgrown folly' by Gervase Jackson-Stops. The rotunda connects through curving pavilions to two Palladian wings, one of which was not completed until 2006. 3 miles SW of Bury St Edmunds.

Kelmscott (Wilmer) is a Cotswold manor built around 1570. It was the home of writer and designer William Morris from 1871 to 1896, and the interior today is largely as Morris left it with Arts and Crafts furniture and textile designs. Near the Thames in Oxfordshire, 16 miles E of Cirencester.

Kimbolton Castle (Greening) began its life in the late lamented county of Huntingdonshire as a Norman castle, was rebuilt as a Tudor manor that served as Catherine of Aragon's final home, and was eventually converted into a stately home for the Duke of Manchester by Vanbrugh and Hawksmoor, with additions by Adam. It is now home to Kimbolton School, 30 miles S of Peterborough.

Knebworth (Gallagher) is early Tudor in origins, but most of the present house is early 19th-century Gothic revival. The interior is largely according to designs of Sir Edwin Lutyens. It has been consistently in the Lytton family since 1490; today it is famous for the summer rock concerts that have been held in its grounds since 1974. In Hertfordshire, 3 miles SW of Stevenage.

Knole (Fuller, Powell) is one of the largest and most storied of English country houses. Built in the mid-15th century, it is the seat of the Sackvilles and the Earls of Dorset and is reputedly a 'calendar house', with 7 courtyards, 52 staircases, and 365 rooms. Virginia Woolf's *Orlando* draws closely on the history of Knole. In Kent, a mile SE of Sevenoaks.

Lanhydrock (Shuttle) is a mostly 19th-century country house with some Jacobean elements. Following a devastating fire in 1881, it was rebuilt with the latest Victorian mod-cons. The estate was in the hands of the Robartes family from the early 17th century until their fortunes declined following the Great War. Now in the care of the National Trust, the public can explore its gardens, staterooms and extensive servants' quarters, which include a gunroom. In Cornwall, 3 miles SE of Bodmin.

Lissadell (Cope, Dallat, Yeats) is a Greek-revival house in County Sligo, Ireland, built in the 1830s for Sir Robert Gore-Booth. It was the childhood home of poet Eva Gore-Booth and her sister, Constance Markiewicz, a leader in the 1916 rising. It was also a frequent holiday retreat of Yeats. Cahal Dallat remarks, 'Aileen Gore Booth, niece of Eva and Constance (Markiewicz) was in the habit of asking visitors to play the family grand (which was, at a time, in the long room with windows to the south in which WBY describes the sisters in silk kimonos)'. The house is a private residence but is open to the public. 10 miles NW of Sligo.

Longleat (Barker), an Elizabethan prodigy house in Wiltshire, has been the seat of the Marquesses of Bath for over 400 years. Its construction was largely complete by 1580. In 1949, Longleat was the first stately home to open to the public on a fully commercial basis – some four years prior to George Barker's visit. It is set in 1,000 acres of parkland designed by Capability Brown and contains the world's largest hedge maze and the UK's oldest African wildlife safari park. 18 miles S of Bath.

Lyveden New Bield (Griffiths, Parker) is an unfinished Elizabethan lodge and moated garden in Northamptonshire, built on the grounds of Sir Thomas Tresham's manor. Tresham, a recusant Catholic, designed the cruciform lodge and had it decorated with religious friezes and religious symbolism. A large labyrinth on the grounds remained hidden for centuries, until it was exposed by photos taken by the Luftwaffe. Grade I listed, it is now in the care of the National Trust. 18 miles SW of Peterborough.

Mapledurham (Blunden) is a Tudor house in Oxfordshire that has since 1490 belonged to the Blounts, a prominent Catholic family who harbored illicit Roman clergy in Mapledurham's priest holes. Alexander Pope, a good friend of siblings Edward, Teresa and especially Martha ('Patty') Blount, was a frequent visitor. In Berkshire, on the banks of the Thames, 5 miles NW of Reading.

Middleton Hall (G. Clarke) is sadly no more. Sir William Paxton purchased the Carmarthenshire estate in 1789 and with eminent architect Samuel Pepys Cockerell (who designed Sezincote) developed an extraordinary water park. The house passed through various hands after Paxton's death, until it was gutted by fire in 1931 and subsequently demolished. 22 miles NW of Swansea.

Milgate Park (Lowell) is a Grade I-listed house in Thurnham, Kent, built in the late 16th century, with significant 18th-century additions. The estate changed hands many times before being occupied in the 1970s by novelist Lady Caroline Blackwood and her third husband, the American poet Robert Lowell. 4 miles E of Maidstone.

Montacute (Aykroyd) is an Elizabethan pile in Somerset and one of England's few prodigy houses to have survived nearly unaltered. It was constructed by Sir Edward Phelps; the mason William Arnold, responsible for Cranborne Manor and Wadham College, Oxford, is believed to have been the architect. It has what is reputedly the longest long gallery in England, and it partners with the National Portrait Gallery as a secondary exhibition space. 5 miles W of Yeovil.

Newstead Abbey (R. Fuller) is best known as the home of the poet Lord Byron. It was originally an Augustinian priory, but at the Dissolution it was given to Sir John Byron and remained in that family until the poet sold it in 1818 to pay off his extraordinary debts. It now houses a museum of Byron memorabilia. In Nottinghamshire, 12 miles N of Nottingham.

Nocton Hall (Waterman) was constructed in the 17th century on the grounds of a former manor and priory. It was occupied by the Earl of Ripon during his period as Prime Minister. During World War I it was converted into a convalescent home for wounded American officers and again became a hospital during World War II. A major fire in 2004 gutted the building, which now stands derelict. In Lincolnshire, 8 miles SE of Lincoln.

Old Gwernyfed Manor (Davies) is a Grade I-listed building in Powys containing medieval, 16th- and 17th-century features and so important as a record of grand domestic building over many centuries. For many years it functioned as a hotel but has recently undergone an extensive reconversion. It is set in beautiful surroundings on the edge of the Brecon Beacons, 5 miles SW of Hay-on-Wye.

Old Hall (Griffiths) is a Grade II-listed Tudor manor in South Burlingham, Norfolk. Renowned for the mermaids depicted in a tympanum on the tower block, 'Mermaid Manor' was rescued from dereliction some 30 years ago by poet Peter Scupham and his wife, Margaret Steward, an artist, playwright, and dramaturge. In 1991, 16th-century hunting scenes were discovered behind coats of plaster on the walls of the long gallery. 11 miles E of Norwich.

Orielton (Mathias) was the seat of the Owen baronets in remote southwest Wales. The Grade II-listed house, a three-storey painted stucco block, was built in the 17th century and modified in the 18th and 19th centuries. It was requisitioned during World War II as a base for Australian airmen, after which it was the home of naturalist and author Ronald Lockley. It now serves as a field studies centre. In Pembrokeshire, 15 miles S of Haverfordwest.

Osterley (Shuttle) is a large house and park in Greater London, near Hounslow. The original house was a manor built for Sir Thomas Gresham in the 1570s. It was extensively rebuilt by Robert Adam 200 years later in the English neoclassical style for Robert Child – whose daughter (mentioned by Penelope Shuttle) eloped with the Earl of Westmoreland. In the 20th century the grounds were used as a training camp for the forerunner of the Home Guard; today it is a popular property of the National Trust. 4 miles E of Heathrow.

Owlpen Manor (Fanthorpe), near Dursley, Gloucestershire, commands a setting of outstanding beauty in a deep Cotswold valley. The house, originally constructed in the 11th century and rebuilt in the Tudor era, remained in the Olpenne and Daunt family for a thousand years. Swinburne referred to Owlpen as 'a paradise incomparable on earth'. 15 miles S of Gloucester.

Oxnead Hall (Stainer) was built by Sir Clement Paston around 1580. It was an elaborate house, and was later expanded after the Restoration to accommodate royal entertainments. It declined in the 18th century and became a ruin. Today all that remains is the east service wing, which has been converted into a popular wedding venue. In Norfolk, 11 miles N of Norwich.

Penshurst Place (Mahon) was first memorialised by Ben Jonson in one of the earliest country house poems ever written. Penshurst was constructed in the 14th century and was the birthplace of poet and courtier Sir Philip Sidney. It is justly famous for its medieval Baron's Hall with a 60-foot beamed ceiling. Its gardens are among the most beautiful in England. In Kent, 5 miles SW of Tonbridge.

Petworth (Warren) is a late 17th-century house with Grinling Gibbons carved interiors, an impressive collection of Turners and Van Dycks, and wall and ceiling paintings by Laguerre. Capability Brown's landscaped park holds England's largest herd of fallow deer. The estate was for centuries the southern home of the Percy family and the Earls of Northumberland but has been occupied by the Wyndham family since 1750. In West Sussex, 23 miles S of Guildford.

Powerscourt (Wingfield) is a large country estate in County Wicklow, Ireland. For many centuries it belonged to the Wingfields (the Viscounts Powerscourt), into which family the poet married. Originally a 13th-century castle, it was completely redesigned in the 18th century. A 1974 fired gutted the house, and it was not restored for another 20 years. The estate is famed today for its gardens, water features and pet cemetery. 5 miles SW of Bray.

Rainthorpe Hall (Thwaite) is a Grade I-listed house near Tasburgh, Norfolk. The E-plan was constructed in the Elizabethan era and is noted for its stonework, wood carvings and leather wall coverings. In 1934 the house was purchased by J. Maurice Hastings, a scholar of medieval architecture. It was eventually owned by his nephew, George Hastings, the aftermath of whose suicide is recorded in Thwaite's poem. 10 miles S of Norwich.

Renishaw Hall (the Sitwells, Woods) has been the seat of the Sitwell family since its construction in 1625. It was built in stages and has an irregular plan. The impressive gardens are open to the public, but the house remains a private residence and has limited openings for guided tours. In Derbyshire, 11 miles SE of Sheffield.

Revesby Abbey (Berkeley) was a Cistercian monastery until the Dissolution; botanist Sir Joseph Banks, who sailed with Cook on the voyage that discovered Australia, grew up at Revesby. By the 1820s, the house had fallen into such disrepair that it was pulled down and a new house was built in the 'Jacobethan' style. Requisitioned for RAF use in World War II, it was later sectioned into flats for families of American officers stationed at nearby air bases. Despite its parlous, 'at risk' condition, it is currently undergoing restoration. In Lincolnshire, 12 miles N of Boston.

Ripley Castle (Fan) is a Grade I-listed 14th-century country house in North Yorkshire. Still privately owned, it is the seat of the Ingilby baronets but is open for guided tours. Among its fascinating features is a priest hole; one 16th-century Ingilby was a Roman Catholic priest and martyr who was hung, drawn, and quartered – and later beatified by Pope John Paul II. 4 miles NW of Harrogate.

Sandringham (Betjeman) has been the royal family's country estate in Norfolk since it was purchased for the future King Edward VII in 1862. George V and George VI both died there. It stands on a massive estate of some 20,000 acres and has long been known for its shooting parties. 8 miles NE of King's Lynn.

Seapark (MacNeice) is an early 19th-century Italianate house in County Antrim, Northern Ireland. It was considerably enlarged and remodelled in the 1850s and is dominated by a four-storey tower. It stands on sweeping grounds overlooking Belfast Lough. 3 miles SW of Carrickfergus.

Shugborough (Lindop) is a Grade I-listed National Trust property built on the remains of a medieval moated bishop's palace. In the 19th century, Thomas Anson, founder of the Dilettanti Society, created the neoclassical interiors to display his extraordinary collection of art, furniture and other treasures, and added complementing monuments and follies to the landscaped grounds. In Staffordshire, 14 miles NW of Lichfield.

Shuttleworth (Gurney), formerly known as Old Warden Park, is a Grade II-listed mansion built in the 1870s and situated in 5,000 acres. The three-storey Jacobean block with Italianate clocktower currently functions as a wedding and retreat venue. The Grotto & Fernery in Shuttleworth's Swiss Garden, dating from the 1820s and restored in 2014, is the likely setting of Gurney's greenhouse, while his 'belvedere' is inspired by Queen Anne's Summerhouse, an 18th-century folly on the Shuttleworth estate built as a miniature mock-military redoubt on a quatrefoil design. It was rescued from near ruin in 2001 and beautifully restored by the Landmark Trust. In Bedfordshire, 9 miles SE of Bedford.

Sissinghurst Castle (Sackville-West) is perhaps more famous for its garden than its house, both lovingly restored by Vita Sackville-West, who grew up at Knole, and her husband, Harold Nicolson. The house itself dates from the late Middle Ages, its most notable feature being a tower that served as Vita's study and sanctum. In Kent, 14 miles S of Maidstone.

Stancombe Park (Ashbee) is known for its gardens – especially its 19th-century 'secret garden'. The Grade II-listed house, dating from 1880 and closed to the public, is small and plain with five bays, a simple Doric portico, and a low hipped roof. The Grade I-listed gardens are open by invitation or appointment only. In the Cotswolds, 16 miles SW of Gloucester.

Stourhead (Beer) is a Palladian mansion designed by Scottish architect Colen Campbell for Henry Hoare, who made a vast profit during the South Sea Bubble of 1720. Along with his descendants, Hoare amassed a fabulous collection of books and art. The estate is perhaps best known for its outstanding gardens and follies. In Wiltshire, 24 miles S of Bath.

Stowe (Salway) is a Grade I-listed Buckinghamshire house made famous for hosting a nearly endless parade of royalty, nobility, early American presidents, and other public figures throughout the 18th and 19th centuries. Its justly praised gardens were laid out initially by Vanbrugh and William Kent, and later redeveloped by Capability Brown. The house was entirely rebuilt in the early 18th century by Sir Richard Temple, Viscount Cobham. He hosted Alexander Pope there, who would dedicate his first Moral Essay to Cobham and praise Stowe in his fourth. Now home to Stowe School but with gardens open to the public. 18 miles E of Banbury.

Swarthmoor Hall (Shuttle) is a rather plain 16th-century house in Cumbria. It was the home of Thomas and Margaret Fell, who were influential in the founding of the Quaker movement, and gave its name (if not quite its spelling) to Swarthmore College in Pennsylvania. Swarthmoor is a Grade II-listed building and is still used as a Quaker retreat centre. 9 miles NE of Barrow-in-Furness.

Thoresby Hall (Waterman) is a 19th-century country house, Grade I listed, now converted to a spa hotel. The original house was 17th century; a new one was constructed in the 18th, with landscaping by Humphry Repton, but was demolished and rebuilt in 1868. In Nottinghamshire, 10 miles NE of Mansfield.

The Vyne (Draycott) was built for Lord Sandys, Henry VIII's Lord Chamberlain. The original 16th-century building has been remodeled several times, such that it represents a hodge-podge of English domestic architectural styles: the diaper-patterned and crenellated brickwork on the Tudor north front, for instance, is mounted by an Inigo Jones-copied classical portico. In Hampshire, 4 miles N of Basingstoke.

Walcot Hall (Garfitt) is a Georgian-period house in Shropshire, designed for Clive of India and famed for its free-standing ballroom built by the Earl of Powis. Currently operating as a wedding and retreat centre, with guest cottages on site and an impressive arboretum. The Grade II-listed building stands approximately 25 miles SW of Shrewsbury.

Walmer Castle (Kavanagh), originally an artillery fort built during the reign of Henry VIII, was converted to a private residence in the 18th century, when it became the official seat of the Lord Warden of the Cinque Ports. Now in the care of English Heritage, it has been occupied by numerous statesmen who served as Lord Warden, including Pitt the Younger, Wellington, Palmerston, Salisbury and Curzon. In Kent, overlooking the channel, 7 miles NE of Dover.

Wells House (Boland) appears to be the property Boland was describing. A 17th-century mansion, it was rebuilt in the 1830s by architect Daniel Robertson (Johnstown Castle, Powerscourt gardens), who designed all interior, exterior, and landscape features of the Tudor Gothic house, including its 550-metre-long tree-lined avenue. Having been in the Doyne family for over 250 years, Wells was sold in 1965 to a German industrialist and is now open to the public. In Co. Wexford, 12 miles S of Gorey.

Wilburton Rectory (Sennitt Clough) is a Grade II-listed house in Cambridgeshire dating from the 15th century, with 17th- and 18th-century additions. Constructed of timber frame and red brick with hipped roof, it may have been a guildhall before becoming a rectory. King Henry VII is reputed to have stayed here with his son, the Prince of Wales and future King Henry VIII; while on pilgrimage to St Ethedreda's Shrine at Ely, they were entertained at Wilburton by the Rector, Alcock. 6 miles SW of Ely.

Wilton House (Brackenbury) has been the seat of the Earls of Pembroke since the dissolution of the monasteries. The present house, designed in part by Inigo Jones, is noted for its magnificent staterooms and gardens and its singular art collection. In Wiltshire, 3 miles W of Salisbury.

Wimpole Hall (Greger), begun about 1640, is the largest house in Cambridgeshire. It has changed hands many times, but the Earls of Hardwicke held the longest tenure there. In 1938 the house was purchased by the daughter of Rudyard Kipling, and royalties from his books helped fund necessary restoration. It contains a chapel by James Gibbs, a plunge bath by Sir John Soane, and landscaping by Humphry Repton and Capability Brown. 11 miles SW of Cambridge.

Winterbrook House (Christie) is a Grade II-listed Queen Anne house, grey brick with red brick dressings. Agatha Christie – who lived there with Max Mallowan and their daughter – describes it in 1934 as having a walled garden, 'gracious windows', a ha-ha and meadows (with the cedar of her poem) sweeping down to 'a pretty bit of river, about a mile out of Wallingford'. 15 miles SE of Oxford.

Woburn Abbey (Cavaliero), set in 3,000 acres of Humphry Repton parkland, is the seat of the Dukes of Bedford. Founded as a Cistercian Abbey in the 12th century, Woburn was granted by Henry VIII to the first earl of Russell in 1547. The present house, a Palladian pile dating from the mid-18th century, holds an impressive collection of art and furniture and, somewhat discordantly, the grounds are home to a safari park. In Bedfordshire, 11 miles SE of Milton Keynes.

Woodtown Manor (Montague) is an Irish country house built in Leinster *ca.* 1700 and expanded in the early 19th century. Architecturally it is unremarkable; historically it is significant only for its associations with American artist Morris Graves, who purchased the house in 1958 and lived there until 1964. 7 miles SW of Dublin.

Wycoller Hall (T. Hughes) was a 16th-century manor house in Lancashire, extended considerably in the 18th century. The last squire to own the manor died deeply in debt in 1818, after which stones were plundered from Wycoller's walls to build nearby houses. The manor soon fell into ruins and is now a Grade II-listed monument – reputedly haunted. 12 miles W of Keighley.

Index of First Lines

A bee in the library 149

A billet-doux. The scent of pinewoods 171

A building on this site existed in 144

A cave of air softens 313

A cock-pheasant on the steaming muckheap 115

A leaf sways gently on a web 312

A lemon bloomed with frost 167

A lodge-house to an estate, once: the front wall 150

A mansion, string of cottages, a farm 329

A peacock feather. And a simple stone 336

A stately home where doves, in dovecotes, coo 294

A tired swimmer in the waves of time 27

After the leaves have fallen, we return 344

All ruffs, and furs, and farthingales 151

All the omens were good, the air smelt of success 283

An estate 337

Any American's likely to entertain 324

'Arithmetic and manners, start with those' 36

As he could not heal his country's disease 214

At six the furniture begins to fade 64

At the sea's edge, near Bray 265

Autumn resumes the land, ruffles the woods 252

Avenues of trees, the route of a wall 216

Awful and artificial 107

Barbarians in a garden, softness does 318

Behind the elms, sunlight on ripe grey stone 83

Believing his mother was named for the passionate countess 245

Birds on the lake; a distant waterfall 139

Brutal shuddering machines, yellow, bite into given earth 231

Byrd composed here 276

Careful not to soil her dainty Ferragamos 322

Chintz, carpets, mahogany, marquetry 147

Clouds make me look as though I disapprove 128

County of squares and spires, in the middle of England 87

Courtesy of a thirteenth Duke 85

Cycles of ulcers, insomnia, poetry 203

Dead pomp sneering underground 198

Deep in a forest where the kestrel screamed 277

Do not reject this fading house 247

Do you remember Lebanon? 347

Down in the fruit-garden the children 254

Down past the Himalayan cedar 333

Drizzle, an oak lined drive, spectres of sheep 346

Easy to pick out, Giaconda-faced 73
English summer, rolling down 298
Estate? It is my world! God knows, I've paid 257
Even when imagined as the place of a caring lord 126
Every night you read yourself to sleep 297
Every sock and collar has a name-tag 134

Families have no beginning, but can end 303
First thing in the morning they went out 109
For taking a trout out of my water: the cold hill 226
For X, in service 58

Gardens, gardens, and we are gardeners 184
God save me from the Porkers 113
good afternoon and welcome come this way 174

Happy New Year to all our ancestors 327
He is wintering out 61
Here is the home of lost romance 40
Here the delicate dance of silence 220
High branches drowse and the leaves press 249
History is silent, the one door 78
How the rich impress us 319

I am folded among my terraces 31
I have come to stand at your border 309
I have nothing to say about this garden 197
I keep everything in its place 118

I know a curious moth, that haunts old buildings 281
I lingered in that unfriended room 81
I meditate upon a swallow's flight 54
I see him in the distance. The stories he tells them 188
I want to leave something behind 191
I was a child but might have been any age 341
I was the brushstroke of light 287
If you arrive by a side road 259
I'm the scullery maid, the skivvy, the flunky 192
Imperceptibly his art has hedged him in 56
In a short time we shall have cleared the gazebo 50
In all those rooms, no light 250
In Casterbridge there stood a noble pile 224
In perfect June we reached the house to let 75
In their great houses there were always tables laid 194
In these old country nooks, it is far from plain to see 86
In these tall trees warbler and wren all day 55
In Wilburton Rectory's green bedroom 169
Incandescence of the triggers 156
Inside the sombre walls the neat quadrangles still are green 162
Is it a great house, opened up now for all 190
It always starts with a dead girl 293
It might have been a wedding, or a wake 180
'It takes several hours to get up here 116
It was a big house, bleak 246
It was a way of punishing the house, setting it ablaze 263
It's a scoop, a coup 111

Laid out in the field 286
Last year we went to Lissadell 244
'Lawrence, of virtuous father, virtuous son 326
Leaves of summer 71
Let nothing be done twice 331
Let oregano – so 60
Like men forced to dig their own graves, my ancestors 205
lime trees in flower   they make you cups of holy tea 280
Limned in the lake the rosy portraiture 267
Lost manor where I walk continually 65

Maybe like this: sunburnt hands 248
Might she have trusted them – the quiet insistence 200
Milgate kept standing for four centuries 236
My first is in sun but not in moon 288
My lady looks across the frozen lake 239

No roving shadow of misfortune stain 168
Not less nor more than five and forty years ago 99
Not quite the meadhall, the ballroom at Walcot Hall 133

O drear, O dreary dreary dirge for this deer 305
Of the old house, only a few, crumbled 79
Oh there hasn't been much change 42
Opening my window for a breath of air 66

Patrons paid – and ill – 196
Places are made of hearsay and story 261
Poetry of the Anti-Jacobin 179

'Prune the roses, plant the lawns with geraniums, shake out the chintzes 211

Rambler, direct your care 314
'Ramshackle loveliness' was the phrase I wrote 30
Remember that house. To what end 77
Rents were collected. Footmen 321
Riders cascade down the valley in the 141

See that my Howse look to the East 223
Shadows the shape of islands paraphrase 72
She had forgotten the bellows again 59
Sir Nameless, once of Athelhall, declared 136
Slim sunburnt girls adorn 302
So now the Victorians are all in heaven 261
So sorry if I have offended you 290
Splitts of well-shot woodcock, partridge, snipe 234
Squire England has grown old 256
Stay traveller! With no irreverent haste 24
Stiffly Sir Frederick 41
Stones only, the disjecta membra of this Great House 229
Such long-ago see-saw of fortunes 120
Suddenly (as when a road steeply rising 89
Sunlight daubs my eye 186
Surely among a rich man's flowering lawns 307

Teas are served in the library 315
That January was a freak-wind 119
The air is sad, but then we laugh 131
The ancient pirouette of trees 80
The arc of the driveway is what's left 219

The Archduke has laid his lap dogs in the grave 304

The avenue was green and long, and green 221

The ballroom is kept shuttered. No one has the key 129

The bright drop quivering on a thorn 88

The child, one evening, looks 123

The coal seam ran under 279

The day dispossessed of light. At four o'clock 137

The dignified gate and driveway through the leafy garden 132

The elongated steeplechaser arches 163

The fire was never lit. Cold, her body 258

The fountains are dry and the roses over 343

The Fourteenth Earl is shivering 34

The gardener and his boy, they found him early 345

The hastening cloud grows thin; the sun's pale disc 272

The Highland-granite walls are three feet thick 173

The house is not locked 157

The house stands as it always has 237

The lawn of marital unhappiness 323

The light of evening, Lissadell 243

The man who takes our coins on the gravel track 316

The old board's not used much: a panel of glass 154

The Sackvilles were mostly mad 338

The sense of unrelatedness that comes 168

The space between the tall plantation firs 270

The Squire is in his library. He is rather worried 291

The steady cedars levelling the shade 240

The tenant absent (Scutcheon Hall is let 238

The trees have all gone from the grounds of my manor 33

The whispering houses have gone 106

There are clues everywhere 67

There has been burning, identifiable still 262

There is a house with ivied walls 289

There was a dining-room, there was a drawing-room 170

There's always been someone to hide 57

There's no-one lounging on the curly iron bed or 300

These are the foundations. Roots of walls 70

These homes in poems 100

They patter from myriad hatchbacks to sit in steam 130

They're dreaming of a garden like the ones they knew 235

This ancient house so notable 93

This autumn park, the sequin glitter of leaves 202

This brand of soap has the same smell as once in the big 74

This is how I wish to remember us 213

This is the gem you cut, Thomas Anson 301

This is the only decaying nineteenth-century house with a stable block 127

Those bad old days of 'rapine and of reif!' 176

Those cherubs on the gate 90

Through the graveyard filled with change-ringing 266

Through the open French window the warm sun 26

Thus spoke the lady underneath the trees 95

Time present and time past 102

Tomorrow. Drive up without lights. Wait for the all-clear. 340

Tomorrow I will order stones 271

Tradition holds that on a wet starless night 155

Tranquillity is only a style, whose glyph 299

Trees, of course, silent attendants 38

Trespassing, we were caught like moths 339

two vizard masks 148

Two years we spent 241

Under my window-ledge the waters race 217

Veins and arteries carry the blood from corner 156

Warm behind curtains drawn to shut out February's cold 160

Watching the doves in the drowned park 32

Water looked up through the lawn 177

We brought up the rear, the army recruiter and I 125

We did not care muchly who, in the murder 296

We walk here 328

Weary we came to it, weary 164

Welcome to my house, this stately home 206

What a night in the vale of Tywi. Guests 110

What a prize prick he's made of himself 306

What I was seeking was a mulberry tree 334

What would they think, those writers, those artists 317

When a thousand coal-gas crocuses ignite like pilot lights 44

When I visited the castle and read about what had happened there 69

When the sun climbed high enough to see into the garden 98

When, to disarm suspicious minds at lunch 48

While cleaning my old six-branched candelabrum 153

White, white in the milky night 274

'Why are you so bent down before your time 260

Why have I never read *Arcadia*? 88

Who will wed the Dowager's youngest daughter 25

Wind slices at the sashes and the double doors, it lashes 135

Yearly, connubial swallows nest 52

You do your work in the small hours 82

You sat sitting in your country seat 209

You will not last. Can't you see the swans circling 253

Index of Titles

Acton Burnell 78
After Mr Mayhew's Visit 261
After the Revolution 324
Alfoxton 89
Ancestral Houses 307
Architectural Masks 289
Artemis Before a Prospect of Blaxter
     Hall 163
Asleep in the Orangery 345
Aspects of a Novel 157
At a Country-House Hotel 131
At a Warwickshire Mansion 203
At Burghley House 328
At Colwick Park 109
At Great Tew 214
At Mapledurham 86
Avington: The Avenue at Dawn 312

Baize Doors 59
The Ballroom at Blaxter Hall 40
A Banquet at Middleton 110
The Belvedere 270
The Blickling Hall Poem 299
Blown Hilcote Manor 75
Blue Bedfordshire 85
The Body in the Library 293
Bolsover Castle 98
Bone China 191
Breaking 341
The Break-up of a Library in an
     Anglo-Irish House in Wexford:
     1964 259
Britannia 322
Brockham End House 326
Burnt Norton 102

Canons Ashby 87
Care-taking 118
Castle Howard 24
The Cedars at Highclere 188
The Changeling 123
The Chaos 257
A Charm for Blagdon 168
The Children and Sir Nameless 136
Cleaning the Candelabrum 153
Colonel Fantock 95
The Conjuror's Trick 248
Conservatism Revisited 190
Coole and Ballylee, 1931 217
Coole Park, 1929 54
Corpus Christi 127
A Country Mansion 93
County 113
Craxton 186

Daisy at the Court 36
Death of King George V 234
The Doll's House 206
Domesday Book 331
Dorothy Osborne in the Country 32
Downe: The Extreme Verge of the
     World 235
The Duke's Pagoda 271
The Dwelling-Place 277

An East Wind 239
Effacements 240
Eighteenth Century Blocks 171
Elizabeth Sweyn, Widow, at Her
     Writing Desk in the Hall 226
Elm End 90
Emma 192

England 309
The English Sweats 286
Enýpnion 149
Erddig 279

Fall Weekend at Milgate (3) 236
Family Seat 128
Felbrigg 303
Final Movement 245
Flensby Hall Day Spa 130
Fore-edge Painting 179
Furlongs 300

Gardeners 184
The Grange 42
Great Edwardian 115
Great Good House 126
Greenhallows 283
Greenhouses 168
Greenway House 297
Guidelines 174
The Gunroom 156

Ha-Ha 304
A Haunted House 67
Haunted House 64
Haydn, in a Neo-Gothic Mansion of
    the National Trust 321
The Hidden 298
Higham Hall 333
Houghton House 83
The House that Was 79
A Household 48
House-keeping 82
A Huntingdonshire Nocturne 135

Ickworth 337
In Blenheim Park 72
In Darley Abbey Park 216
In Heytesbury Wood 99
In Memory of Eva Gore-Booth and
    Con Markiewicz 243
In the Castle 69
In the Formal Garden 336
In the Grounds 318

Inheritance 334
The Inherited Estate 329
Interior at Petworth: From Turner 263

J.P. 339
The Jacobean Mansion 213

A Kind of Jericho 254
The King's Bed 155
Knebworth Park 313
Knole (Fuller) 162
Knole (Powell) 338

The Laird's Lug 173
The Lakes at Blenheim 249
The Landowner 314
Landscape 202
The Landscape Gardeners 231
Landscape Poem 205
Late Elizabethan 151
The Laurel Axe 252
Letter of Notice to the Country
    House 253
The Library 258
Lines on a Tudor Mansion 302
Lissadell 244
Lord and Lady Romfort 211
Lyveden New Bield 107

A Man 224
The Manor 306
The Manor Garden 343
Manor House 247
The Manor House 30
The Mansion 237
Mappa Mundi 194
Metamorphoses 116
Meteor 287
Milgate 52
Mistress 57
Moonlight 340
Mr Gradgrind's Country 170

Name-Tag 134
The National Trust 144

Newstead Abbey 139
Night-Scented Stock 274

October in Clowes Park 137
The Old Bell-board 154
The Old Squire 256
The Old Workman 260
Open Day at Stancombe Park 316
Open Gardens Scheme 315
Open to the Public 317
Order to View 246
Orielton Empty 262
The Ornamental Water 267
Osterley Park: Summertide Trees 280
Our Weird Regiment 319
The Owl Writes a Detective Story 294
Owlpen Manor 31
The Owner Instructs the Master
    Mason 223
Oxnead Hall, Norfolk 276

Parson's Castle, Birr, Ireland 147
Penshurst Place 88
Peter Wentworth in Heaven 33
The Pier-Glass 65
The Plain Sense of Things 344
Plas Difancoll 38
Plumbing 167
The Property of the Executors 180
A Property of the National Trust 125
Prospect of Ditchley 80

Real Estate 164
Rest on the Hunt 141
Revesby 129
Ridge-Foot House 132
Ripley Eels 119
Romance of a Youngest Daughter 25
The Ruined Garden 70
Ruins of a Great House 229

A Sad Story 261
Saltatorium 305
Send for Lord Timothy 291
Servant Boy 61

Service 58
Shrine for a Young Soldier, Castle
    Drogo 73
Shugborough Eclogues 301
Sir Frederick 41
Sir Osbert's Complaint 44
Sissinghurst 27
Soap Suds 74
Somewhere 250
Song of a Past Scullery-Maid 60
Song to Mark a Boundary 55
The Space 133
St Botolph's 266
Stanzas on a Visit to Longleat House
    in Wiltshire, October 1953 198
A Stately Exterior 238
Stately Home (Grigson) 196
Stately Home (Harrison) 176
Staying with Friends 323
Still-Life 26
Stourhead 327
Swans 219
Swarthmoor Hall, Cumbria 148

Tapestries 81
Tapestry 156
Tapestry Moths 281
That House 77
These Homes 100
Three Riddles 288
To a Cedar Tree 347
To a Stately Home 346
The Topiarist 56
Tresham's Fancy 106
Twilight 34
The Two of Us 209
Two Versions of Pastoral 200

Unexpected Visit 197
The Uninvited 296
Up at the House 290

A Vacant Possession 50
A Valentine for John and Margaret
    160

View 265
A Visit to Castletown House 221

Walmer Castle 71
The Washstand 169
Water-Gardens 177
While Reading a Ghost Story 66
Wilton Park 88
The Woods 241

Woodtown Manor 220
Wycoller Hall 120

The Young Duchess Walks with Mr
    Brown To Discuss Improvements
    111
Youth Revisited 272

53° 09′33.17″ N, 0° 25′33.18″ W 150

Index of Poets

Adcock, Fleur 33, 197
Agbabi, Patience 206
Armitage, Simon 209, 306
Ashbee, David 316
Auden, W. H. 48
Aykroyd, Juliet 223

Barker, George 198
Bartlett, Elizabeth 127
Beer, Patricia 327
Bennet, Peter 40, 163
Berkeley, Anne 129, 322, 340
Betjeman, John 24, 113, 234
Bidgood, Ruth 247
Binyon, Laurence 79
Blunden, Edmund 86, 267
Boland, Eavan 259
Boxall, Penny 155, 173
Brackenbury, Alison 88
Brookes, James 286
Brown, George Mackay 226

Caldwell, Roger 151
Causley, Charles 41
Cavaliero, Glen 85, 304
Christie, Agatha 347
Clarke, David 346
Clarke, Gillian 110, 167, 261
Clegg, John 287
Connor, Tony 137
Conquest, Robert 83
Cope, Wendy 244
Crucefix, Martyn 319

Dallat, Cahal 245
Daryush, Elizabeth 26

Davies, Hilary 116, 213
Davis, William Virgil 156
Day Lewis, C. 81, 202
de la Mare, Walter 277
Didsbury, Peter 194
Downie, Freda 56, 239, 317
Draycott, Jane 290, 315
Dunn, Douglas 184, 318

Eliot, T. S. 102
Evaristo, Bernardine 147, 192
Ewart, Gavin 294

Fan, Kit 119
Fanthorpe, U. A. 31, 64
Fenton, James 50
Fowles, John 131
Fraser, G. S. 326
Fuller, John 271
Fuller, Roy 139, 162, 203, 272

Gallagher, Katherine 313
Garfitt, Roger 133
Gowrie, Grey 157
Graves, Robert 65, 93
Greening, John 135, 188, 279, 297
Greger, Debora 125
Griffiths, Jane 67, 107
Grigson, Geoffrey 196, 231, 321
Grosholz, Emily 324
Gross, Philip 58, 257, 336
Guest, Harry 171
Gunn, Thom 329
Gurney, John 168, 270

Hall, J. C. 89

Hamburger, Michael 164, 190
Hardy, Thomas 136, 224, 260, 289
Harrison, Tony 176
Hartnett, Michael 221
Heaney, Seamus 61
Heath-Stubbs, John 291
Henson, Stuart 34, 345
Hill, Geoffrey 252
Hooker, Jeremy 312
Hughes, Glyn 205
Hughes, Ted 120

Jenkins, Alan 200
Jones, Brian 77, 214

Kavanagh, P. J. 71
Kelly, Lisa 305
Khalvati, Mimi 100
Kramer, Lotte 328

Lerner, Laurence 144
Levi, Peter 249
Lewis, Alun 302
Lindop, Grevel 301
Lomas, Herbert 132
Lowell, Robert 52, 236, 331

MacBeth, George 250
Mackinnon, Lachlan 323
MacNeice, Louis 74, 246
Mahon, Derek 88, 241
Mansfield, Katherine 274
Martinez de las Rivas, Toby 309
Masefield, John 75
Mathias, Roland 80, 262
Maxwell, Glyn 296
McAuliffe, John 219
McKendrick, Jamie 134
Minhinnick, Robert 36, 237, 254, 339
Montague, John 220
Moraes, Dom 186
Morgan, Esther 57, 82, 118, 191
Motion, Andrew 341
Murphy, Richard 128

O'Brien, Sean 177
Padel, Ruth 235
Parker, Rennie 78, 106
Plath, Sylvia 343
Porter, Peter 32
Powell, Neil 70, 338

Raine, Craig 59
Raine, Kathleen 160
Ransom, John Crowe 25
Raymond, Vicki 298
Redgrove, Peter 149, 281
Reed, Henry 123
Reeves, James 283
Ridler, Anne 55
Rivière, Michael 303

Sackville-West, Vita 27
Sail, Lawrence 174
Salway, Sarah 111, 248, 288
Sassoon, Siegfried 66, 99, 153, 238
Scammell, William 333
Schroeder, Corinna McClanahan
    253
Scupham, Peter 154, 179, 240
Selby, Robert 266
Sennitt Clough, Elisabeth 169
Sheppard, Robert 299
Shuttle, Penelope 148, 156, 280
Sitwell, Edith 95
Sitwell, Osbert 211
Sitwell, Sacheverell 98
Smith, Ken 261
Smith, Stevie 42
Sprackland, Jean 69
Stainer, Pauline 276
Stallworthy, Jon 90
Stevens, Wallace 344
Szirtes, George 109, 141

Thomas, R. S. 38
Thwaite, Anthony 180
Tomlinson, Charles 334
Towers, Katharine 300

Vince, Michael 126

Walcott, Derek 229
Warner, Sylvia Townsend 170, 256
Warren, Rosanna 263
Waterman, Rory 73, 130, 150
Watts, Rebecca 337
Whistler, Laurence 168
Wilkins, Paul 216
Williams, Tony 115

Wilmer, Clive 30
Wingfield, Sheila 60, 265
Winn, Kieron 72
Wong, Alex 314
Woods, Gregory 44
Wright, David 87

Yeats, W. B. 54, 217, 243, 307
Yeh, Jane 293
Yoseloff, Tamar 258